An Illustrated History of

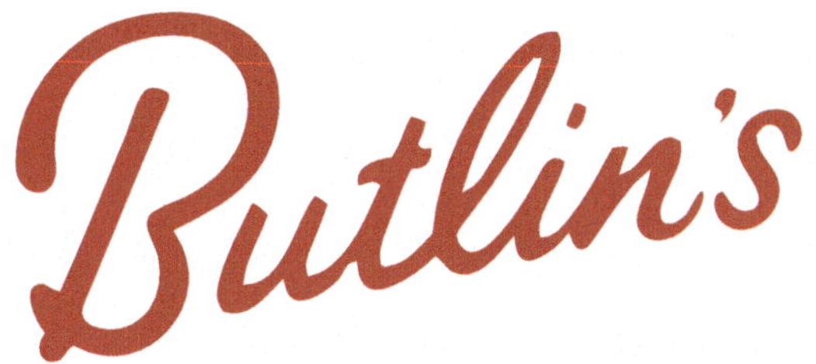

Derek Tait

AMBERLEY PUBLISHING

Acknowledgements

Thanks to Andy King, Rocky Mason, Sylvia French, Kerry Conroy, Butlin's, Butlin's Archive, Sylvia Endacott, Roger Billington, Ron Breedon, Geoff Burgess, Lesley Penniston, Kathryn Leaver, Vanessa Morgan, Dave Bashford, Alan Tait, Ellen Tait, John Cole, Joyce Cole, Simon Knott, Penny Corner (née Holmes), the Holmes Family, David Brierley, David Denny, Alan Peach, David Hammonds and 'Skippy'.

Thanks also to Tina Cole and Tilly Barker.

I have tried to track down the copyright owners of all photographs used and apologise to anyone who has not been mentioned.

Please check out my website at www.derektait.co.uk

Further Reading

Books

Hello Campers by Sue Read (Bantam Press 1986)
The Billy Butlin Story by Sir Billy Butlin and Peter Dacre (Robson Books 1998)
Here Come the Redcoats by Rocky Mason and Frank McGroarty (Authorhouse 2010)
Gumshield to Greasepaint by Rocky Mason (Authorhouse 2010)
Butlin's 75 Years of Fun by Sylvia Endacott and Shirley Lewis (The History Press 2011)

Website

Butlin's Memories at: www.butlinsmemories.com

First published 2012

Amberley Publishing
The Hill, Stroud
Gloucestershire, GL5 4EP

www.amberley-books.com

ISBN 978 1 4456 0806 8

British Library Cataloguing in Publication Data.
A catalogue record for this book is available from the British Library.

Typeset in 9.5pt on 12pt Celeste.
Typesetting by Amberley Publishing.
Printed in the UK.

Introduction

The name Butlin's has been synonymous with seaside holiday camps and wholesome family entertainment for generations.

Billy Butlin opened his first holiday camp at Skegness during the Easter holiday of 1936. It was a low-key affair and the accommodation was basic. There was no heating in the chalets and no hot water. Butlin guaranteed free entertainment to all of his campers, no matter what the English weather threw at them. As well as their accommodation, they had access to bars, dining halls and theatres. To keep out the cold, campers ate their breakfast dressed in warm clothes and danced in their overcoats. As the first campers arrived, the camp was still incomplete and didn't have its own water supply. Water was discovered three weeks later after many bore holes had been sunk on-site. Previous to the camp opening, Butlin had taken out a half page advert in the *Daily Express* offering accommodation, four meals a day and free entertainment. He was soon inundated with enquiries and 500 campers were expected on the day of its opening. The first campers played table tennis while the building of the camp continued around them. Even with its teething problems, over half of the people who stayed the first week booked to stay again. The popularity of the camp led to another being built at Clacton in 1938 and the construction of a third camp at Filey began in 1939.

When the Second World War broke out, completion of the Filey camp was postponed and both the camps at Skegness and Clacton were taken over for military use. The Admiralty asked Billy Butlin to build two more camps for them to be used by military personnel. These were constructed at Ayr in Scotland and at Pwllheli in Wales. Butlin deliberately built the camps to a design which would make it relatively easy to convert them into a holiday resorts after the war. When the war was over, the Navy moved out of the camp at Ayr in 1946 and ownership reverted to Butlin who quickly brought the camp up to holiday standard and opened it to the public the following year.

When it first opened, it could accommodate 2,000 visitors but this later increased to over 5,000. The camp at Pwllheli opened in March 1947 and would eventually accommodate a total of 8,000 guests. Butlin went on to open a camp at Mosney in Ireland in 1948. Three more camps opened in the 1960s and these included one at Bognor Regis in 1960, another at Minehead in 1962 and finally one at Barry Island in 1966.

As well as holiday camps, Billy Butlin also owned hotels which welcomed holidaymakers in Blackpool, Cliftonville, Llandudno, London, Saltdean, Scarborough and Spain.

In 1983, both the camps at Clacton and Filey were closed and in 1986, the camp at Barry was also closed. The camps at Ayr and Pwllheli were re-branded in 1998 and became Haven Park. Bourne Leisure took over the remaining camps in 2000. Today, the Butlin's name lives on with camps at Bognor Regis, Skegness and Minehead.

For generations, Billy Butlin welcomed campers with his own brand of entertainment, amusements and competitions. This book takes a nostalgic look back at those 'Hi-De-Hi' days of yesteryear when most people holidayed at the seaside and everyone joined in enjoying bingo, Knobbly Knees competitions, beauty pageants and Glamorous Grandmother contests.

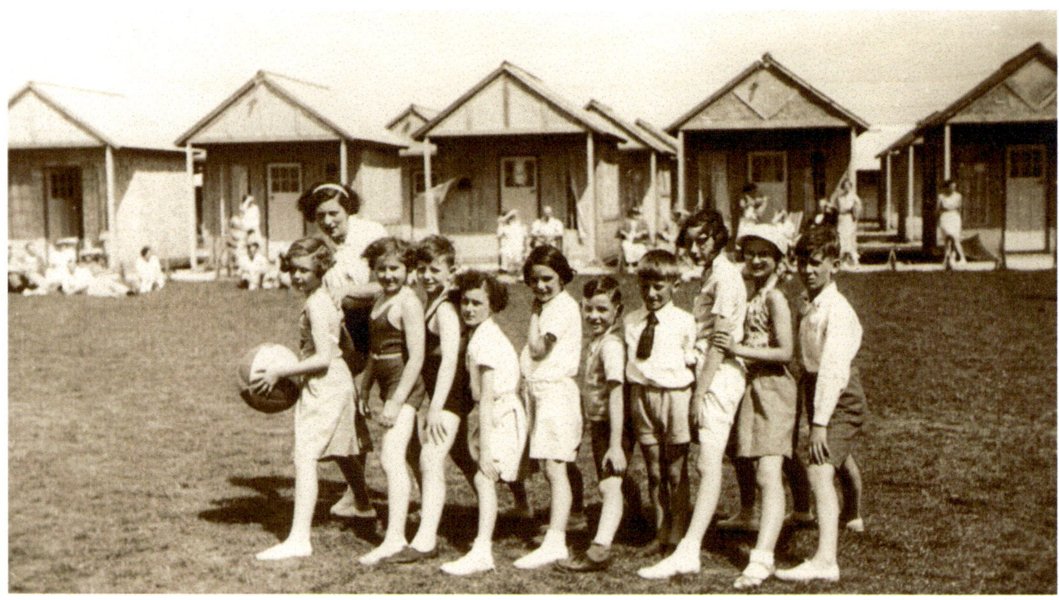

Children playing in front of their chalets at Butlin's in Skegness in 1936.

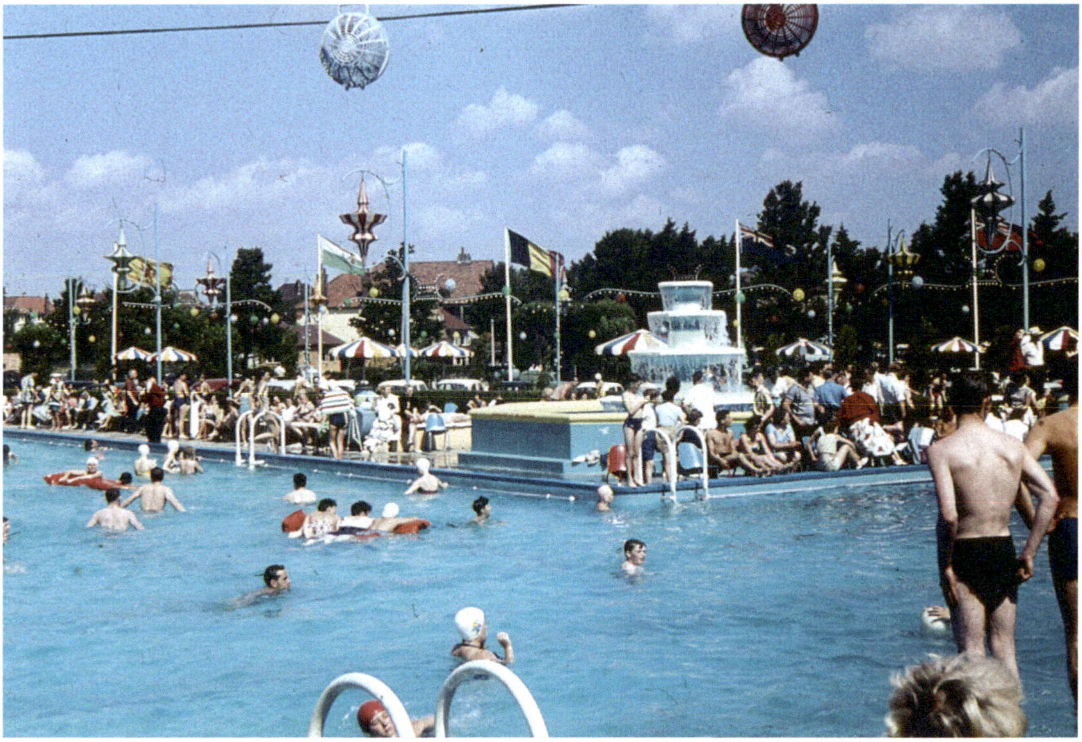

The building of the camp at Skegness commenced in 1935 and opened the following year. Billy Butlin conceived the idea for the holiday camp based on his experiences as a boy at a Canadian Summer Camp. The camp at Skegness included entertainment halls, sports fields and dining facilities. During the Second World War, the camp became a Naval training base but reverted back to a holiday camp in 1946. The two photographs from 1959 show busy activity around the pool and the entrance to the camp.

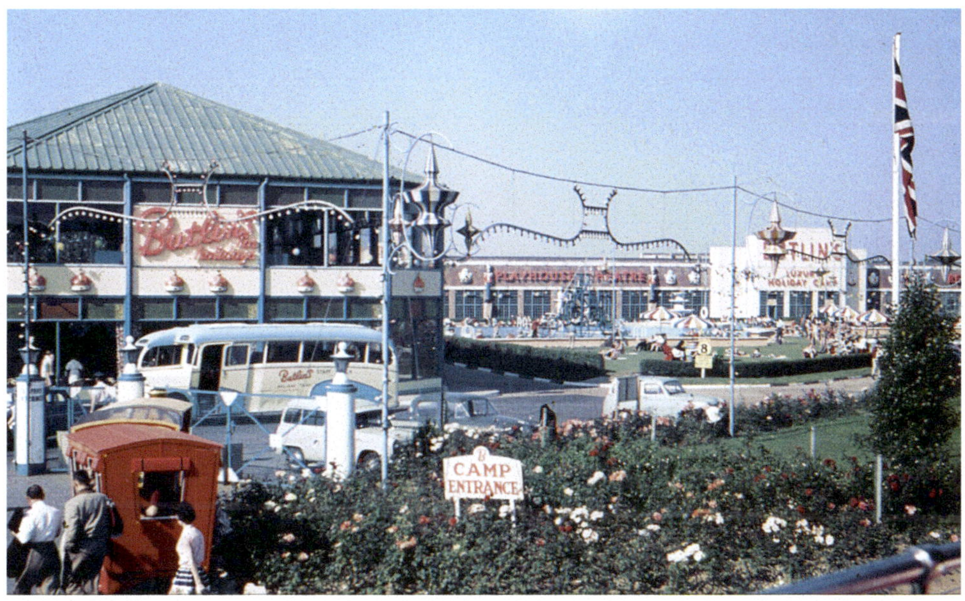

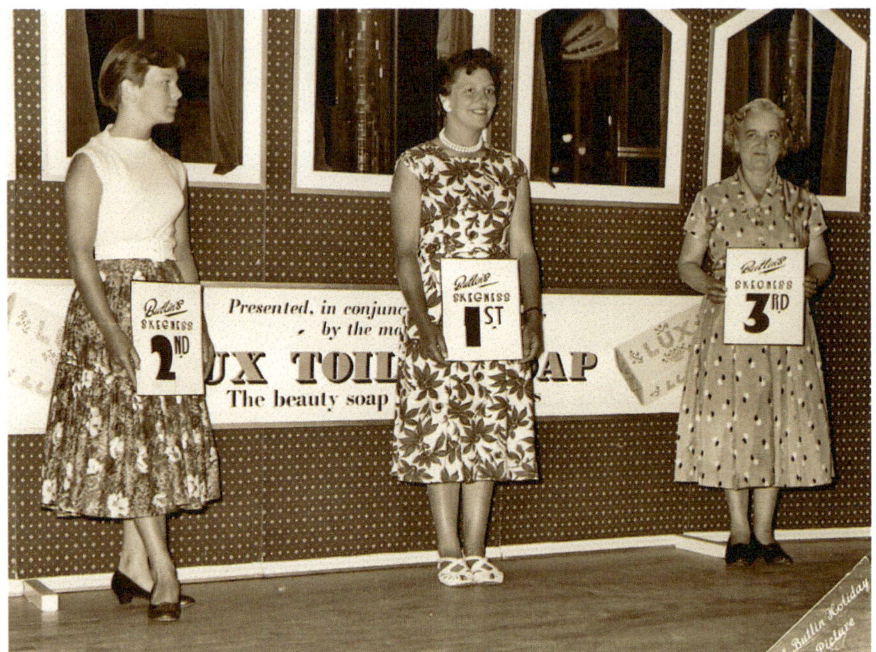

There were regular contests that campers to take part in during the week. These included talent shows, beauty pageants, the Junior Miss Contest, Tarzan contests for the boys and the Glamorous Grandmother Competition for older female campers. In 1955, Billy Butlin met Marlene Dietrich in America and found her very glamorous for her age. This gave him the idea for the Glamorous Grandmother Competition and soon weekly contests commenced. The finals were held at the end of the season. Early contests were supported by national newspapers. By the 1980s, the top prize for winning the competition was £2,500 together with a holiday to the Seychelles.

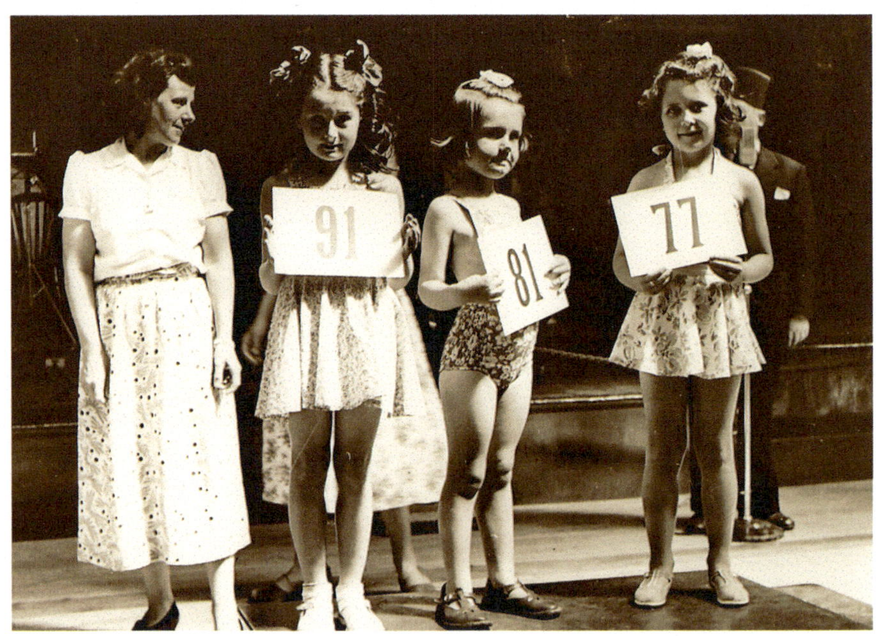

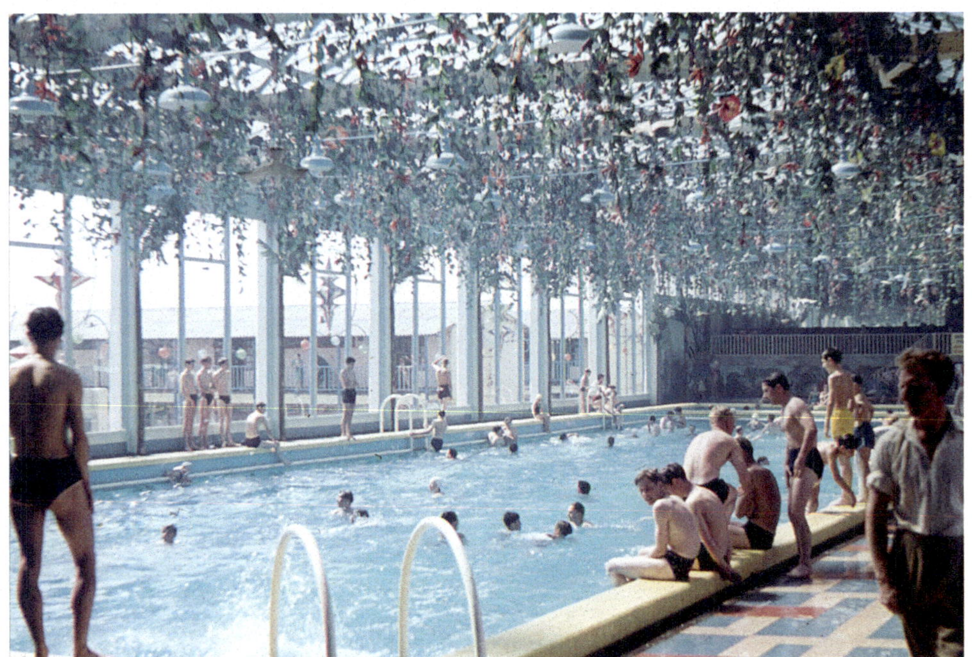

These two photographs show the busy pool areas at Skegness in 1958. As well as swimming areas, the camp included a theatre, a gymnasium, a boating lake, tennis courts and bowling and putting greens. In 1948, Billy Butlin opened a small airport nearby which offered pleasure and sightseeing trips. The Butlin Theatre, which was later renamed the 'Gaiety', was open to both holidaymakers staying at the camp and to the general public. In 1962, a chairlift was installed which ran from the south side to the north side of the site. The futuristic monorail opened in 1965 and took holidaymakers for trips around the camp.

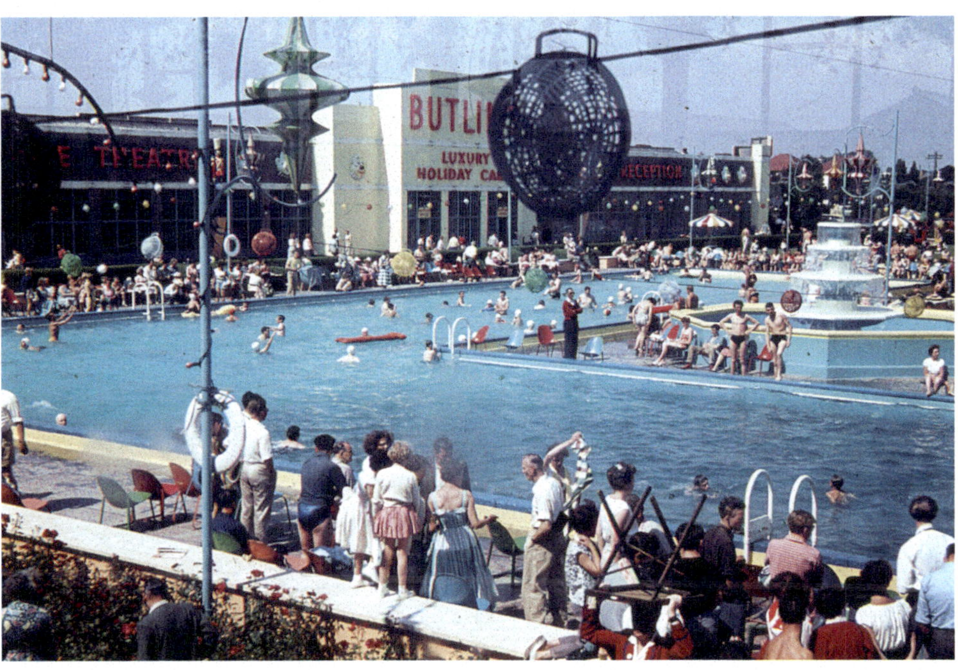

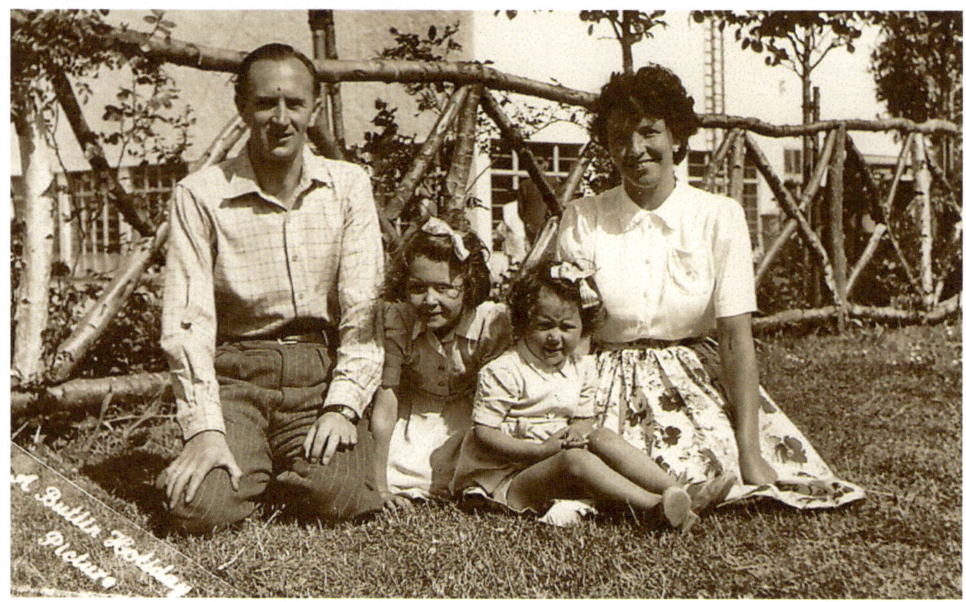

Family holidays in the 1950s would often include a trip to the seaside. The introduction of Butlin's camps meant that people could have a week's holiday for as little as 35 shillings, which included board, entertainment and three meals a day. Before Butlin's, a holiday to the seaside would mean days indoors when it rained. Guesthouses would have no entertainment and, in the days before television, there was little to occupy children. Many guesthouses would only allow visitors in at lunch or tea time so holidaymakers would walk the streets. The Butlin's pledge in the 1930s was to provide entertainment no matter what the English weather threw at them.

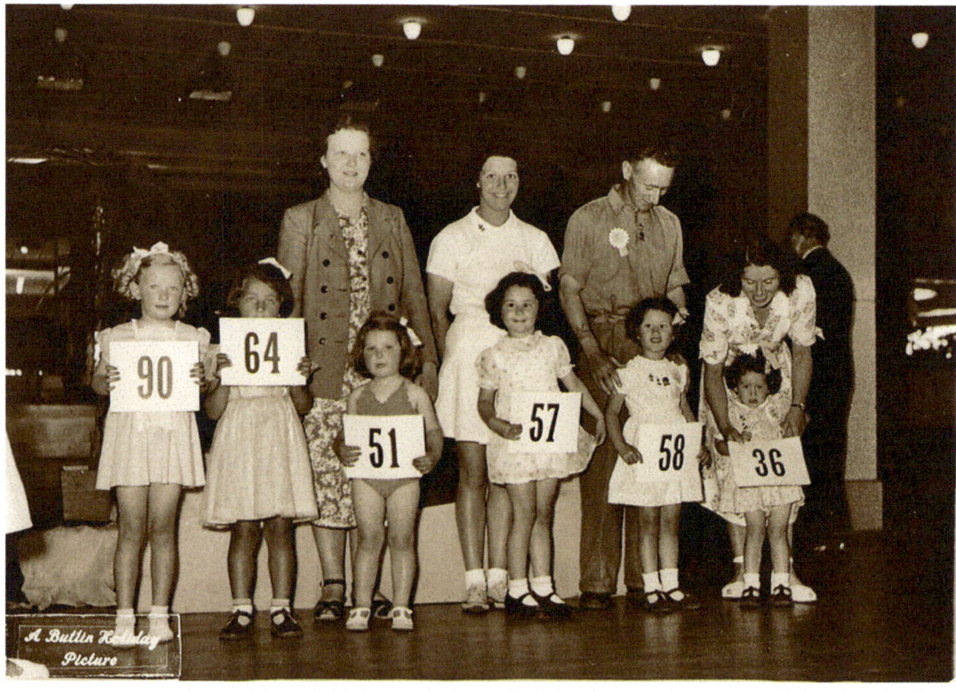

Children loved Butlin's and there was much entertainment laid on for them. In 1951, the 'Beaver Club' was started for children under nine years old. Children who joined got a metal badge as well as a sew-on cloth badge. Back home, they would receive birthday and Christmas cards reminding them of the fun they had at the camp. The membership card stated that all 'Beavers' should:

Be kind to dumb animals.
Eager always to help others.
Aim to be clean neat and tidy.
Victory by fair play.
Energetic at work and play.
Respect for parents and all elders.
And in all things BE AS EAGER AS A BEAVER.

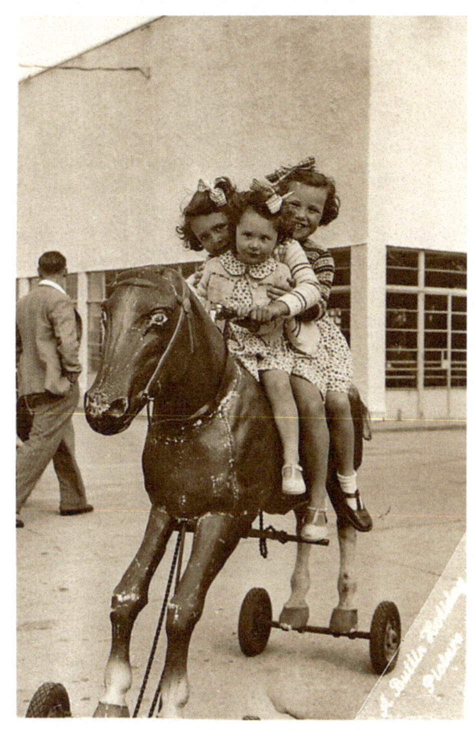

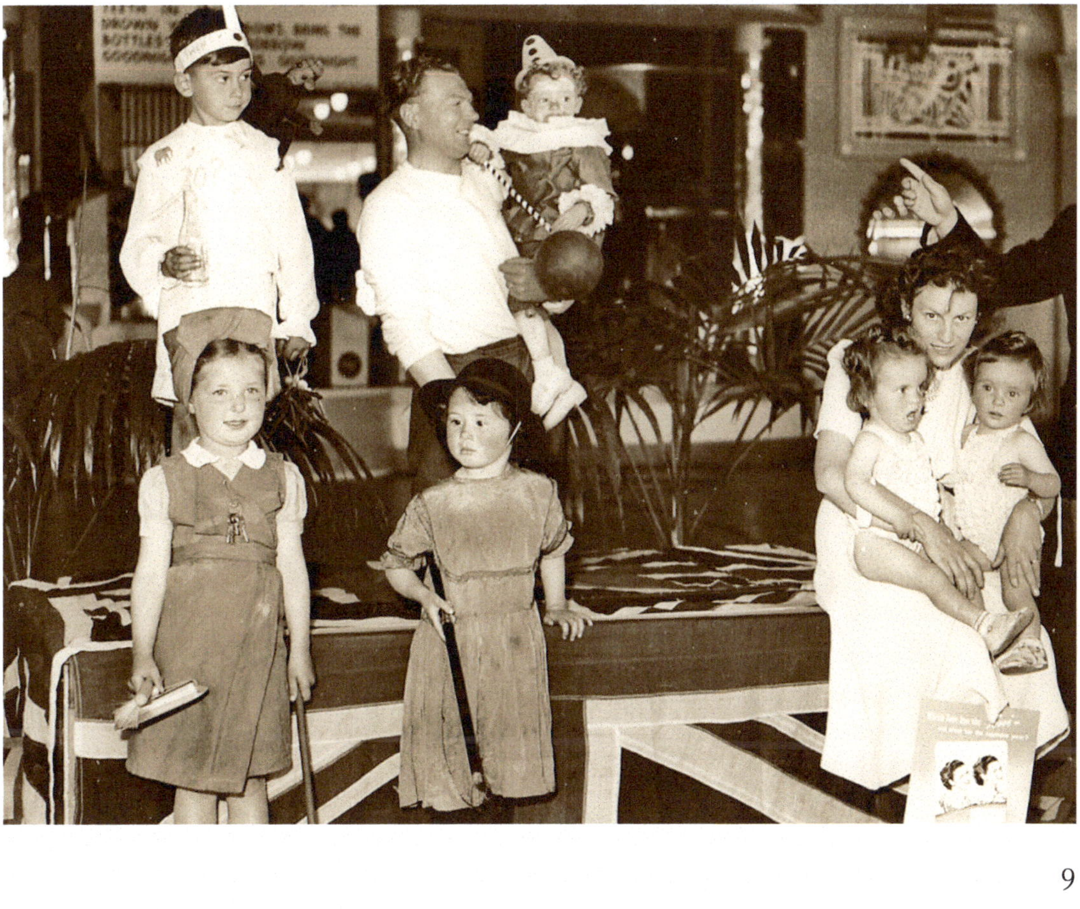

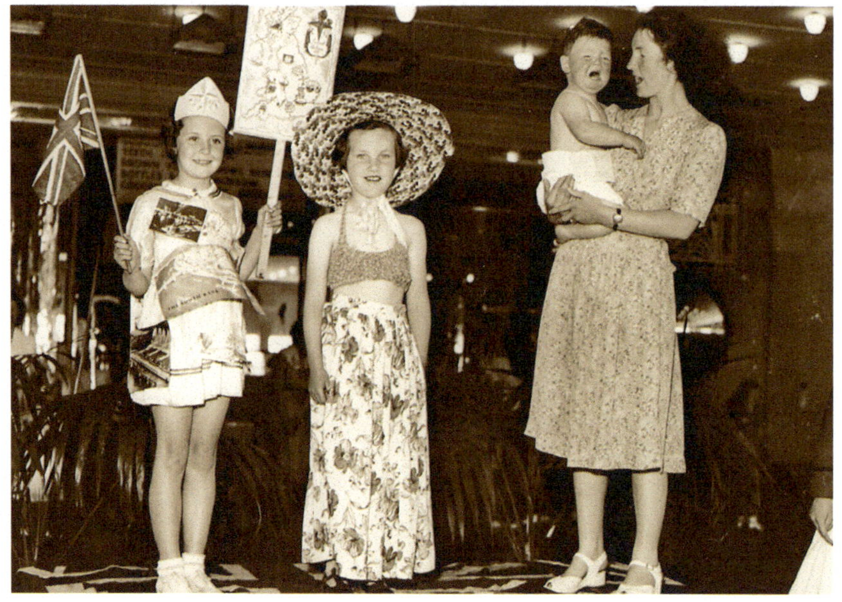

A shop on site would hire out fancy dress costumes for competitions but many campers came well prepared and made their own such as the contestants shown in the first photograph. Penny Holmes is on the left dressed as the Festival of Britain. The little boy doesn't look too happy about taking part. His sash reads, 'Baby Sunlight'. In 1939, a contestant won the Fancy Dress Competition after dressing up as Adolf Hitler. With many items still rationed after the war, contestants would make their costumes out of anything available. These included pirate costumes made from tied handkerchiefs worn on the head with curtain rings used for earrings. Often the more ingenious a costume was, the more chance it had of winning.

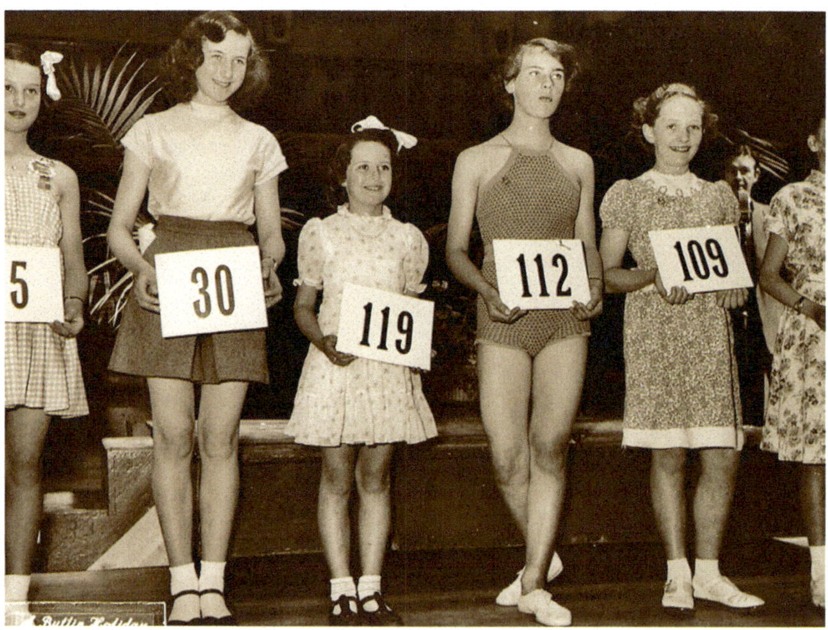

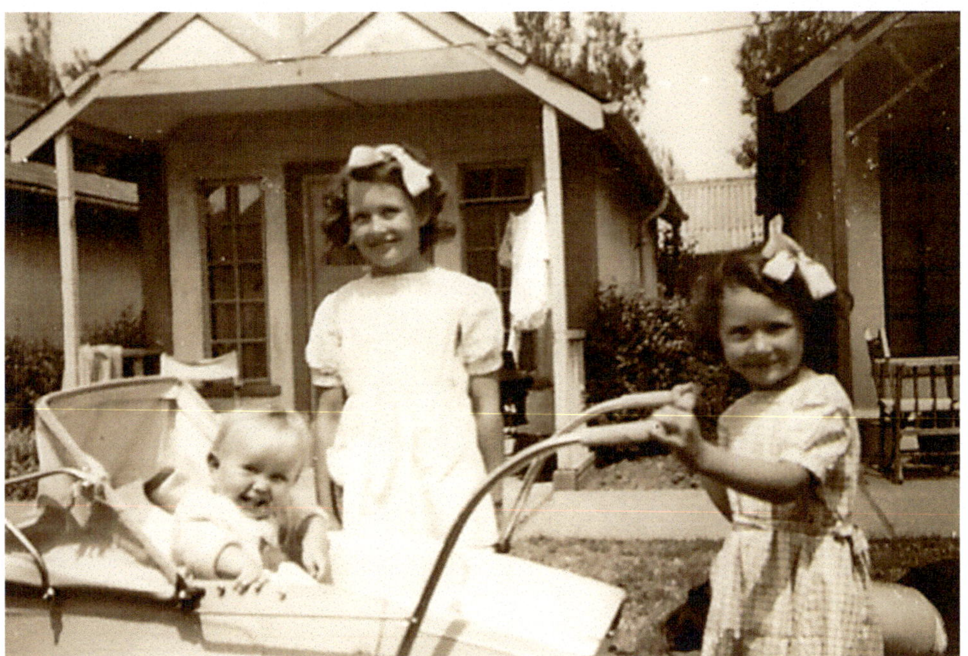

Smiling children enjoy their holiday at Butlin's at Skegness in 1952 in the earlier photograph. Their chalet can be seen in the background. In the second photograph Penny Holmes enjoys a donkey ride on the beach. Donkey Derbies began at the Minehead camp in the 1950s after the idea was suggested by Don Trapnell who also provided the donkey rides on the beach. The idea soon caught on and weekly derbies were held at all the camps. Two-shilling tote tickets could be bought for the race and a staggering £1,249.35 was won by a Mrs Arkwright in 1984.

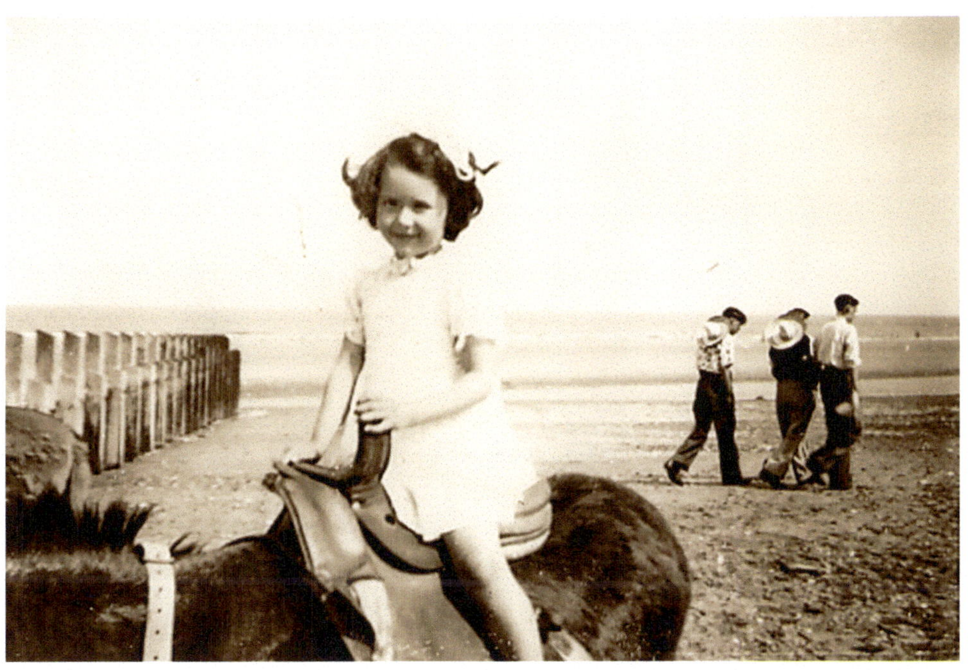

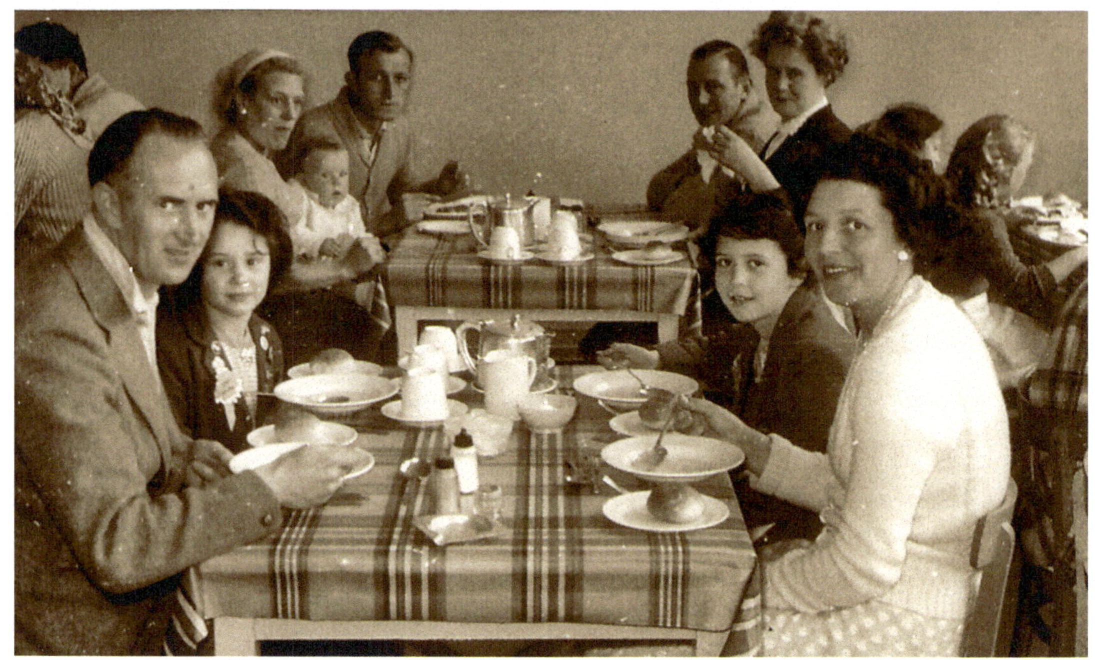

The advert for Butlin's offered three meals a day. The camps all had two or more dining areas with two sittings for each meal, usually an hour apart. It was quite a task to organise with the larger camps preparing approximately 200,000 meals a week. Everything was prepared on site and the staff comprised of a large number of chefs, kitchen workers, waiters and waitresses. Campers would be fed and out within the hour so that the next lot of hungry campers could take their place. Cheers would go up if anyone dropped a plate. Within the pages of their brochure was the slogan, 'Mother gets a real rest at Butlin's'.

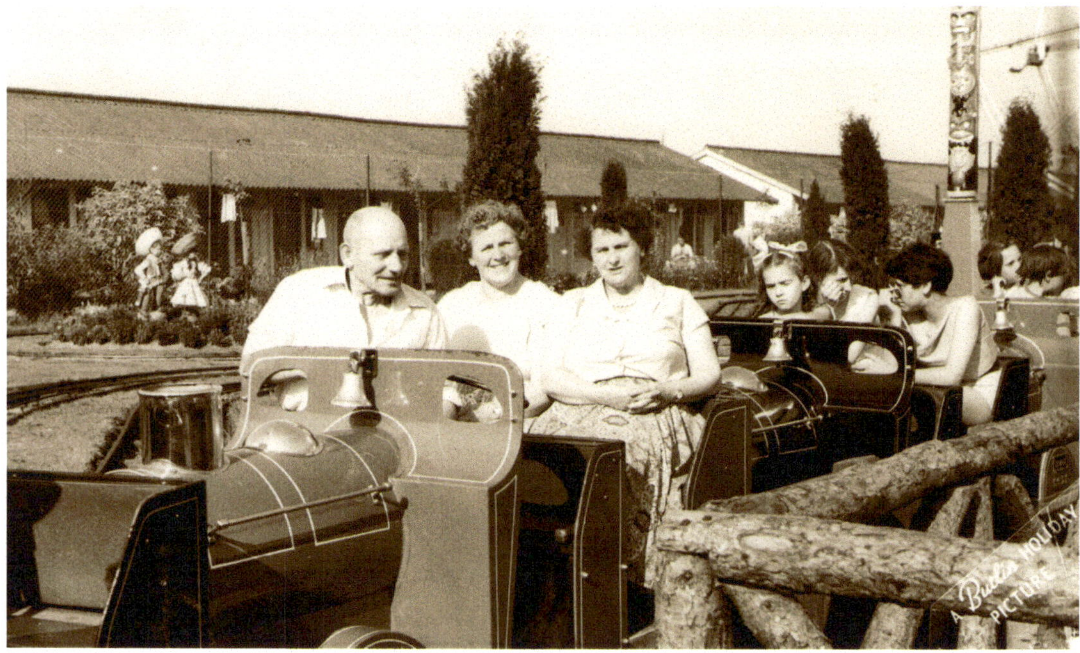

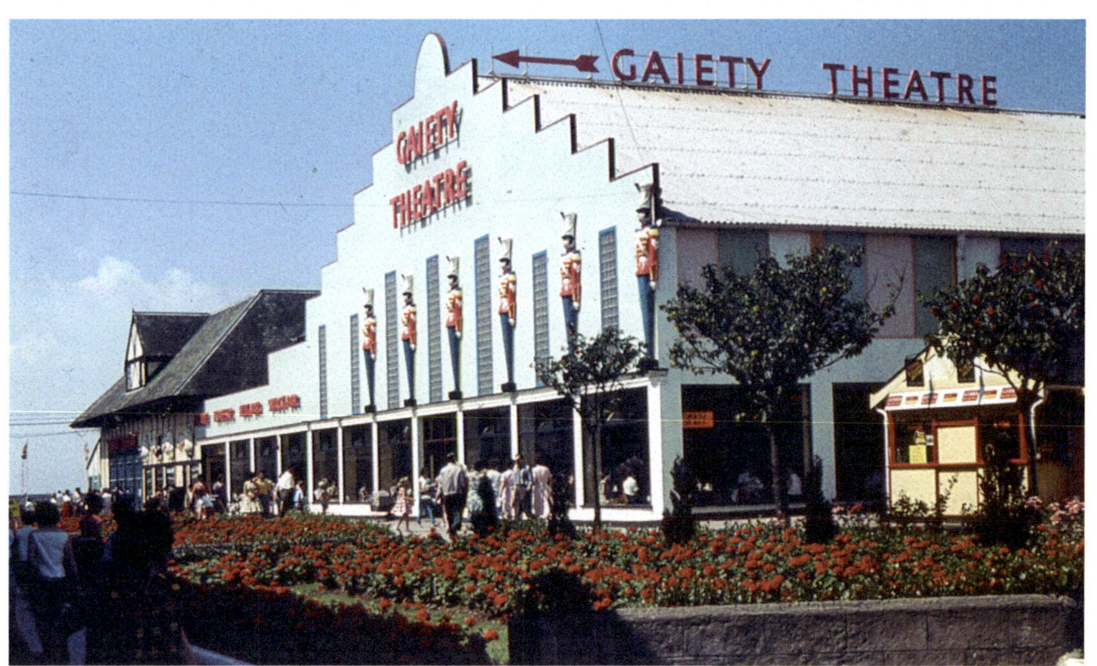

All camps had at least one theatre which would host talent, film and children's shows. The larger theatres could hold up to 2,000 and boasted facilities only found in London's West End. The Gaiety at Filey, which was built in 1960, could seat over 3,000 people and offered top entertainment including early performances from people who would later become huge television stars. There were daily shows with the main show performed each evening. 'Sunday Night Showtime' became a popular event each week with big stars from television appearing regularly. Talent contests and Redcoat shows were also extremely popular.

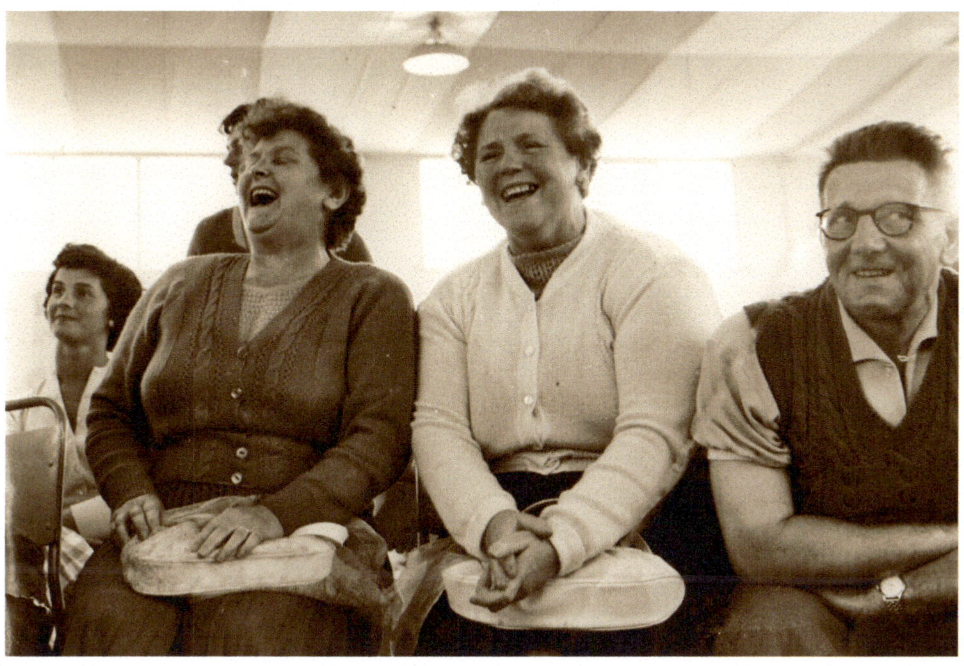

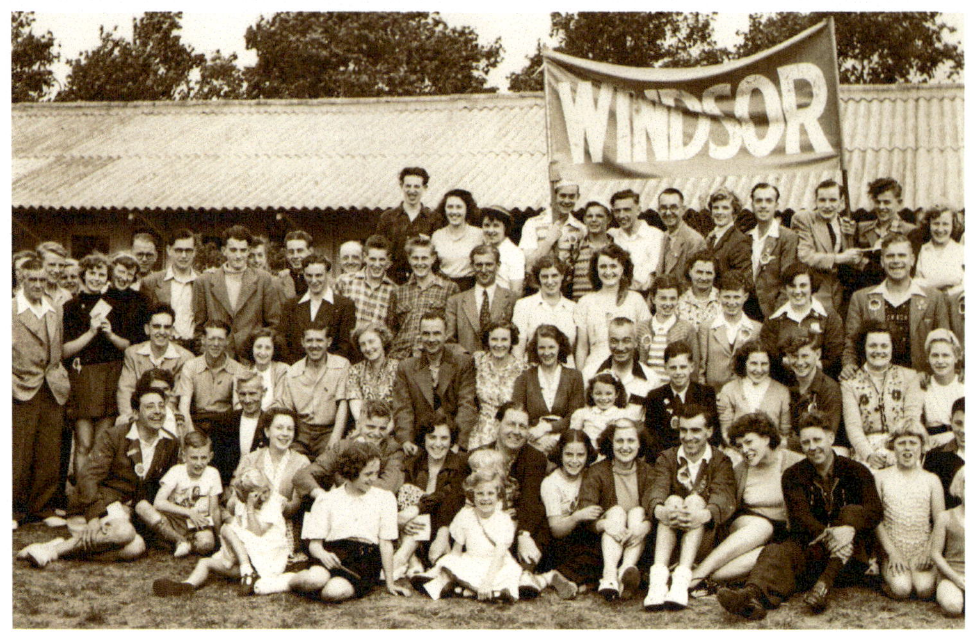

When arriving at Butlin's, campers were allocated to a particular 'house' which included Kent House, Windsor House, Gloucester House, Connaught House, Edinburgh House or Lincoln House. The teams would take part in events and everyone was encouraged to enter to win their particular house points. The Windsor House team, together with their allotted Redcoats, are shown in the earlier photograph taken at the Skegness camp in 1952. A photographer would take group photographs, family shots and pictures of any event around the camp and the photographs would be available to buy the next day.

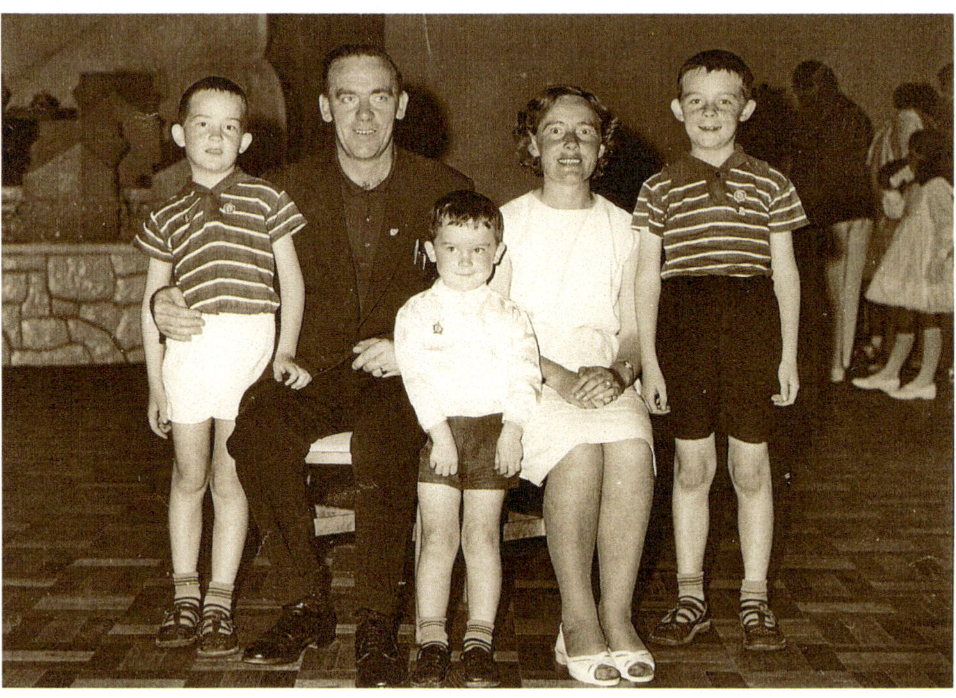

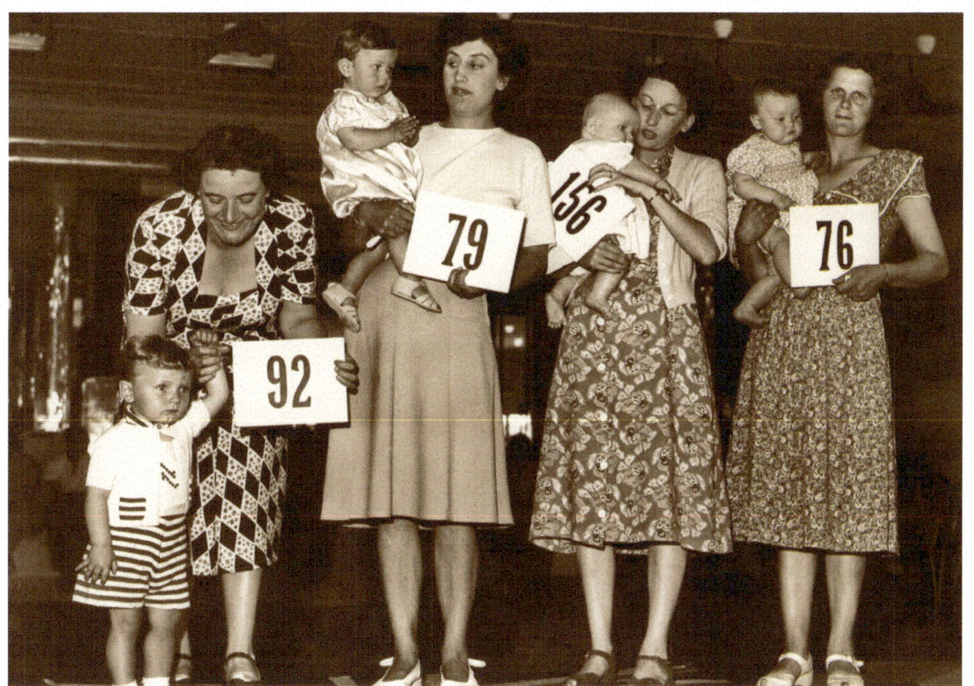

The Bonny Baby Competition started after the war and proved very popular. The age of the babies ranged from nought up to three years old. The judging panel consisted of a vicar, the person in charge of the nursery and a member of the camp committee. *Nursery World* magazine sponsored the competition in the 1960s and *Gerba* took over sponsorship in the 1970s. At many competitions, a Redcoat would join the competitors, complete with a large nappy and dummy. Prizes would be awarded to the winners and points would be added to the total collected by the house in which the winner was a member. Older children could enter the 'Kiddies Holiday Lovelies Competition'.

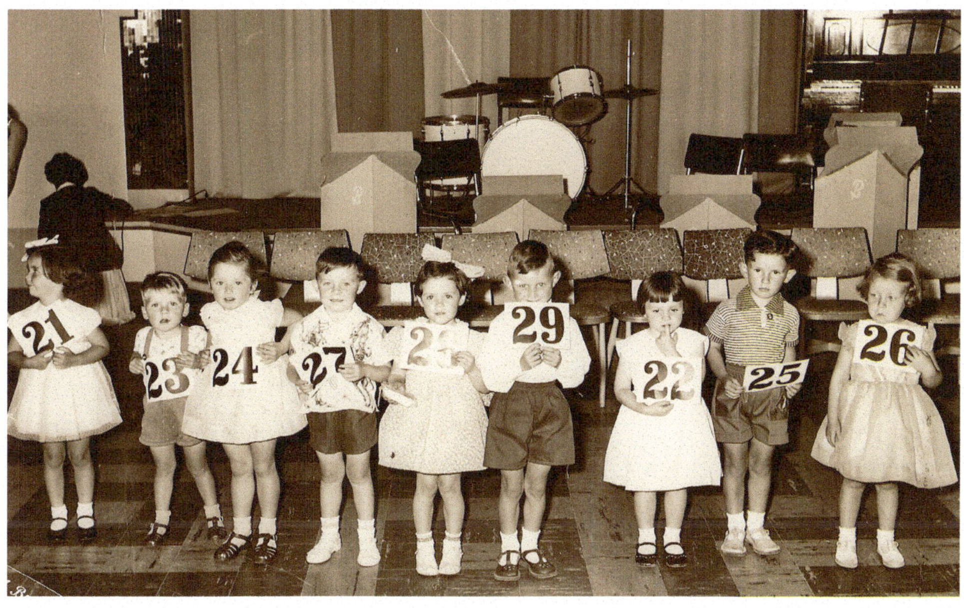

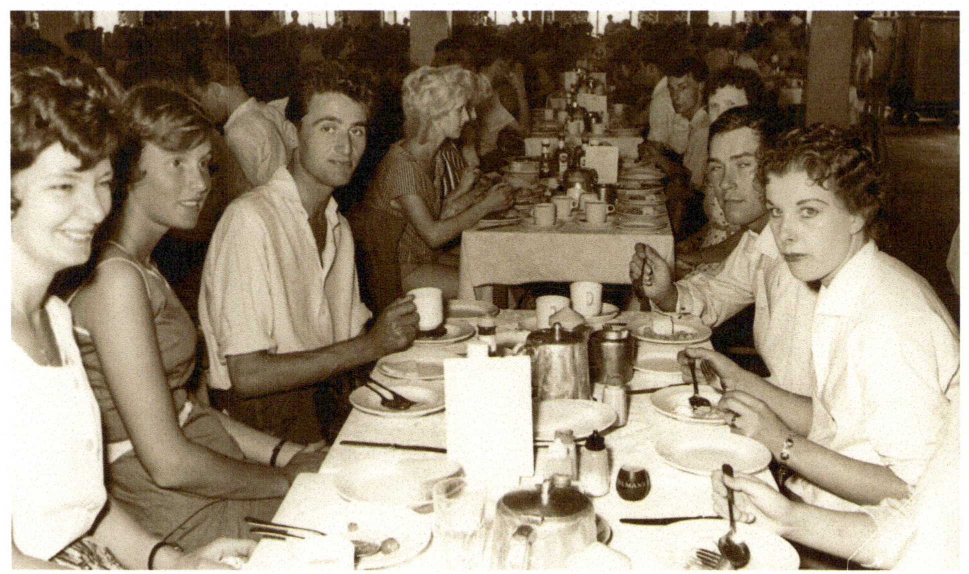

After the war, the luxury of a full cooked breakfast including eggs and bacon became something special. Many didn't eat so well at home. Rationing meant that catering for the many campers proved difficult. The fresh eggs needed came from local farmers and powdered egg was used for making cakes and sandwiches. Campers were served with 'Canadian wind-dried steak', which, because of the shortages, was actually whale meat. Potatoes, spam and fish, which were more readily available, were used in most meals. The top photograph shows mealtime in the 1950s complete with tomato sauce, OK brown sauce and Colman's mustard.

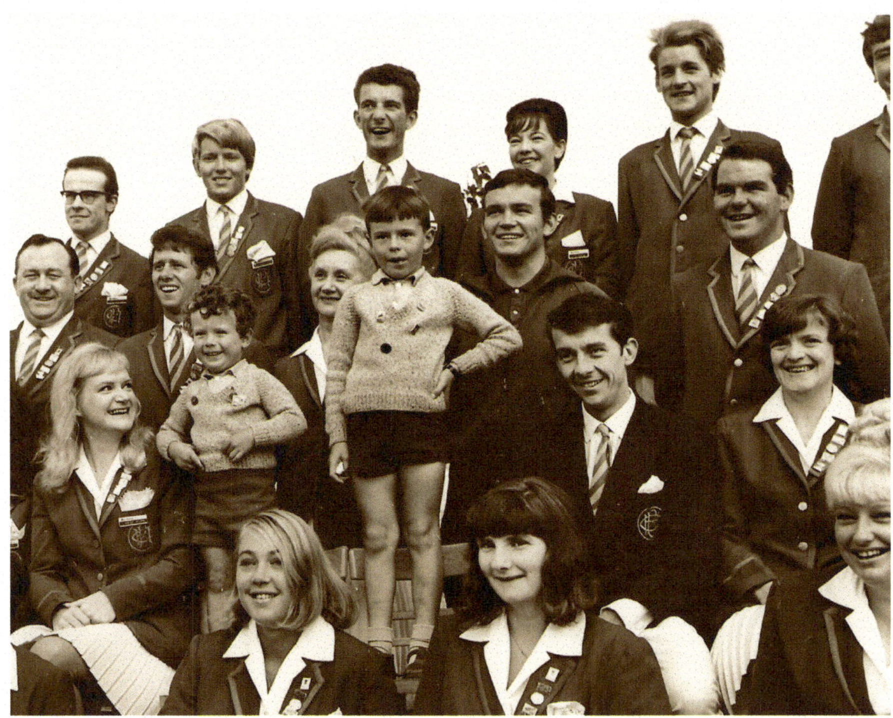

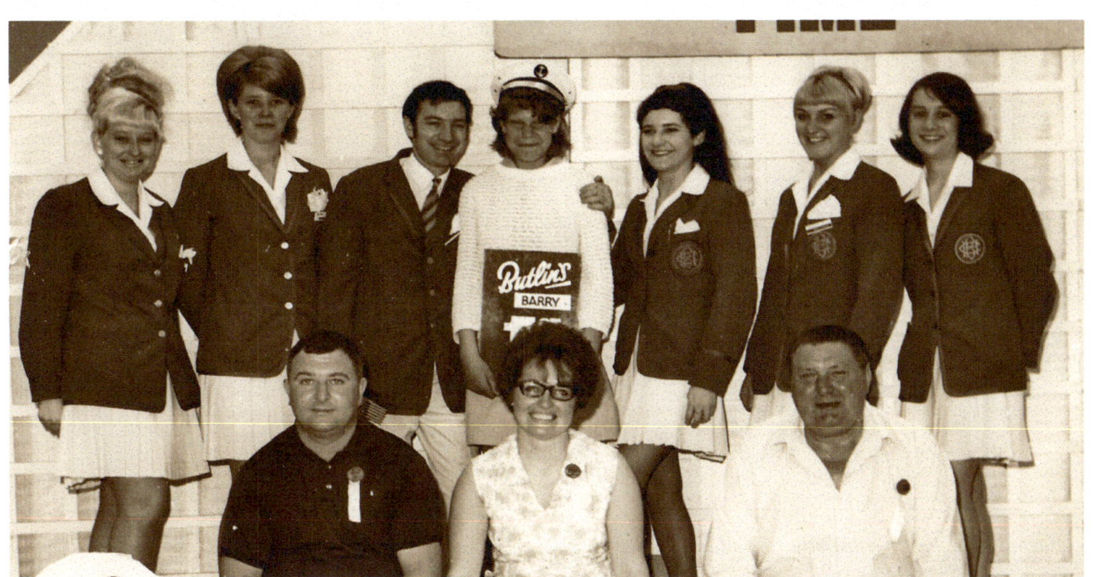

Both photographs feature Sylvia French (née Varney) who was a Redcoat at Butlin's Barry Island camp between 1966 and 1969. The campsite at Barry was opened in 1966 and covered 45 acres. It was the last camp to be built and also the smallest. It consisted of over 800 chalets and could accommodate 5,000 people. The Beachcomber bar, which was said to be the largest bar in Europe, was destroyed by fire two years after the camp opened. The first campers were given a free bottle of champagne because the site wasn't completed. The camp closed in 1996.

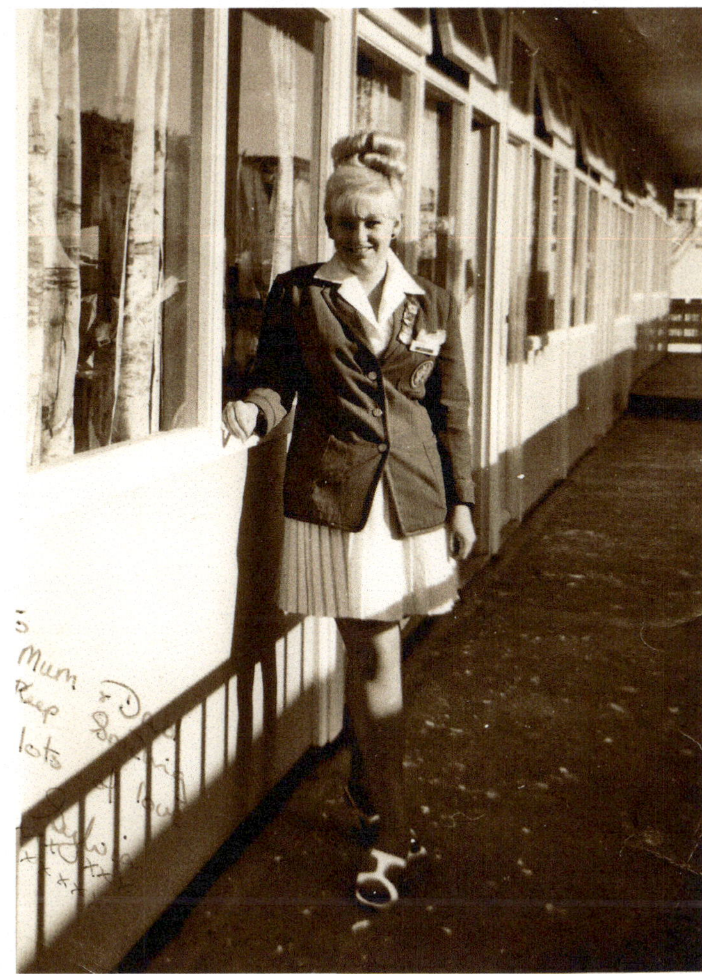

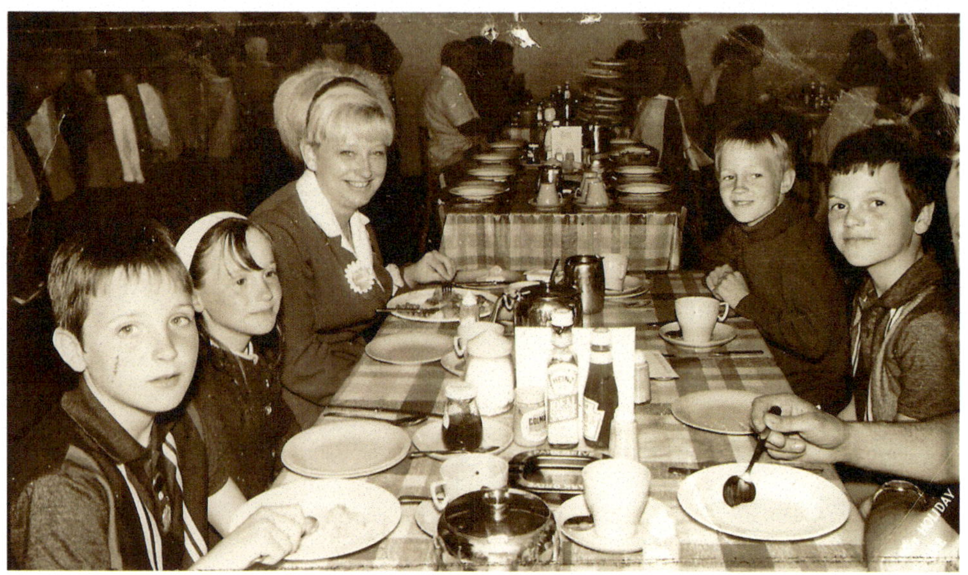

Norman Bradford became the first Redcoat after Billy Butlin asked him if there was a way to encourage more campers to join in with all the activities available. Norman was a maintenance man by day but entertained the campers by night with his stage act. One evening, he asked all campers to shake hands with the person on their right and to introduce themselves. This they did, some reluctantly, and very soon, everyone was happily chatting away to each other. Billy Butlin liked this approach and sent Norman to Skegness to purchase a bright jacket so that campers could easily recognise him. Norman returned with three blazers, bought at Allan Wildman's clothing shop, in white, yellow and blue. However, Billy wanted something brighter and different from the rest of the staff and so the 'Redcoat' was born.

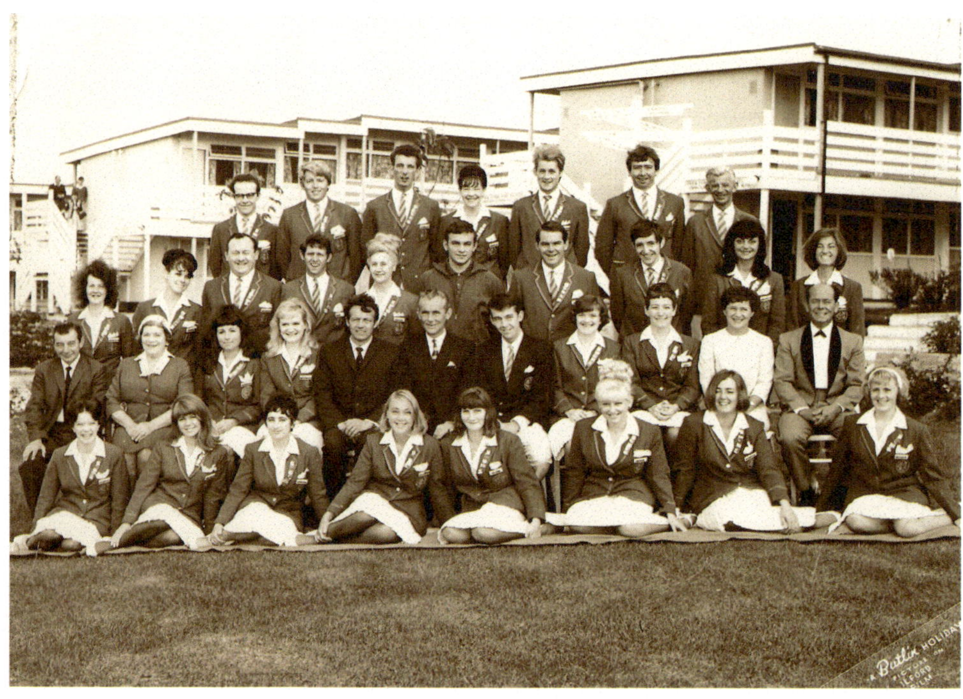

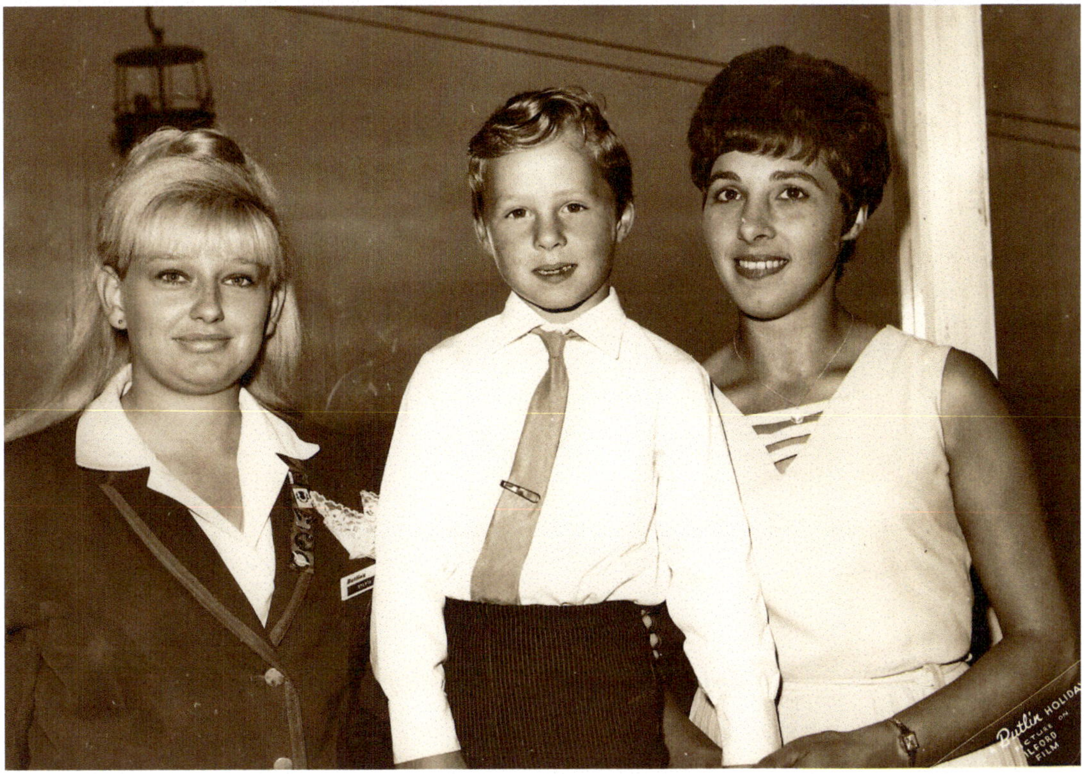

Barry Island's chairlift stretched 430 yards and opened in 1967. A total of six camps had chairlifts or cable cars including Ayr, Filey, Minehead, Pwllheli and Skegness. Some were practical and transported campers around the site while others were used solely as amusement rides. Originally called the Butlin Rope Railway, the first was opened at the Ayr camp by Eve Boswell in 1959. It proved very popular with campers and the idea soon spread to the other camps. They allowed campers to get a birds-eye view of both the camp and the surrounding countryside. The one at Pwllheli was opened in 1960 and the round trip covered one and a half miles.

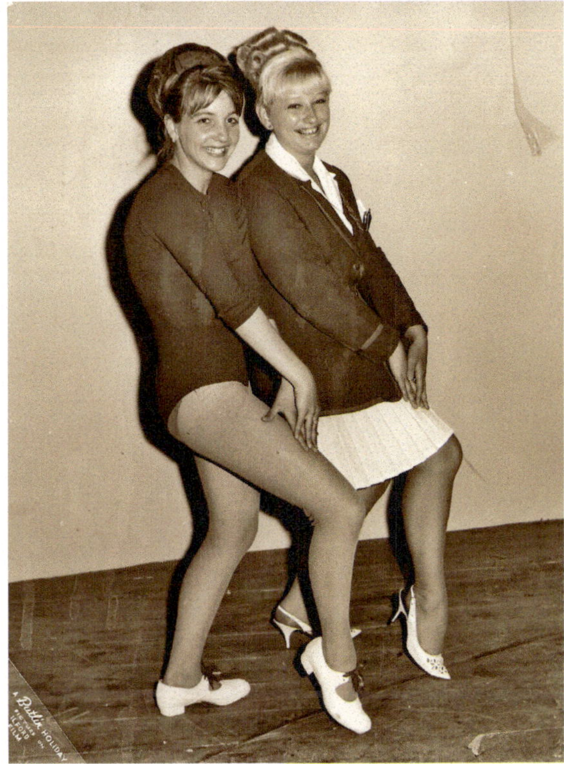

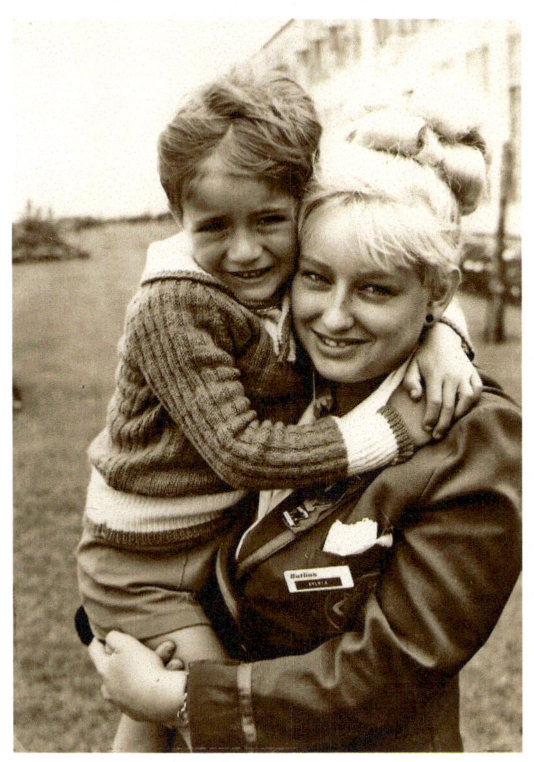

After Norman Bradford's popularity as the first Redcoat, Billy Butlin purchased more red blazers and white flannels from Allan Wildman's shop and selected ten of his friendliest and most popular staff to wear them. Their job was to encourage the campers to join in as much as possible and many games and contests were organised. Midnight hikes were popular and several hundred campers would follow Norman Bradford on a walk along the beach before setting up a huge bonfire. Musicians would also tag along and entertain everyone. A sing-song would ensue which would go on for well over an hour before campers returned to their chalets in the early morning.

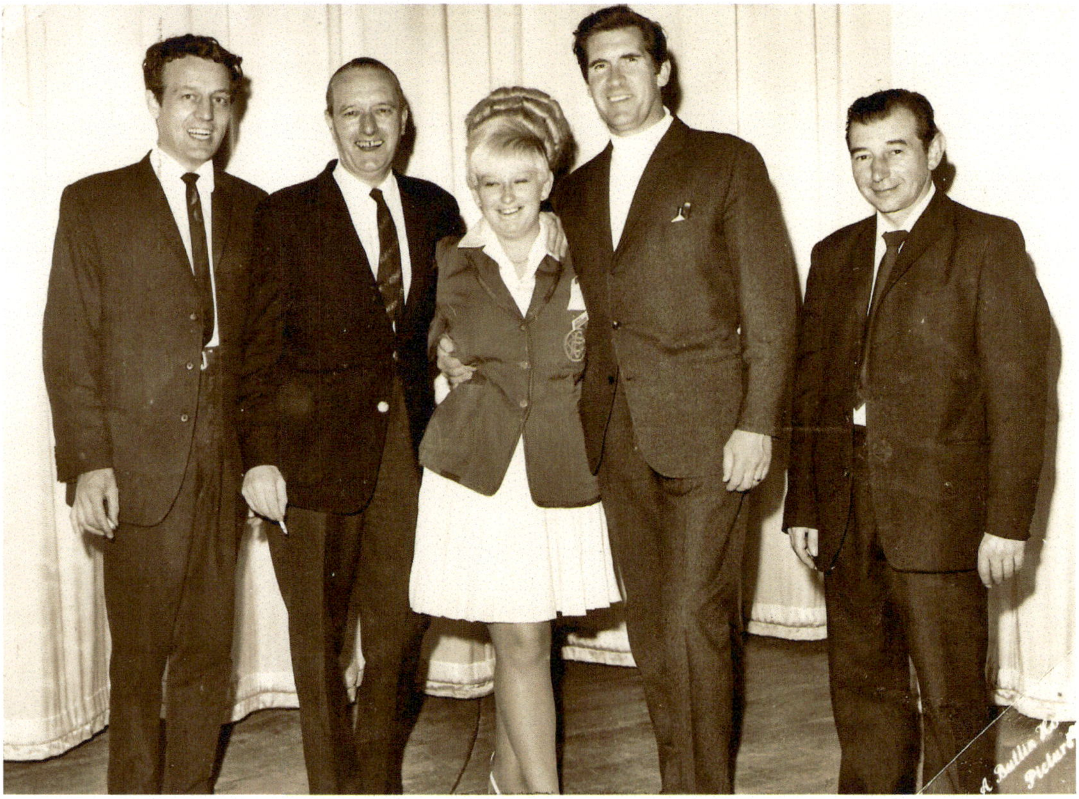

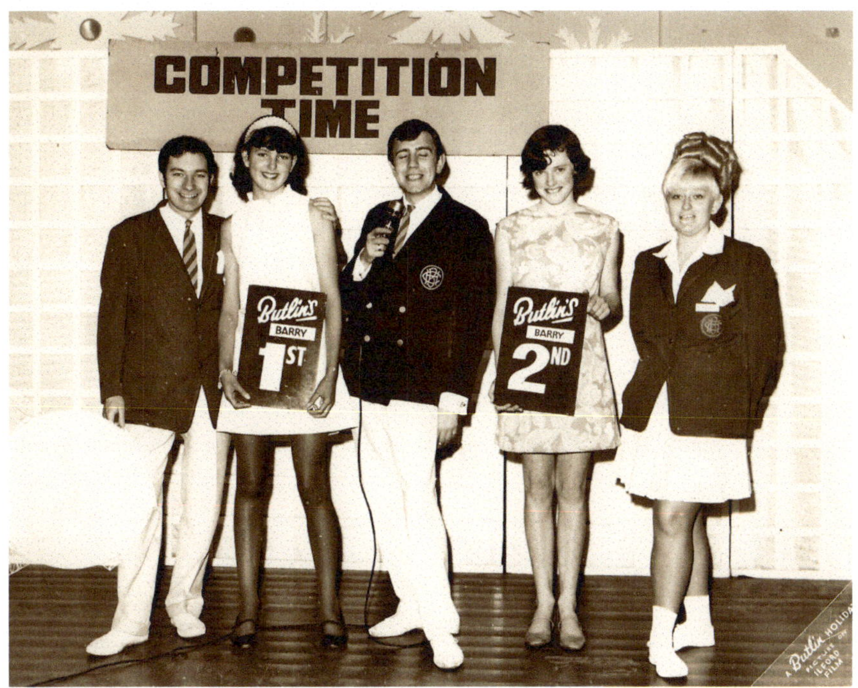

Competition Time pitted the various 'houses' within the camp to compete against each other. Sylvia Varney appears in both photographs and is representing Kent House. Campers would get together on a Sunday morning and follow the banners, carried by their allotted Redcoats, towards one of the large bars for a lunchtime concert. All sorts of competitions would be laid on and the winners would gain points for their allotted house. This made the campers quite competitive and eager to enter the many contests held throughout the week. The plan was to get everyone to join in and even the reluctant campers were encouraged to take part.

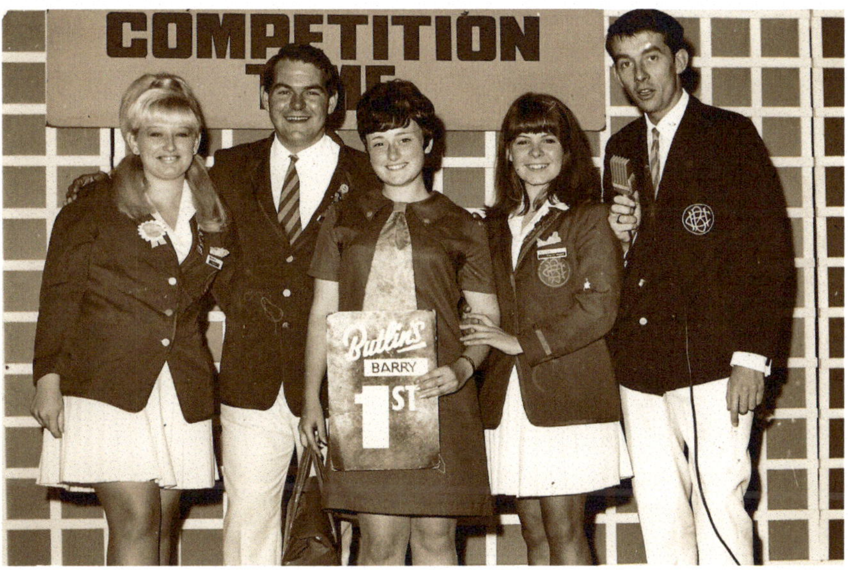

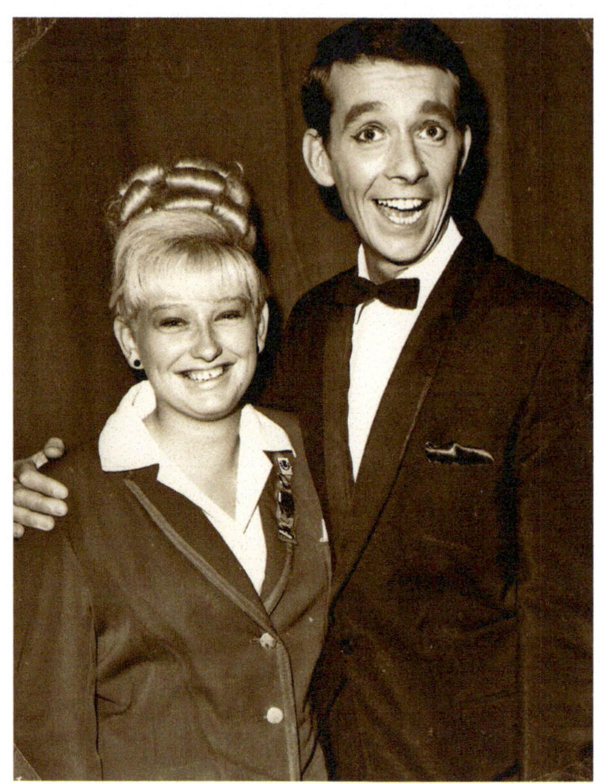

The first photograph shows Sylvia Varney at Barry with Manchester comedian, Dave Thomas. Many household names started at Butlin's. Des O'Connor was a Redcoat at Filey, Ted Rogers was a Redcoat at Butlin's Ocean Hotel at Brighton and Cliff Richard and the Drifters played in the Pig and Whistle Bar at the Clacton camp in 1958. Other Redcoats who would later become famous included Charlie Drake, Roy Hudd, Dave Allen, Freddie 'Parrotface' Davies, Isla St Clair, Russell Grant, Jimmy Tarbuck, Rod Hull and Michael Barrymore. Glenda Jackson worked as a waitress at the coffee bar at Filey. Rory Storm and the Hurricanes, featuring Ringo Starr, played at Butlin's in Pwllheli in 1960 before taking their act to Skegness.

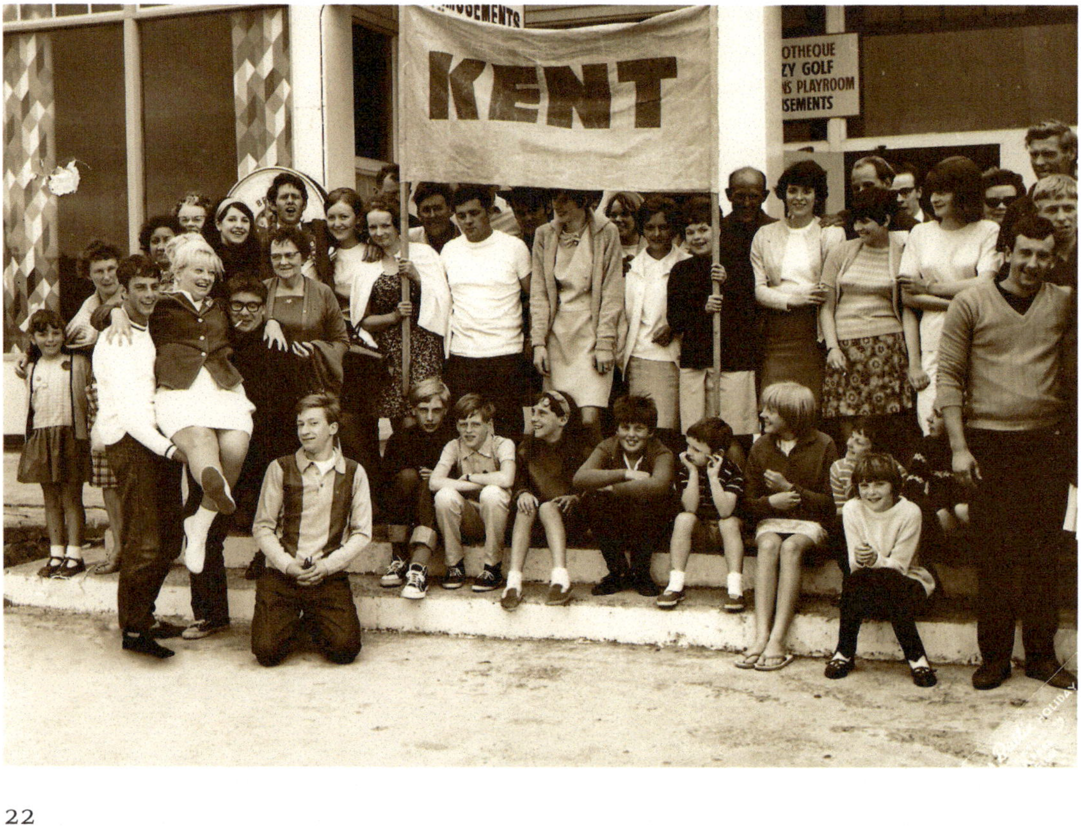

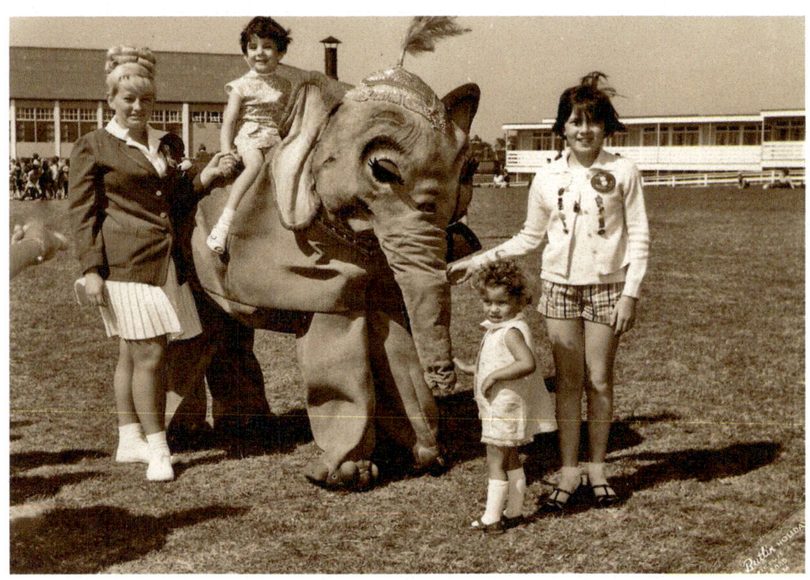

The top photograph shows a pantomime elephant, which proved very popular with the children at Barry. A real elephant, called Charlie, was bought by Billy Butlin from Craigend Zoo who couldn't afford his upkeep. Charlie was described as the biggest bull elephant in captivity. Charlie, along with his keeper, Shaik Ibrahim, became a big hit with campers at Ayr. The camp was considered too small for him so, in 1957, Charlie was moved 300 miles to the camp at Filey. It was a difficult operation transporting an elephant from one camp to the other and on the morning that he arrived, he was greeted by the camp mayor, in full regalia, together with hundreds of children waving Union Jacks.

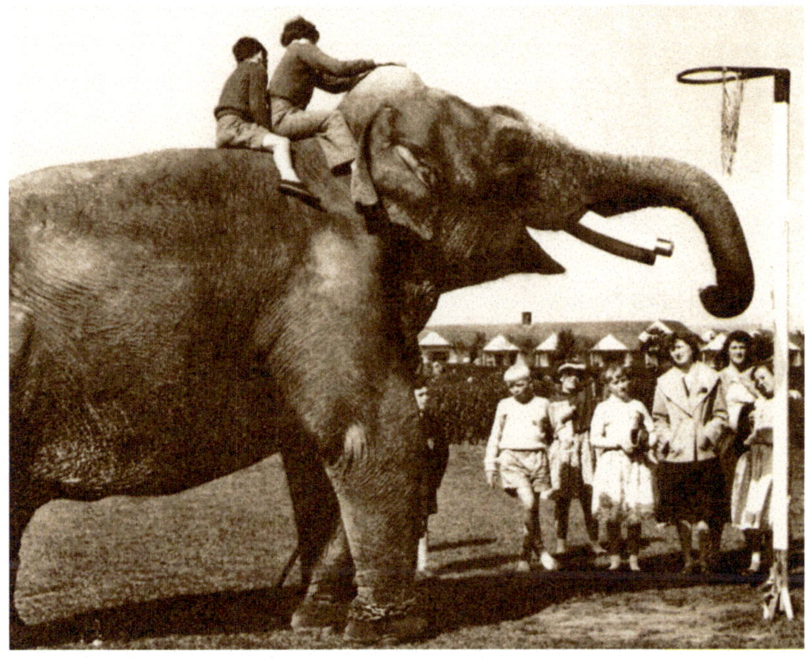

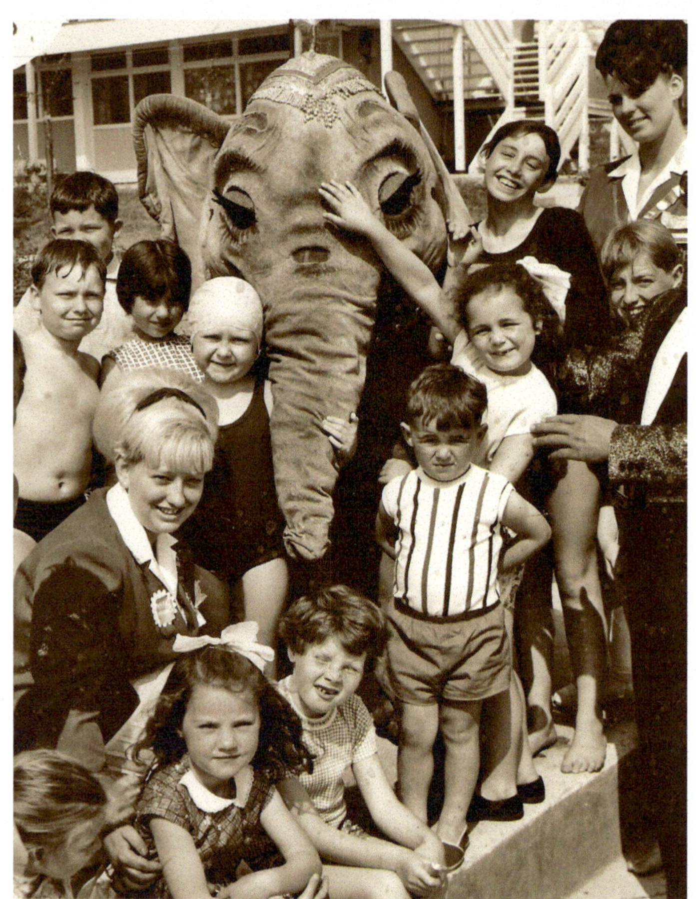

The pantomime elephant in the top photograph had two people inside operating it. Charlie the elephant, on the previous page, and his trainer, Shaik Ibrahim, were inseparable. When Ibrahim became ill and died, Charlie grieved so much that the RSPCA had to put him down. During the 1960s, Billy Butlin bought another elephant called Gertrude from London Zoo. Gertrude arrived at the camp at Pwllheli but proved difficult to handle (she would run through the camp, trumpeting, with her trainer running behind her) and was moved to the Skegness camp where there was an elephant trainer. Unfortunately, Gertrude had a heart attack in the swimming pool while being washed and died.

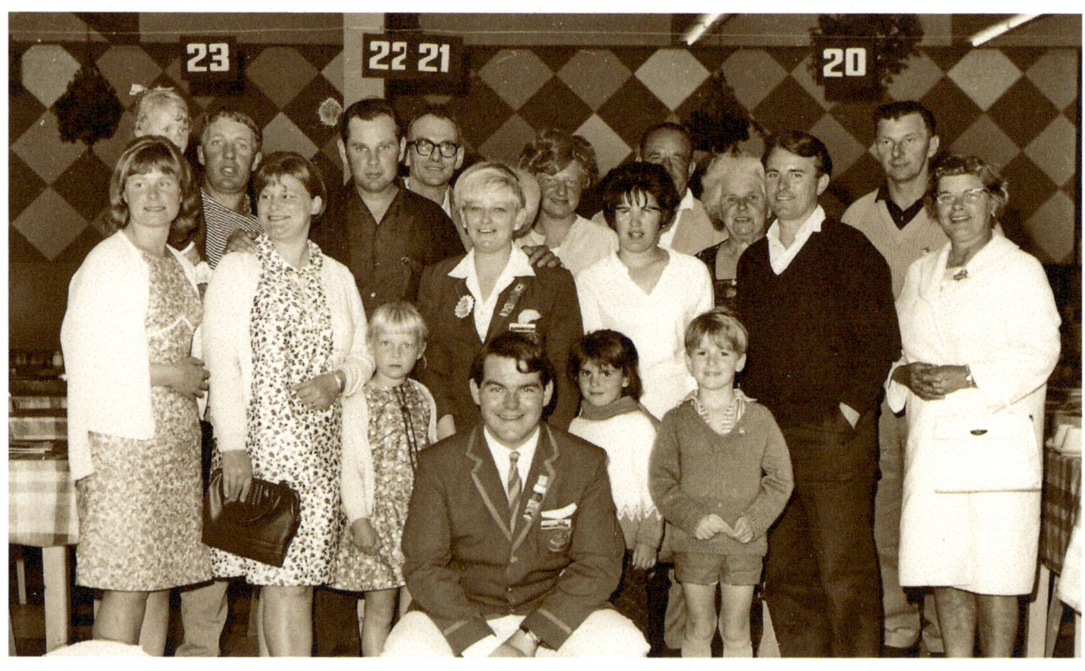

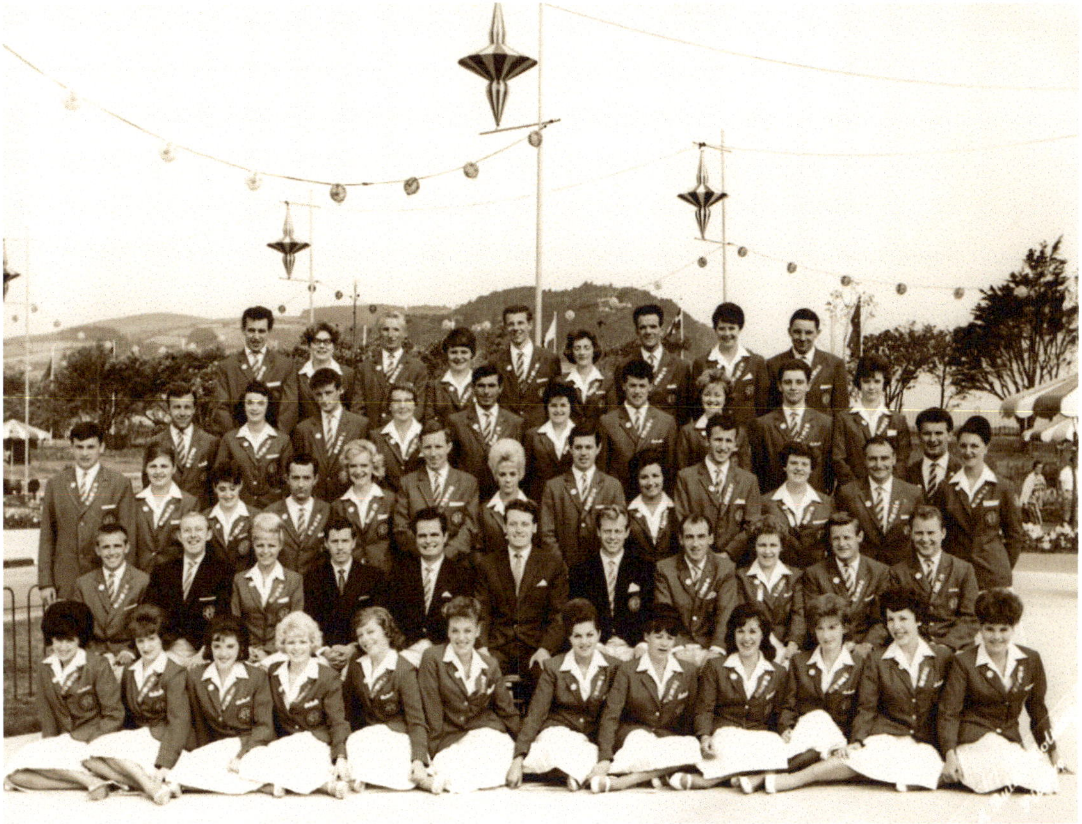

Billy Butlin also had lions on his amusement sites and would drive his Austin Seven around the camp at Skegness with a lion cub on the back seat. One lion, called Rex, was due to be transported from Skegness to the Butlin's zoo at Bognor. Rex was mistakenly not loaded onto the lorry and when it arrived without him, a local newspaper reported, 'Butlin's Lion on the Loose'. There was much press coverage and the Territorial Army joined the hunt as local people panicked. This went on for several days and, when it was discovered that Rex was still at Skegness, Billy Butlin, the reporter at the local paper and a farmer who claimed the lion had attacked his sheep, were all charged with 'conspiracy to commit a public mischief by certain false statements that a lion had escaped'. It had all been great publicity. Billy Butlin was found not guilty although the reporter was fined £30 for exaggerating the story.

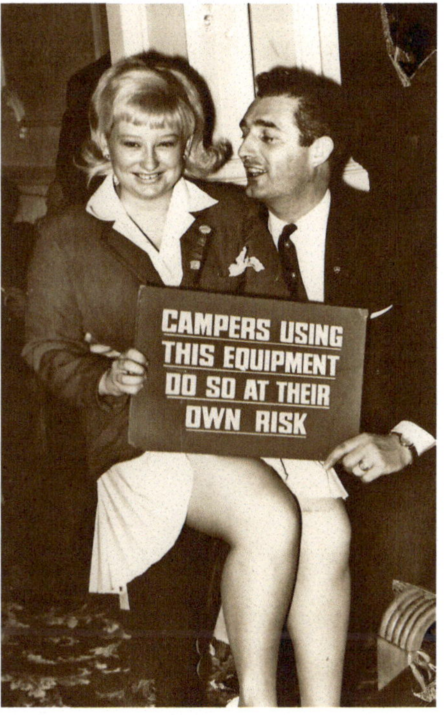

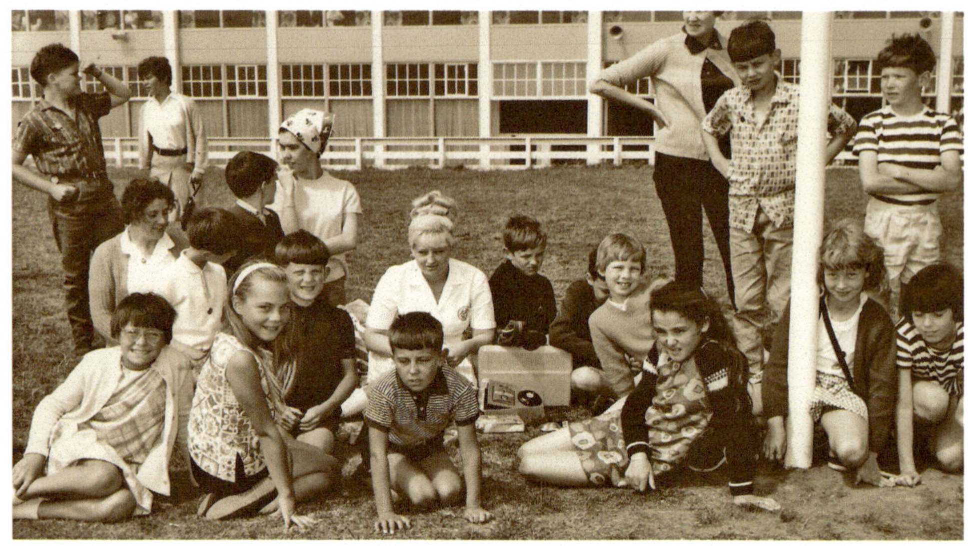

Children's entertainment at Butlin's included a full programme of shows and competitions including the Bonny Baby Contest, fancy dress competitions and square dance instruction. The Beaver Club was for children up to twelve years old and, later, there were other clubs such as the 913 Club for children between nine and thirteen years old, Whizzkids for children between the ages of six and nine and Teamsters for children aged between nine and twelve. Entertainment also included a daily Punch and Judy show and regular magic shows. Children's activities at Pwllheli in 1955 included team games, a boat trip to Seal Island, Junior Cinema, Panto Time, Grand March Past, Exercise to Music, Fun with Uncle George, the Boating Regatta, a Scavenger Hunt, Playtime in the Nursery, Children's Television, Treasure Hunt and a Junior Concert.

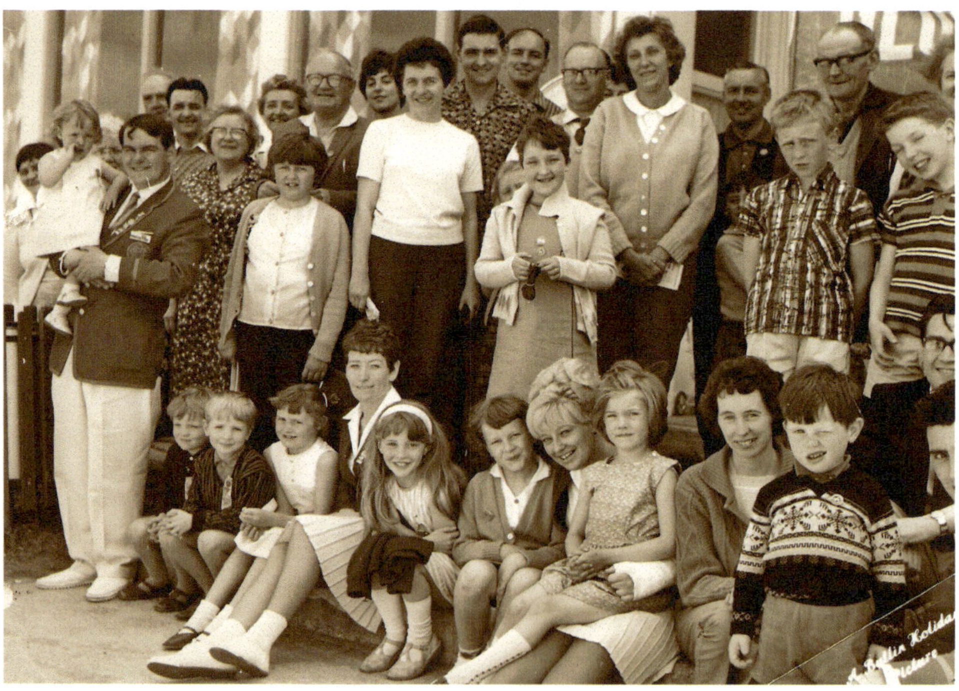

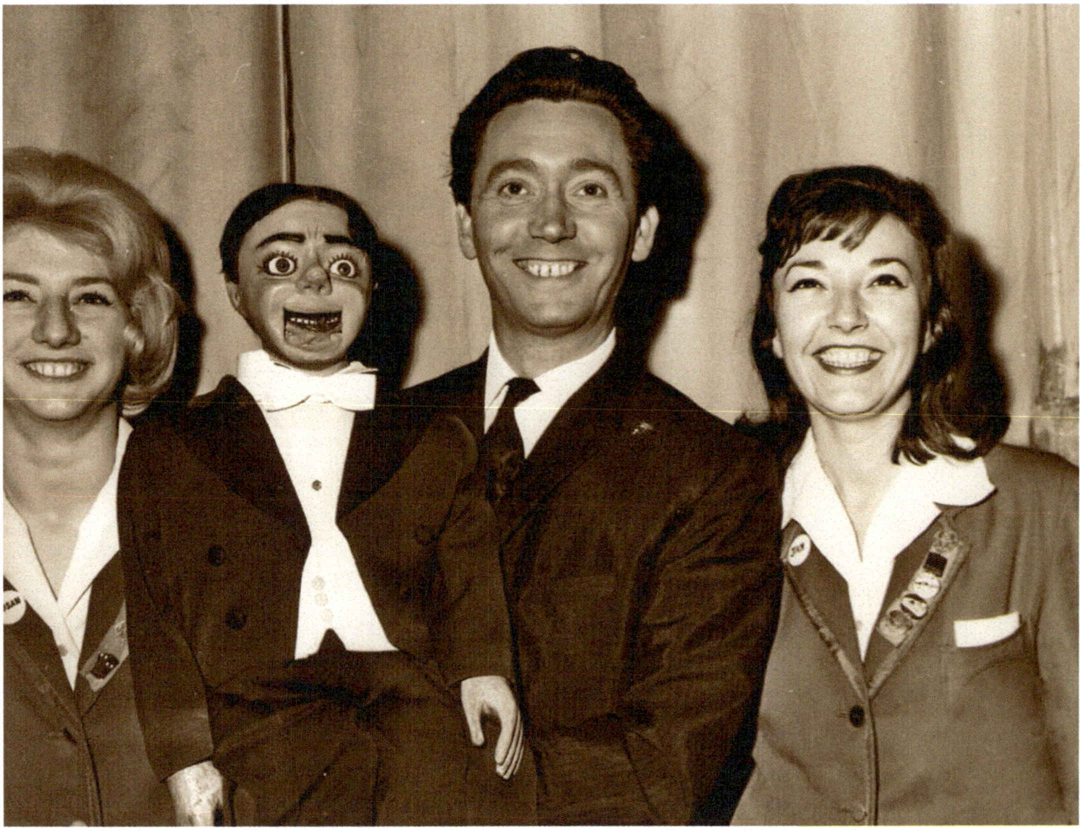

Ventriloquist acts proved very popular not only with children but also with adults at Butlin's. The top photograph shows Arthur Worsley with Redcoats Val and Heather at the Sunday Night Variety Show at the Gaiety Theatre. Worsley's dummy was called Charlie Brown and it would turn and look at him and say, 'Look at me, son, when I'm talking to you' and would regularly insult his owner. Worsley appeared on most popular British variety television shows and also appeared on the Ed Sullivan show in America with Sullivan commenting that he was 'the world's greatest ventriloquist'. The bottom photograph shows the very popular Ken Wood who was a Redcoat at both Skegness and Filey before he turned professional. He featured on both television and in theatres around the country.

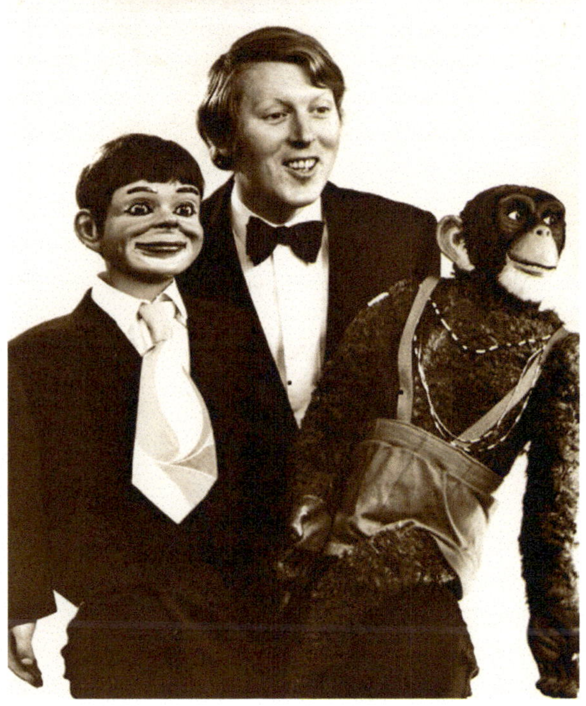

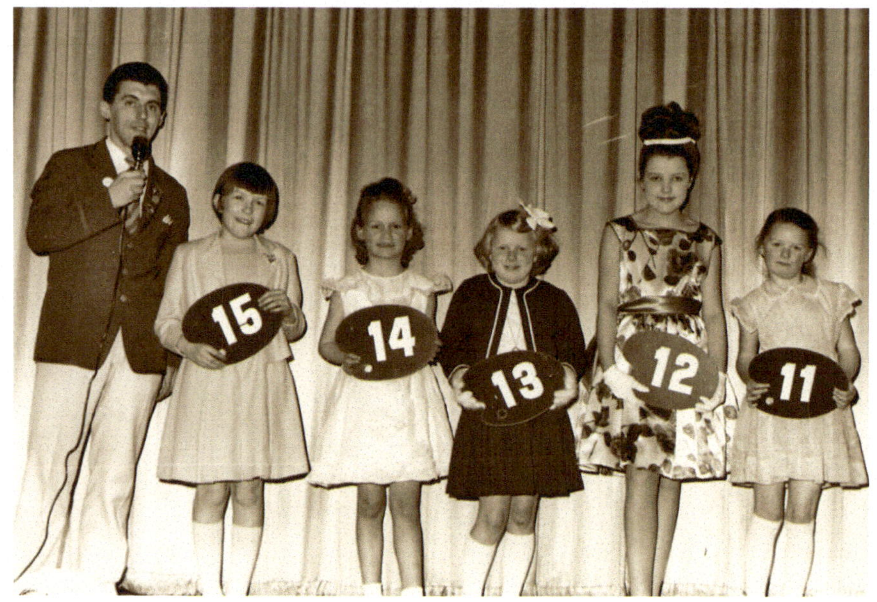

Children loved Butlin's and there was so much for them to do there. As well as the many competitions, there was also the Beaver Club with its regular shows. Funfair rides included the ever popular dodgems which were brought to Britain by Billy Butlin in 1928 and used at his funfair site at Skegness. He bought his first dodgems from an American manufacturer for £2,000 and they proved to be hugely successful. Butlin went on to acquire the sole rights for supplying dodgems this side of the Atlantic. News of their popularity spread and very soon, he had sold hundreds of the little cars all over Europe.

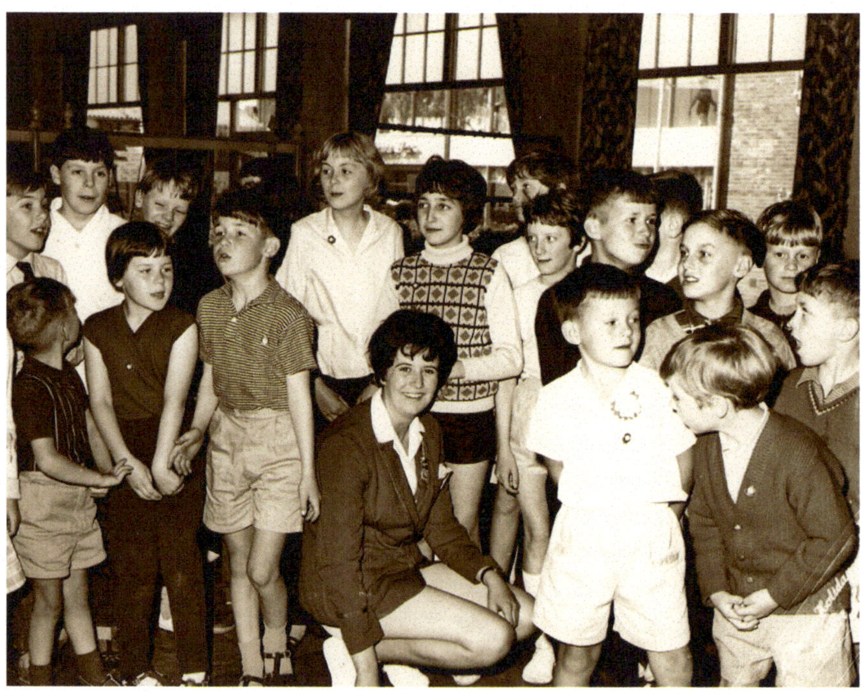

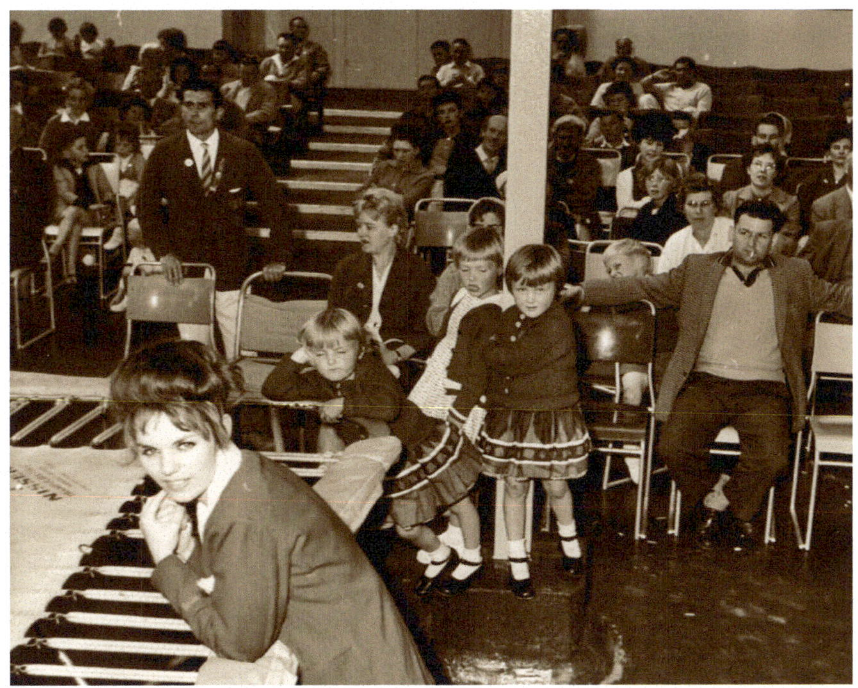

On days when it rained, many of the indoor activities would become very popular, including bouncing up and down on the trampoline. These activities are commonplace for children nowadays, but back in the 1960s, if you were a child, the only time you were likely to go on one was either at school or at Butlin's. Redcoats would adjust the day's entertainment if the weather was predicted to be bad. Films would be shown and extra entertainment would take place in the ballroom. Other popular indoor entertainment included ping pong, darts, billiards and snooker.

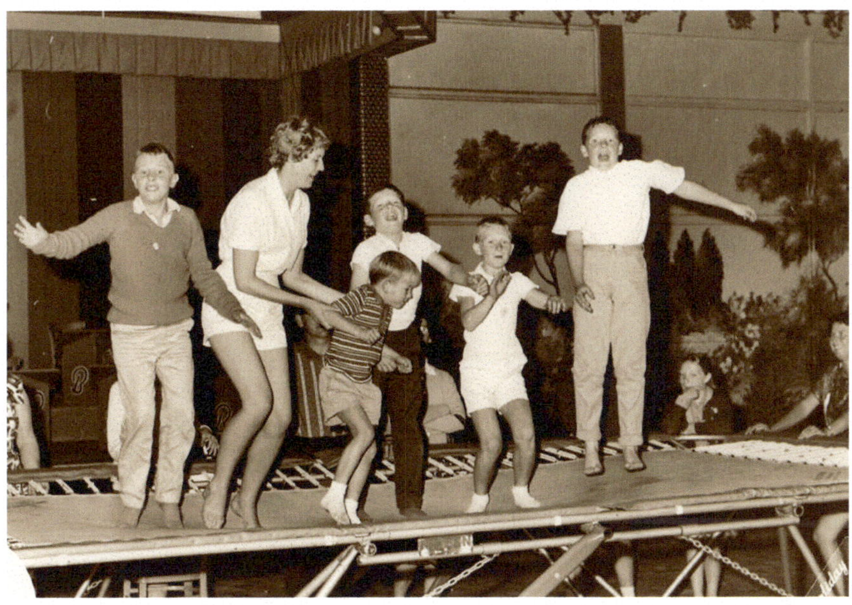

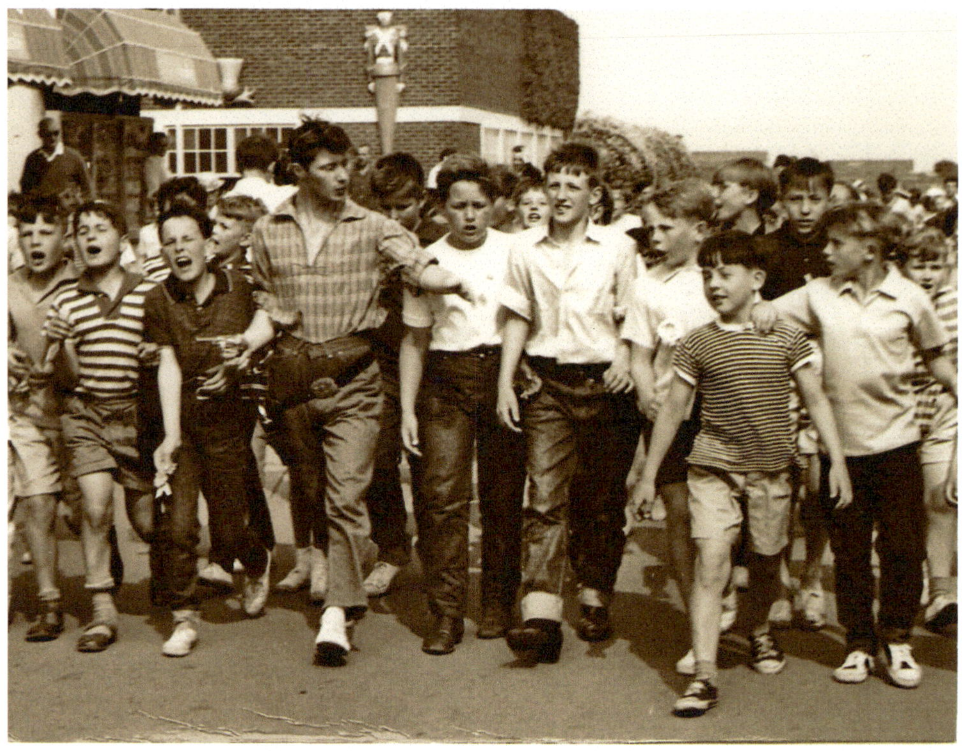

The top photograph shows members of the Beaver Club searching for 'Chief Running Bear'. In the 1950s, 1960s and early 1970s, Westerns were incredibly popular on the television and at the cinema so getting members of the Beaver Club to form a posse, while a Redcoat dressed as a cowboy, was very exciting. Trying to locate Chief Running Bear, also a Redcoat, and taking him to the pool before chucking him in, added greatly to the excitement. In later years, the children would gather to track down 'Captain Blood' and, again, his fate would be to end up in the pool.

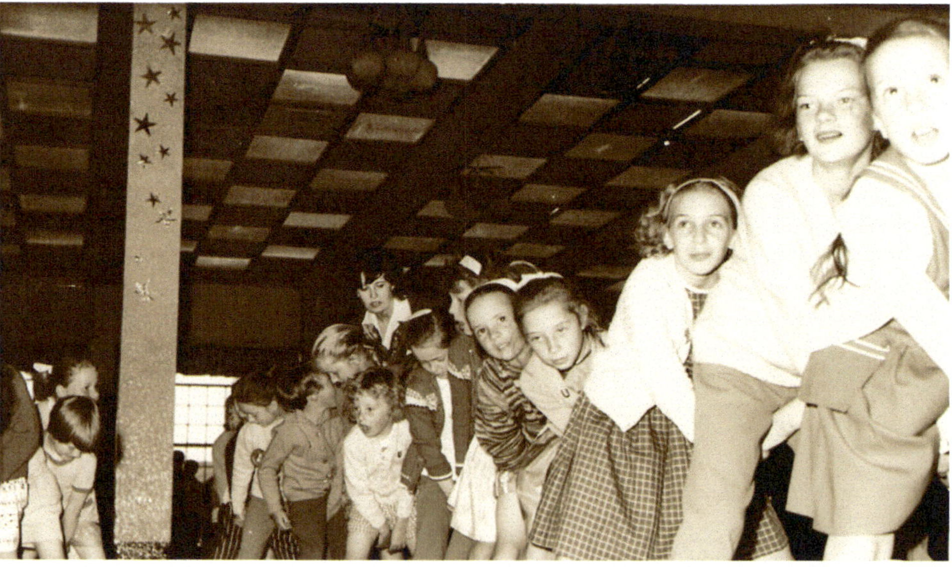

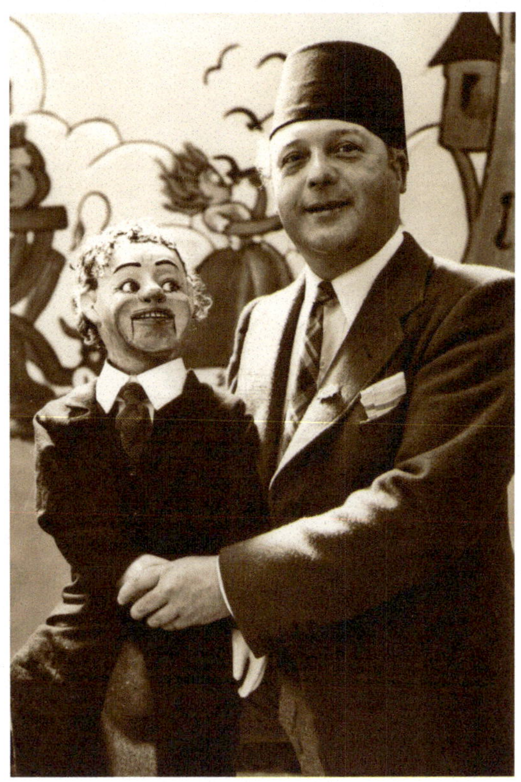

Uncle Boko can be seen in the top photograph complete with a ventriloquist doll. He was very popular with both children and adults. Even his closest friends knew him only as Uncle Boko although his real name was Frank Keep. He worked at the Skegness camp for twenty-one years and was proud in later years to be entertaining the children of parents who he had entertained as children themselves many years before. He was always the professional and put on excellent shows for the children. He was also 'Master of Ceremonies' at all the children's competitions.

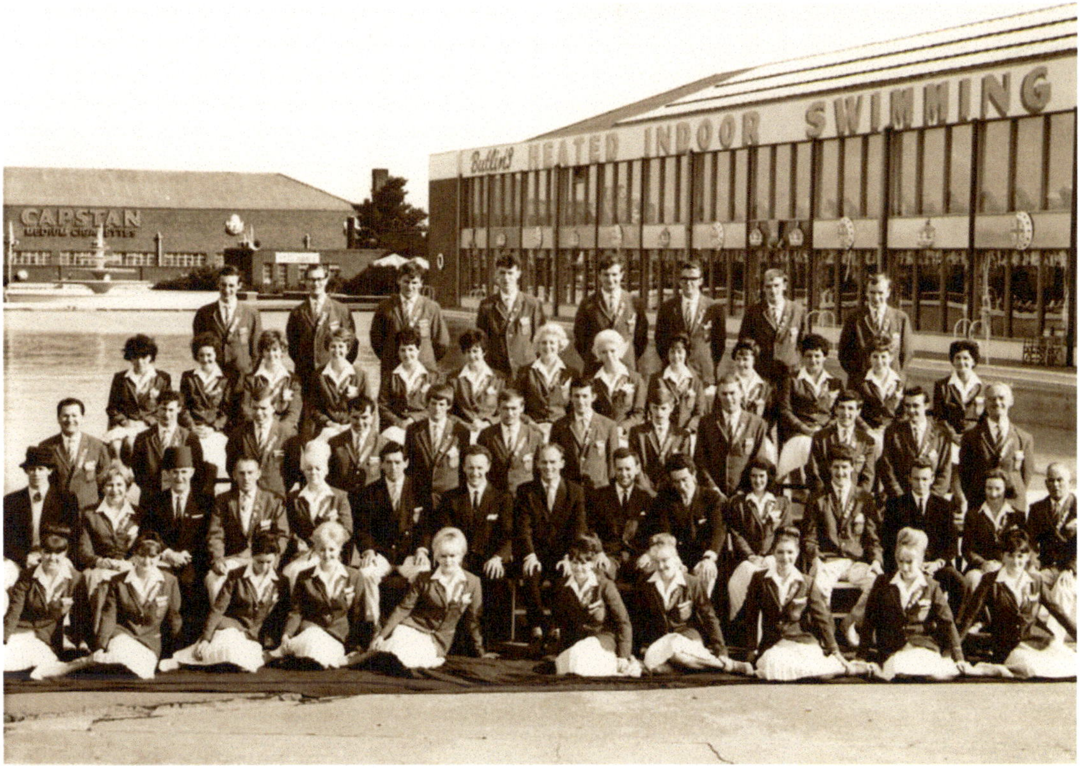

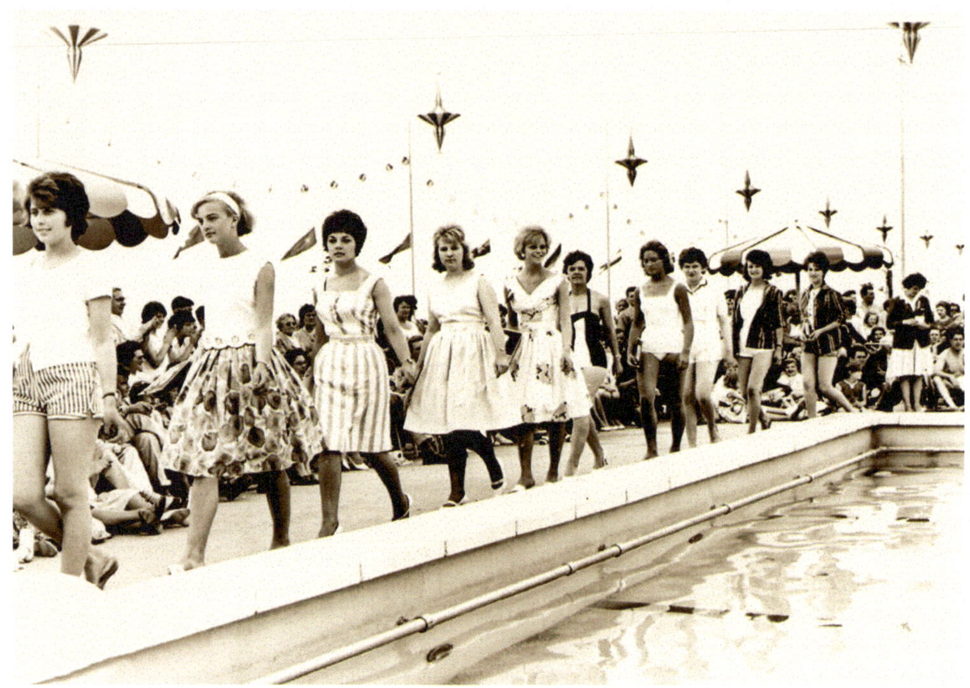

A beauty pageant takes place around the pool in the top photograph. The 'Miss She Competition' was billed as a contest for 'ladies in day wear' and became very popular in all of the camps and attracted thousands of entrants. Ladies from eighteen to eighty took part in the weekly contests and entries grew steadily to over 10,000 a year. The winner in 1964 was Ann Sidney who also won the Miss World Contest in the same year. In the second photograph, Lou, the Skegness camp comic, lines up the competitors in the Holiday Princess Competition of 1962.

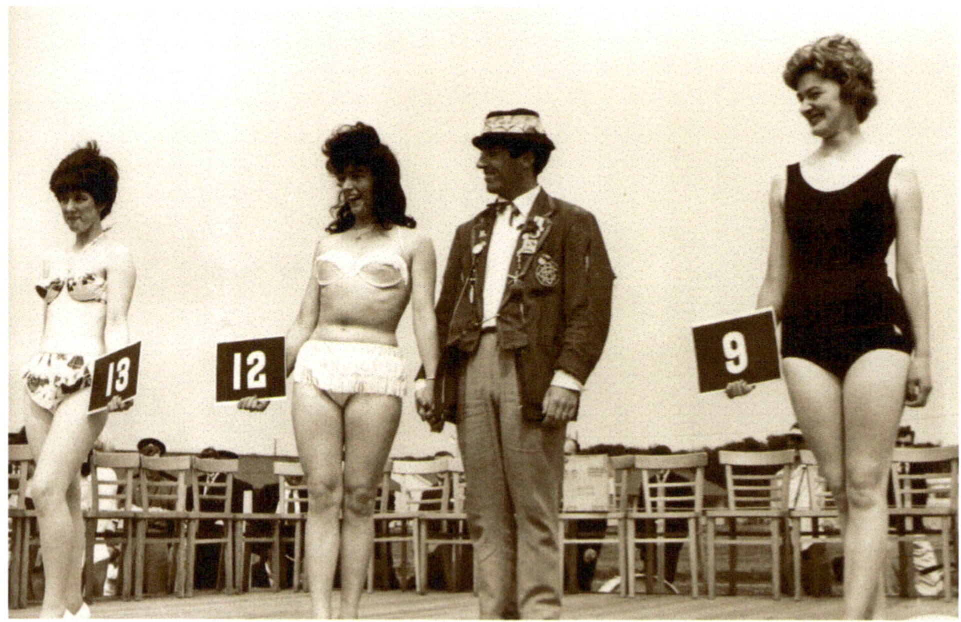

Nursery care was provided on all sites so that children could be looked after while their parents were elsewhere. An evening chalet patrol was also operated while their parents enjoyed the on-site entertainment. Nurses listened out for any distressed babies or young children within the chalets and a message was relayed over the tannoy if a baby was crying. Stories are told of comedians, just about to deliver the punch line to jokes, who were interrupted by announcements over the tannoy such as, 'Baby crying in chalet R52!'

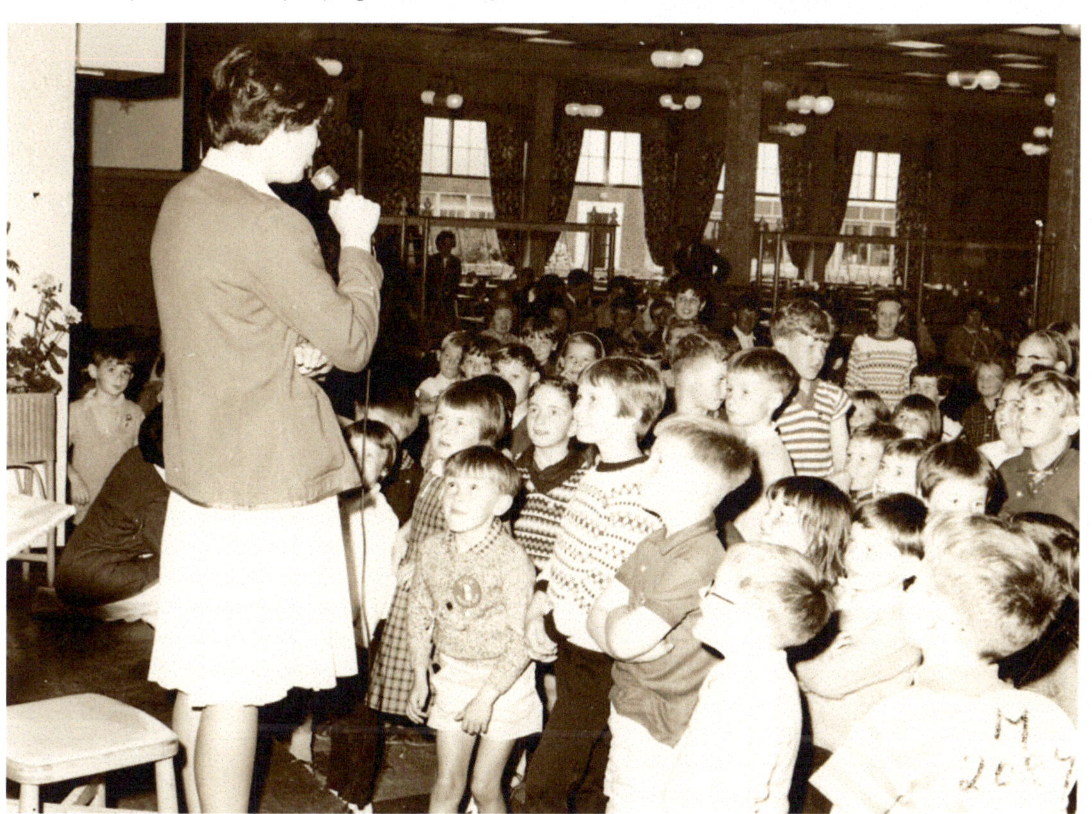

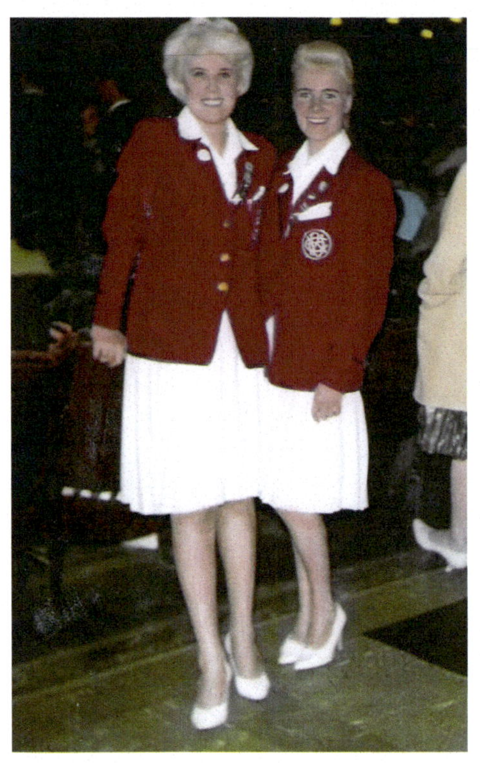

Both photographs show Redcoats at Skegness in the 1960s. The first photograph shows Redcoats Doreen Shaw (née Barker) and Pat. The second photograph shows Redcoats Doreen, Larry and Tina. In the background of the second photograph is one of the soldiers at the entrance to the Skegness camp. Never one to miss a bargain, Billy Butlin bought up a selection of old Christmas lights, previously used on shops in London, and used them to decorate several of the camps.

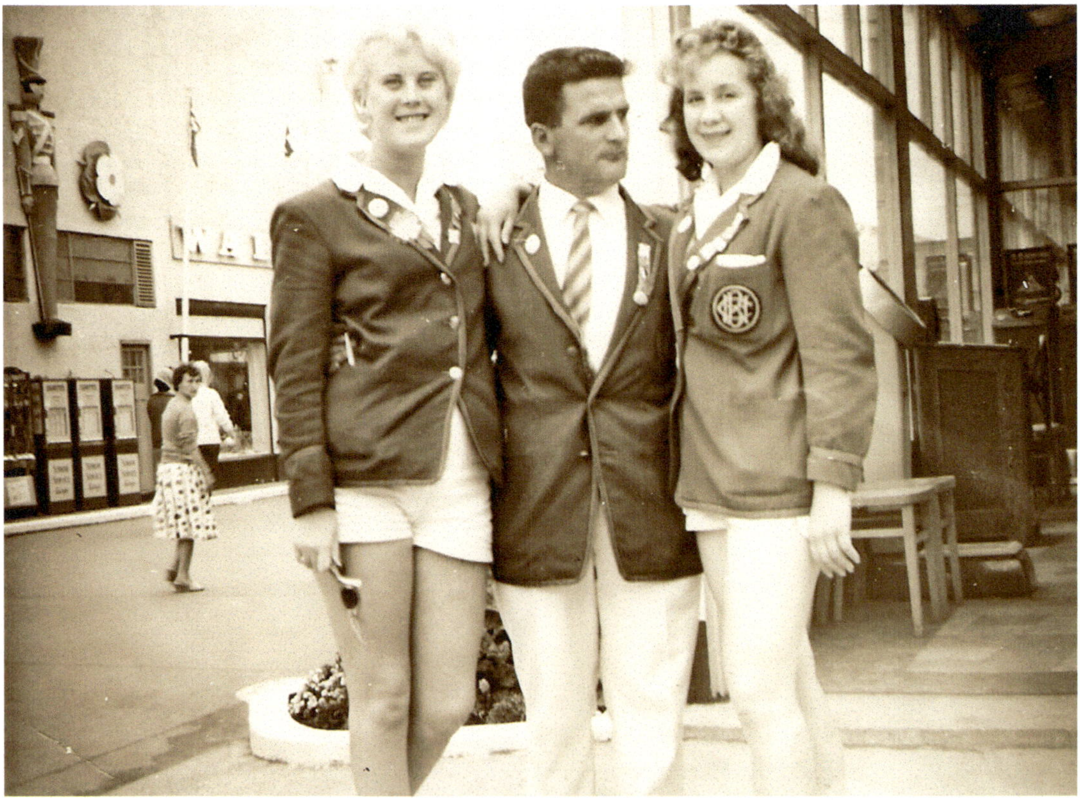

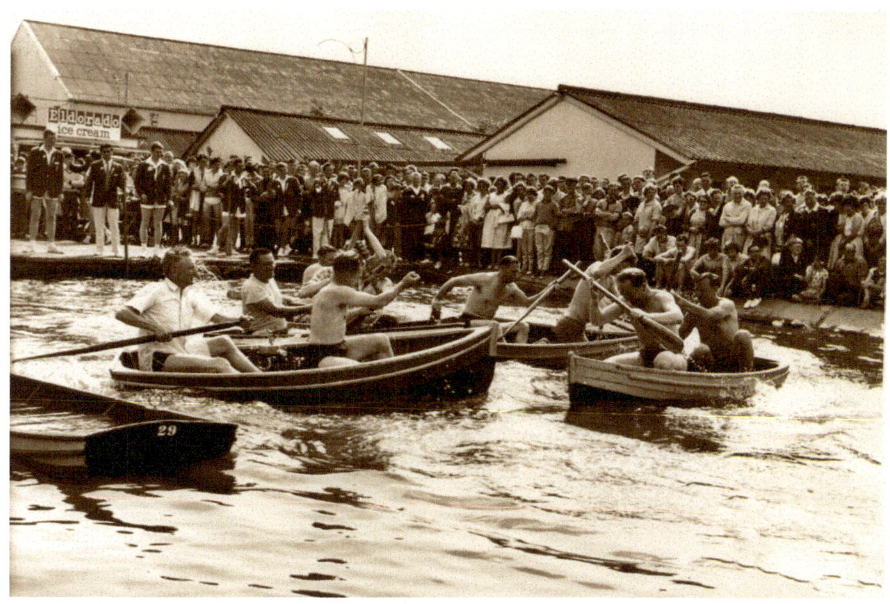

The boating lake was very popular in all of the camps and was used for leisurely rowing and also for inter-house competitions such as the one shown in the top photograph, taken at Skegness in 1963. The boating regatta was very popular. The lake was included as part of the programme of children's entertainment. It would open at 9 a.m. in the morning and other attractions were staggered throughout the day, with the skating rink and the indoor pool opening at 10 a.m. and the amusement park opening at 11 a.m. A film would be shown in the Empire Theatre in the afternoon. The second photograph shows Redcoats posing for the camp photographer at Skegness in 1963.

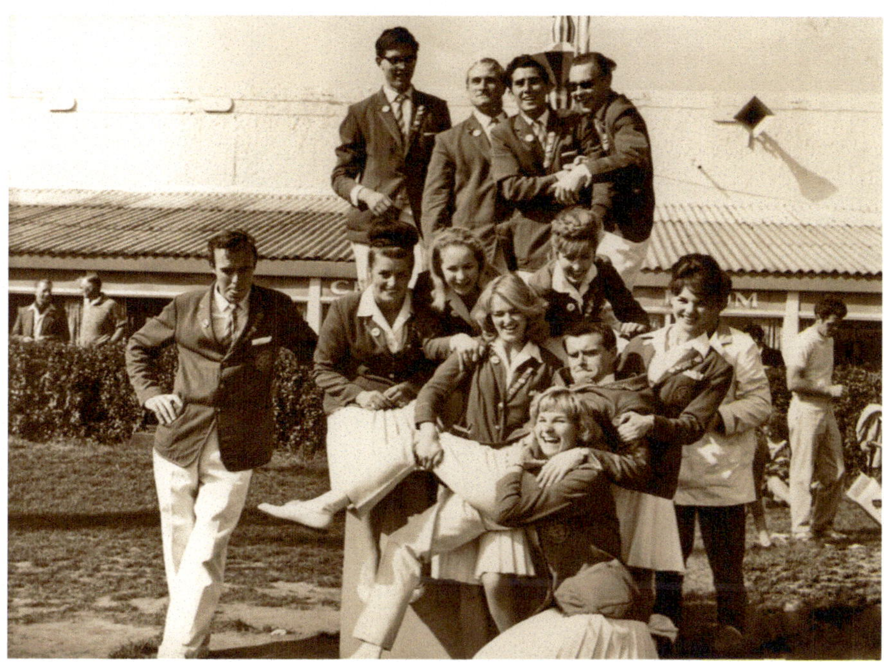

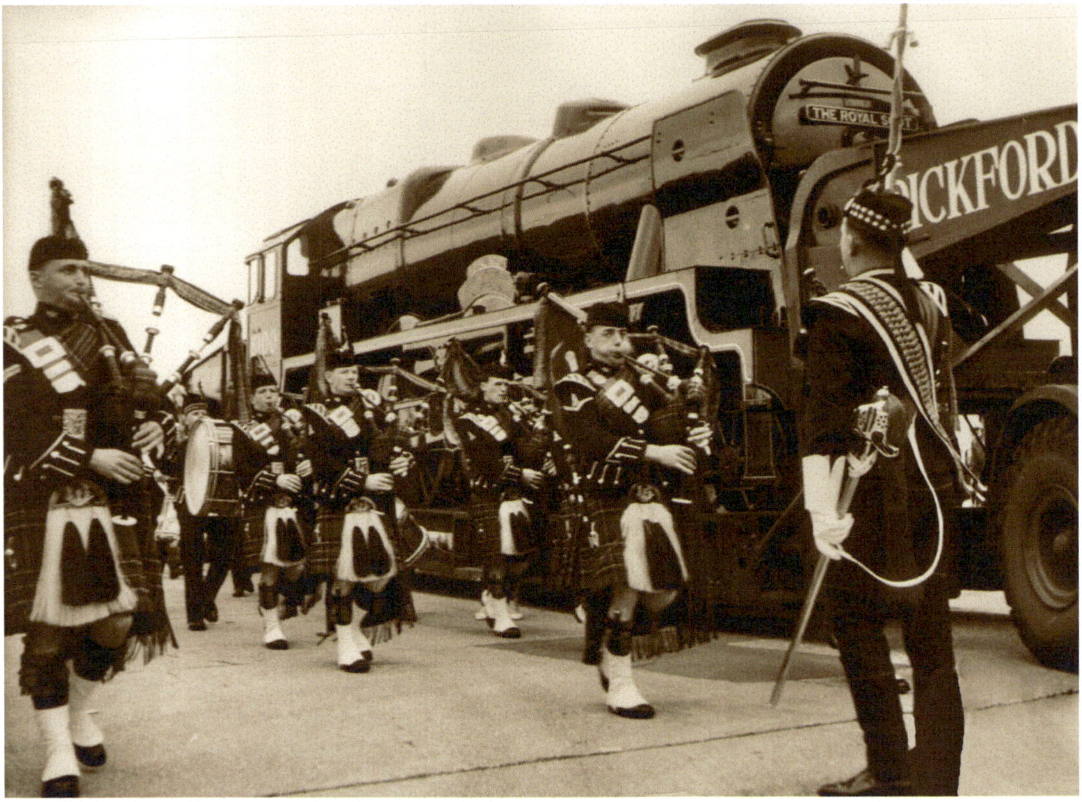

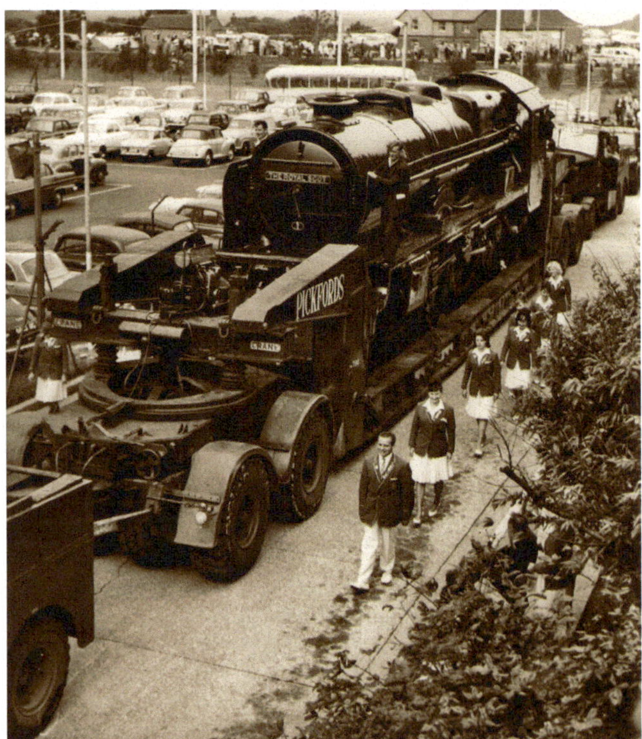

In 1963, several steam locomotives were displayed on-site and Redcoats would arrange for groups of children to see then up close. The trains included the Duchess of Hamilton which was displayed at Minehead, the Duchess of Sutherland which appeared at Ayr, the Royal Scot which was stationed at Skegness and the Princess Margaret Rose which appeared at Pwllheli. The Royal Scot is seen welcomed to Skegness by Scots pipers and drummers. Although a great draw for young children, trains suffered from the effects of salt air and were removed from camps between 1970 and 1974.

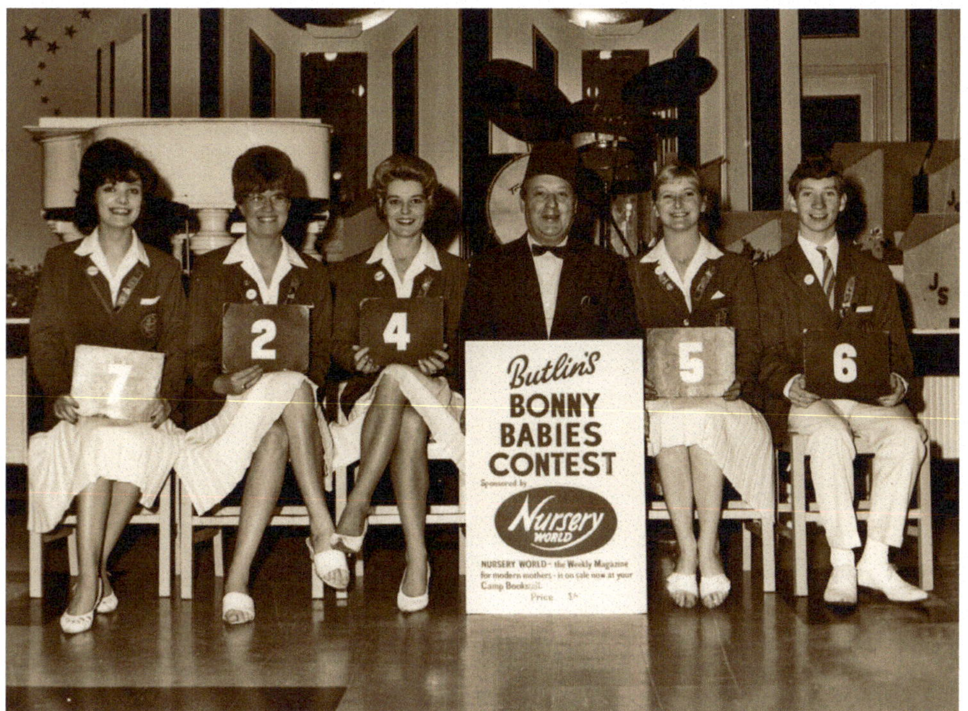

Uncle Boko, complete with fez, can be seen in the top photograph taking part in the Bonny Babies Competition. The contest was sponsored by *Nursery World* which was a weekly magazine for 'modern' mothers. The photograph shows Uncle Boko's Redcoat Aunties and Uncles team who entertained the juniors and Beavers at Skegness in 1961. The second photograph shows Redcoat Andy King being helped out of the pool by Auntie Betty at Skegness in 1962 after being thrown in by the Beavers.

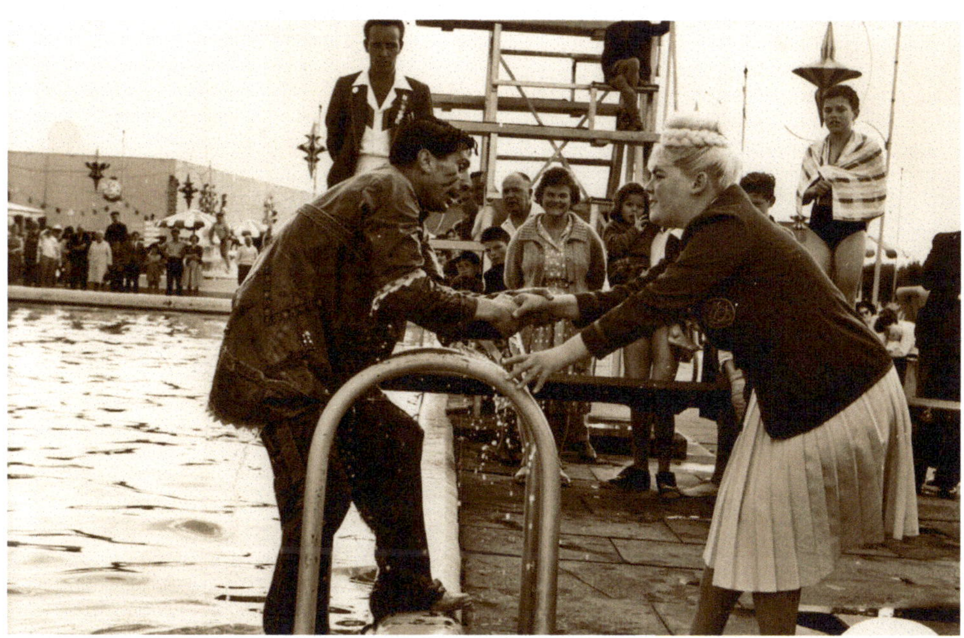

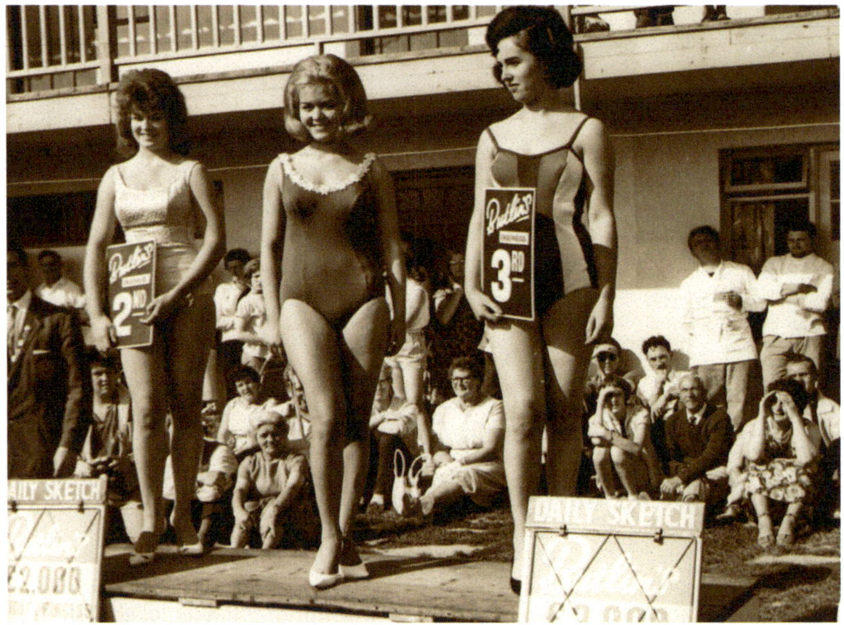

The top photograph shows the 1st, 2nd and 3rd winners in the Holiday Princess Competition at Skegness in 1963. The *Daily Sketch* advertises the top prize as £2,000 in both photographs. There were many sponsors of the competition over the years. Apart from the *Daily Sketch* there was also *Chrysler, Weekend Magazine*, Babycham, the Ford Motor Company, the Austin Motor Company and Southern Comfort. The Royal Marines became involved in the competition in 1979 until it ended in the late 1990s. During those years, the winner of the Holiday Princess Competition would be invited to become Miss Globe and Laurel, the Royal Marines pin-up, and would visit troops all over the world. The competition ended in 1997.

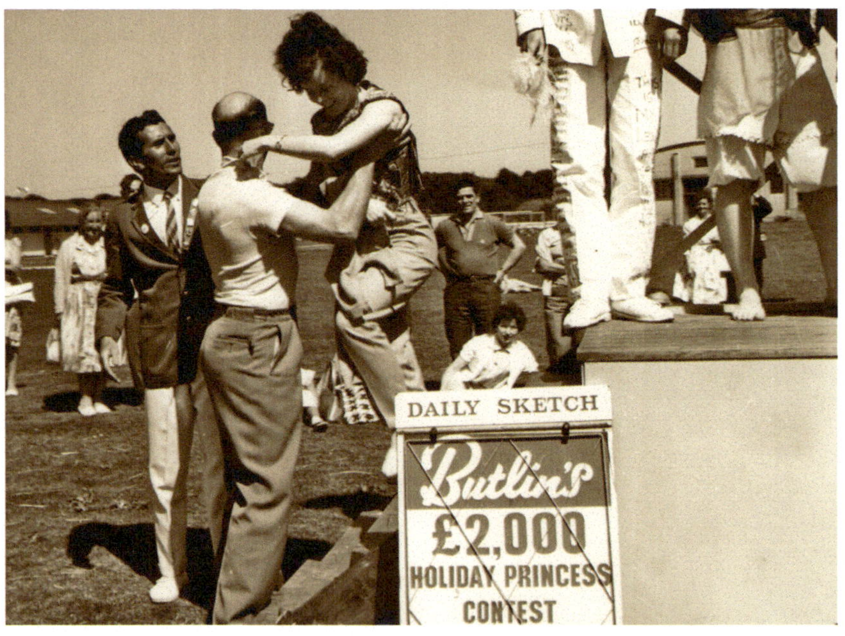

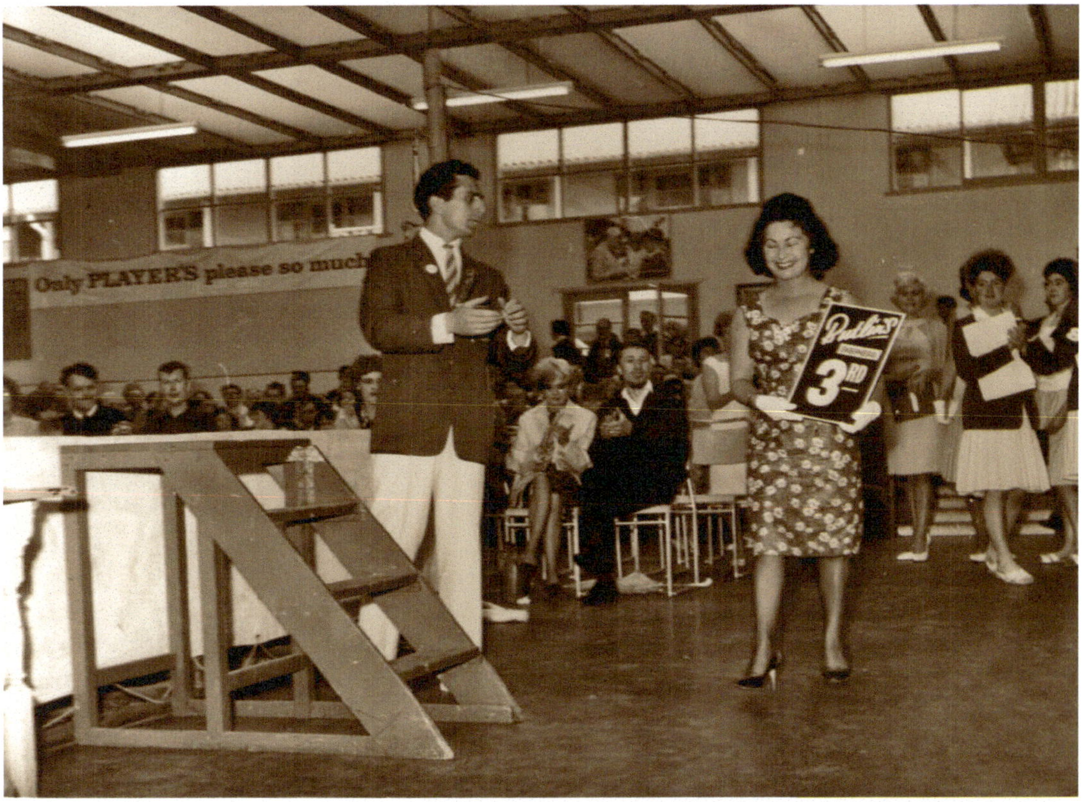

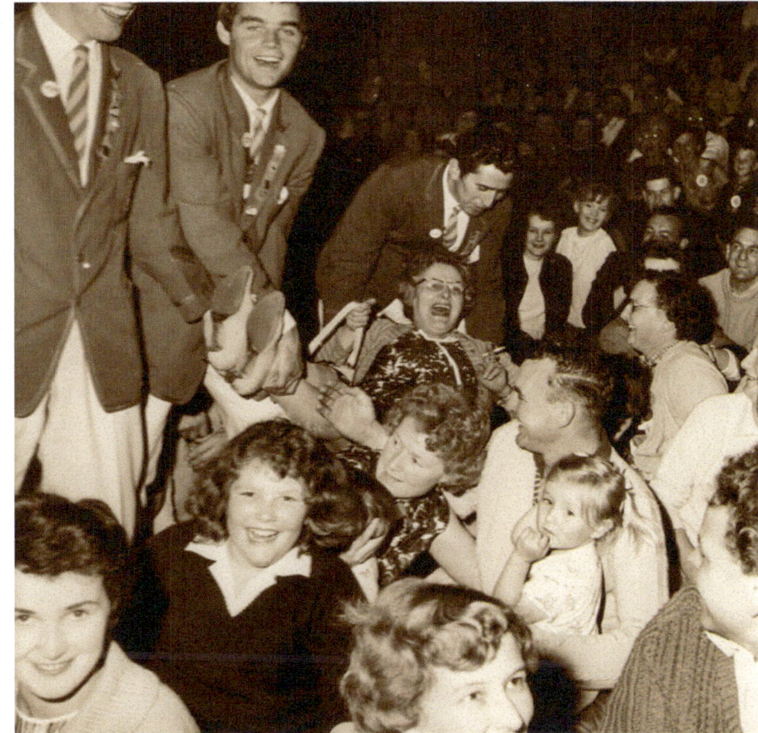

The top photograph shows Redcoat Andy King at the Glamorous Grandmother Competition at Skegness in 1963. By 1975, the top prize for winning the Glamorous Grandmother Competition was £1,000 in cash together with a holiday to the Seychelles. In the bottom photograph, Redcoats encourage a reluctant camper to enter the contest. During the 1970s and 1980s, the competition attracted over 10,000 entries a year. In 1995, the competition was renamed, the 'Super Gran Competition' and two years later, the competition came to an end although it was, for a short time, resurrected by Grand Hotels Ltd who purchased the Butlin's Hotels in 1999.

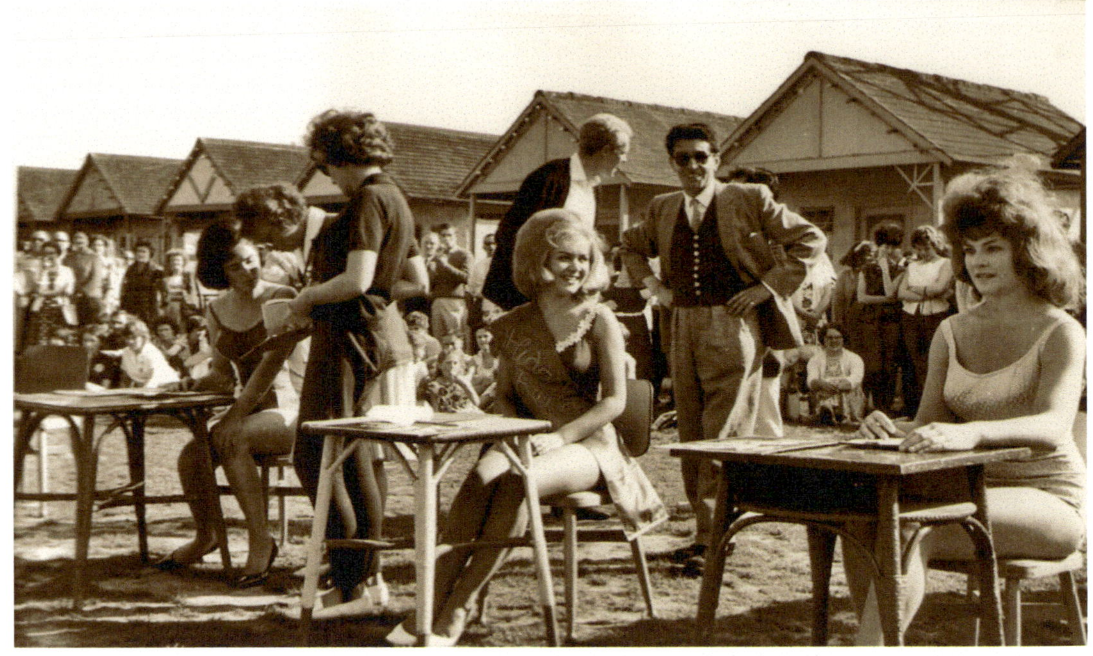

In the top photograph, the winners from the Holiday Princess Competition can be seen judging the Knobbly Knees Competition at Skegness, in 1963. Beauty contests started at Butlin's almost as soon as it opened. The first competition was judged by Gracie Fields in 1938 and the winner received a powder compact. The name 'Holiday Princess' arose in 1955 and was named after the two Royal Princesses, Elizabeth and Margaret. The Royal Albert Hall hosted the finals. The competition was sponsored by the *Empire News* in the 1960s and the overall prize winner received £1000.

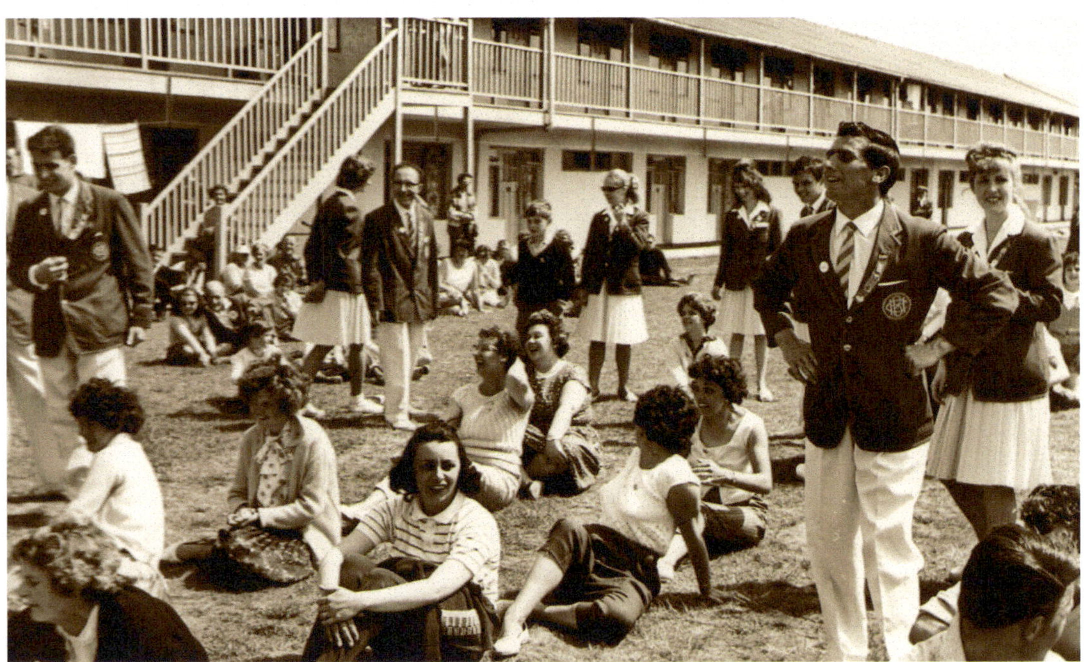

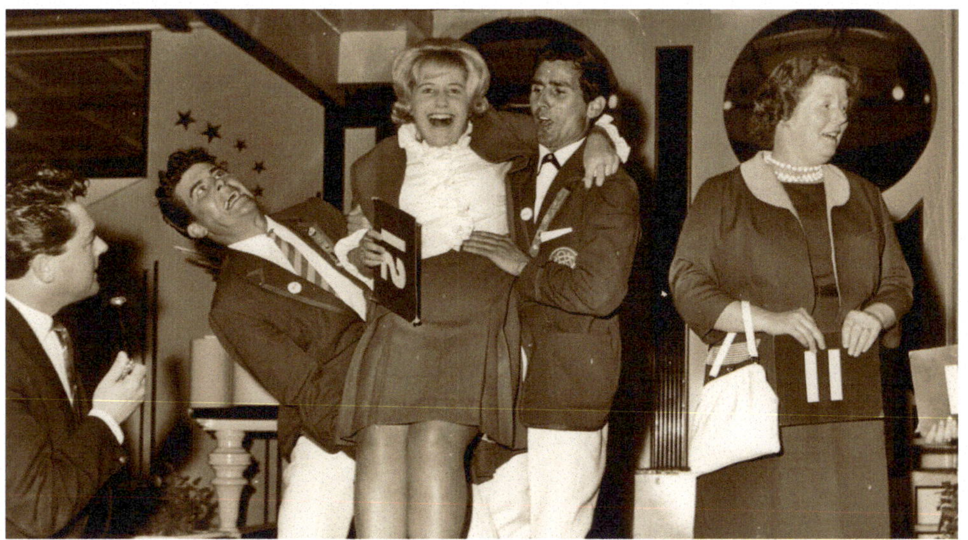

The first photograph shows the Cheerful, Chubby and Charming Competition which was held in the Princes Ballroom at Skegness in 1963. The title of the competition probably wouldn't be seen as being politically correct nowadays and many other competitions would probably be seen in the same light including the Ugly Face Competition and the Cigarette Rolling Competition sponsored by Rizla. There were many other weird and wonderful competitions including the 'Snorer of the Week', the 'Shiniest Bald Head' and 'Shaver of the Week' contests. In the 1950s, there were also lookalike competitions, with the winner being the camper looking most like Princess Elizabeth, Marilyn Monroe or other celebrities of the day.

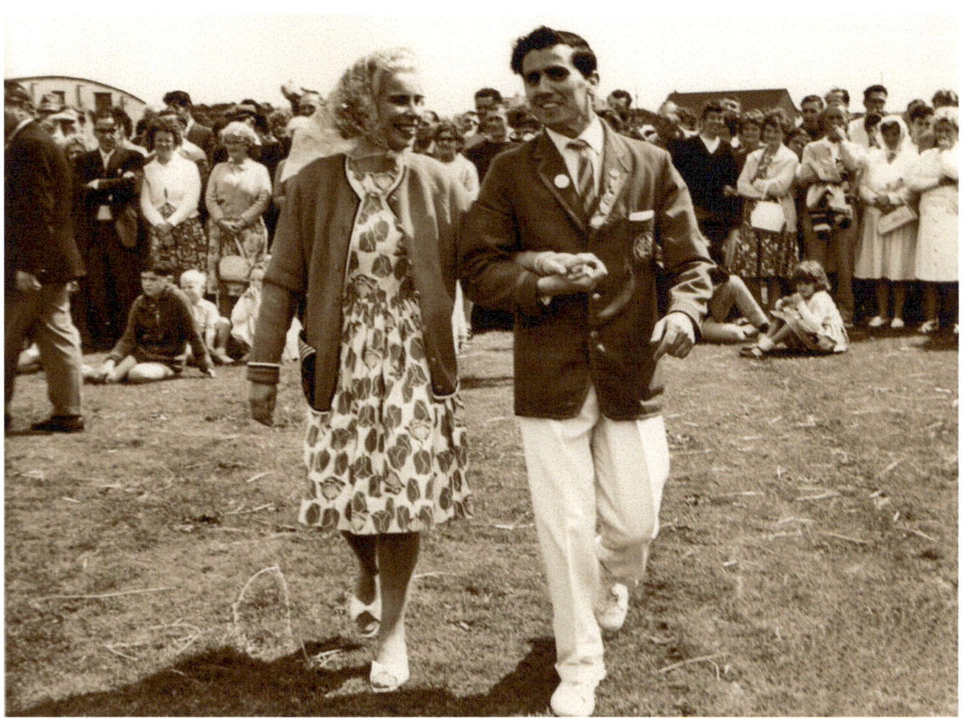

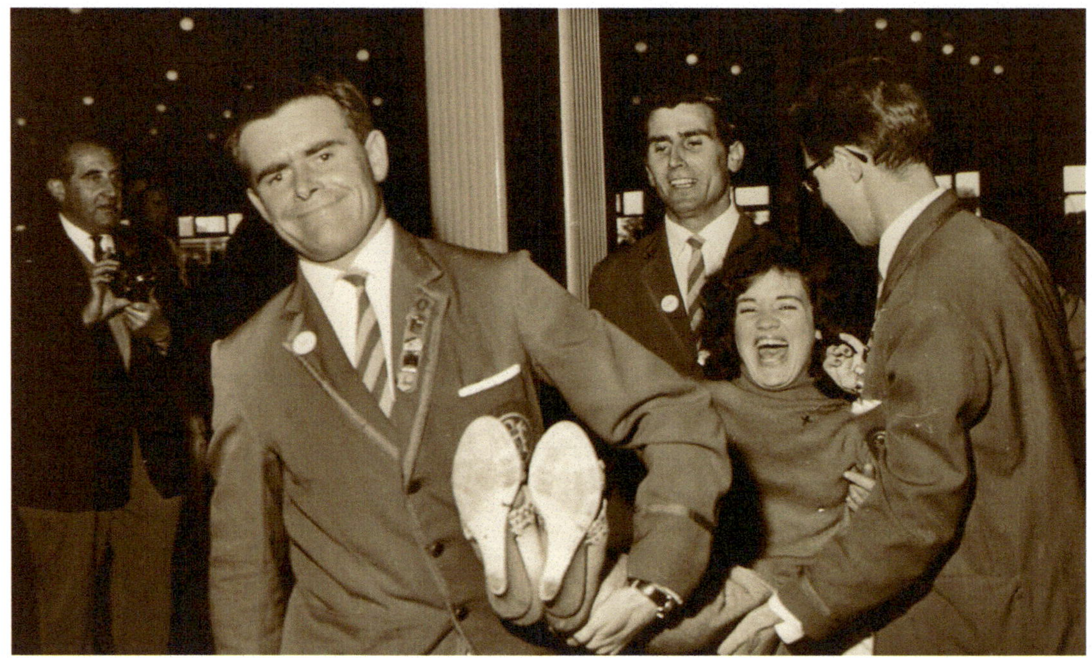

Both photographs show Redcoats recruiting shy volunteers for the Holiday Princess Competition. The overall winner in 1963, when this photograph was taken, was Nanette Slack of Ipswich. Everyone was encouraged to join in and enjoy themselves. Many were reluctant to take part, in fear of embarrassing themselves, but were given a helpful hand by friendly Redcoats. Another similar contest was for 'Girls with the Best Cared for Complexion' which was sponsored by Lux soap.

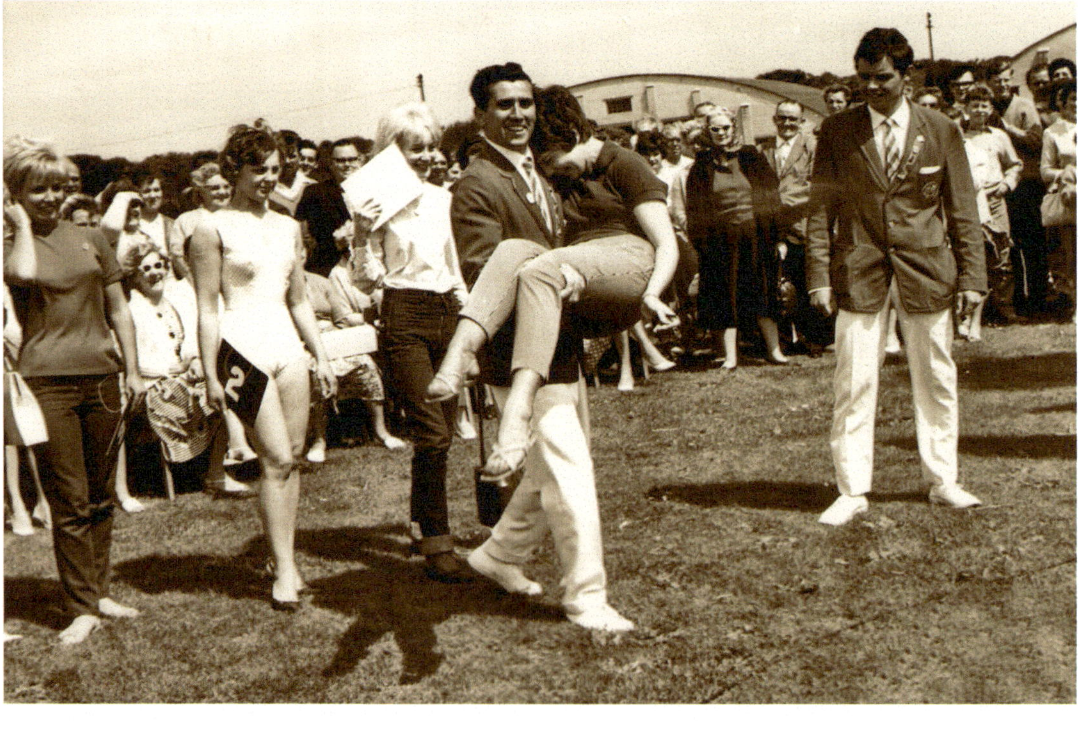

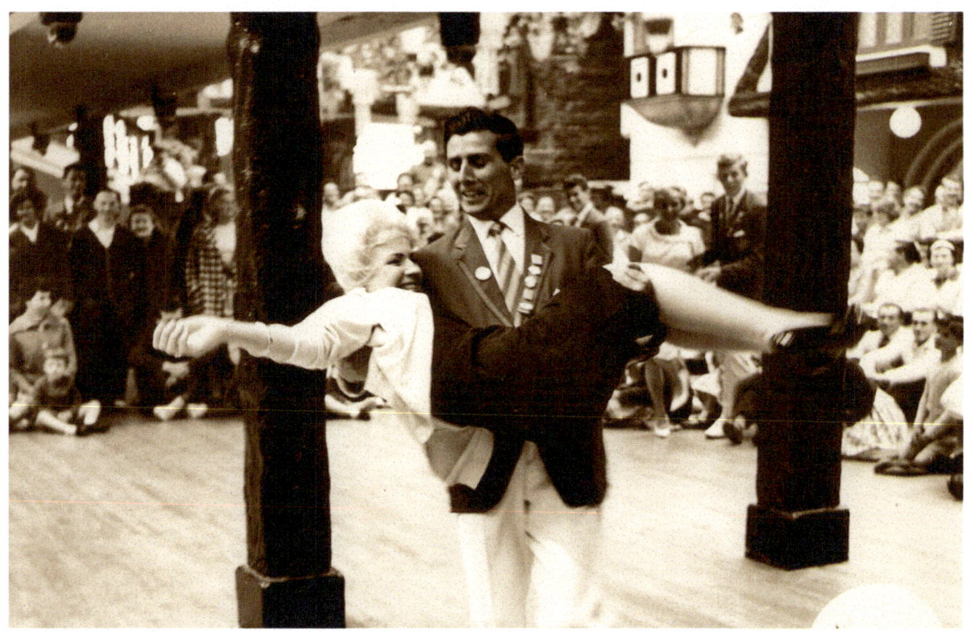

The top photograph shows a volunteer for the Holiday Princess Competition. She later won the week's heat at Skegness in 1963. A tannoy system ran close to the chalets announcing competitions and announcements about various activities. Speakers were placed on large poles and would broadcast details of meal times, lost children or important messages. Radio Butlin was run by the Redcoats and originally included 'wakey-wakey' calls announcing that breakfast was due to be served. There were also announcements about early morning 'keep fit' classes which took place on the sports field.

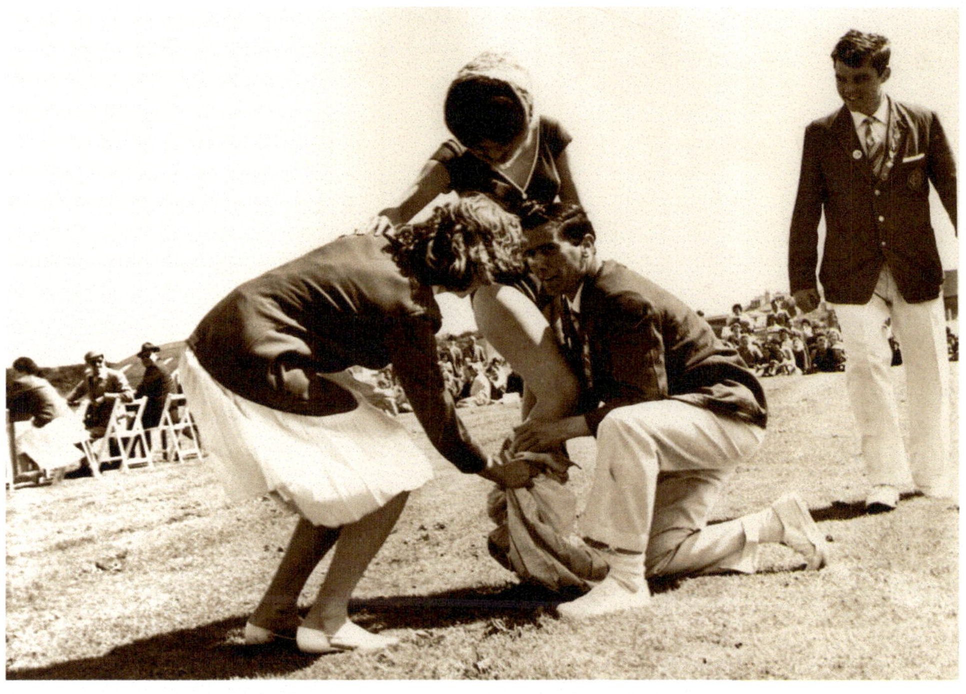

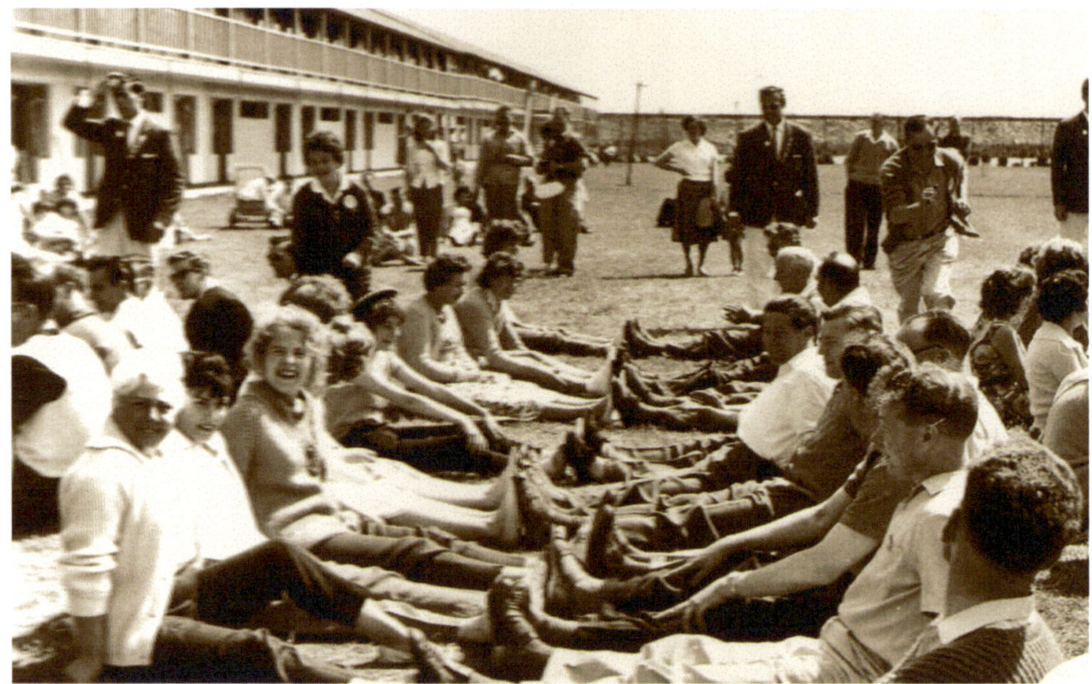

All Butlin's camps were emblazoned with the slogan, 'Our True Intent is All For Your Delight'. The original phrase came from Shakespeare's play, *A Midsummer Night's Dream*. Billy Butlin had seen the words, years before, written on a fairground organ and had used them on his camps without realising that they had originally been written by Shakespeare. At Skegness, the words were above the main entrance to the camp.

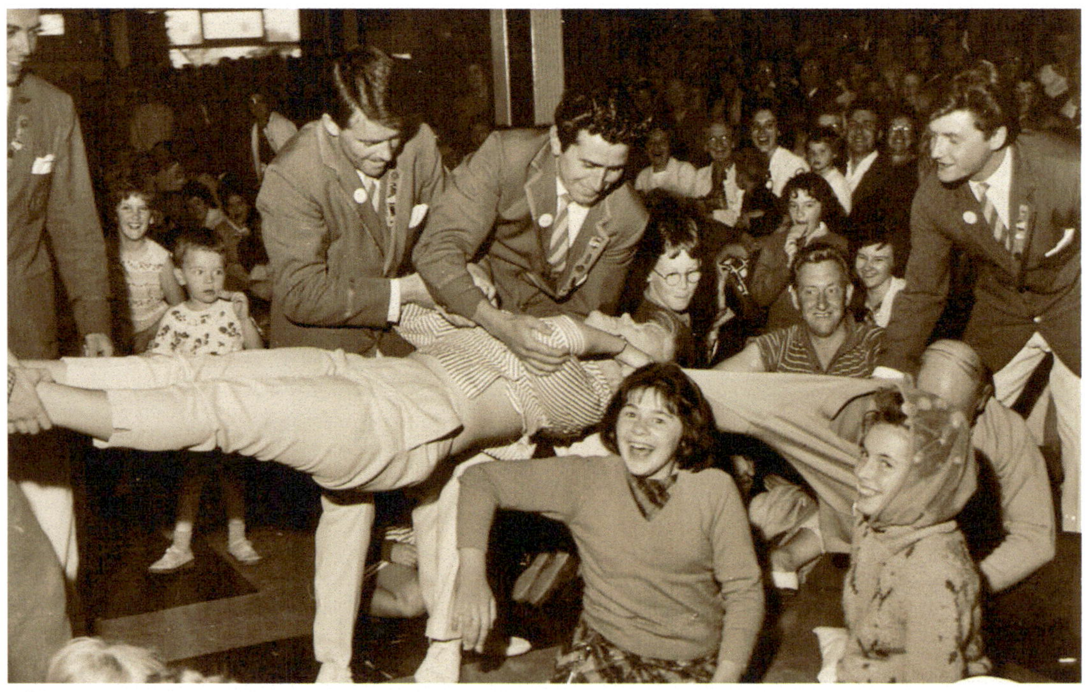

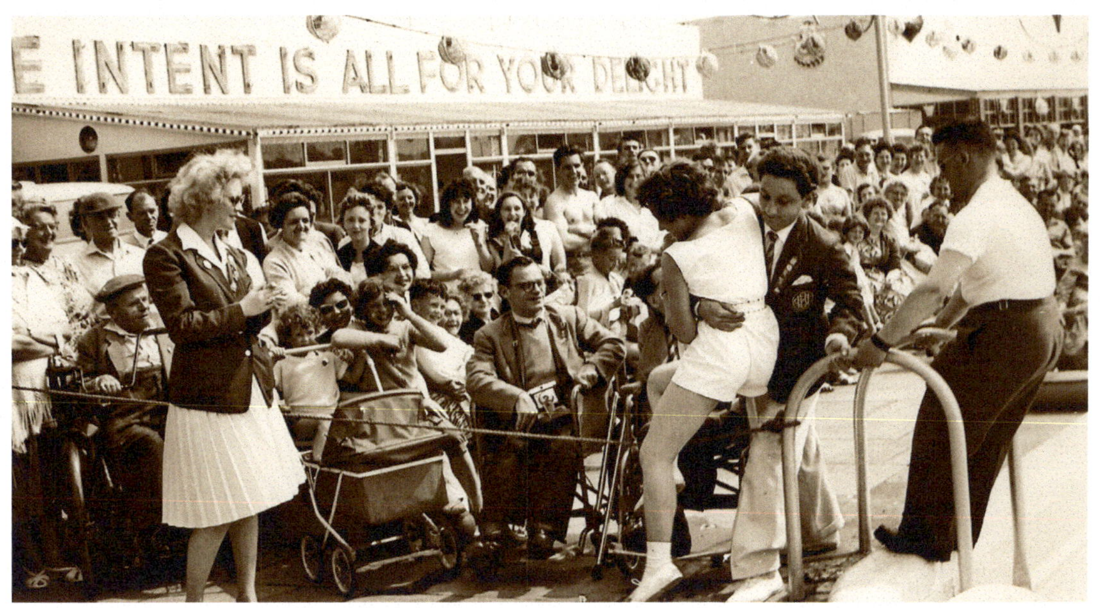

The first photograph shows Freddie Davies helping a reluctant camper to volunteer at Skegness in 1961. Freddie would later find fame on television as comedian and actor, Freddie 'Parrotface' Davies. While Freddie was at Butlin's, he performed a comedy and magic show but didn't perform his 'parrotface' act until after he left. Later, on television, his catchphrase was, 'I'm thick, thick, thick up to 'ere!' In the background of the top photograph, the Butlin's slogan can be seen clearly displayed. The second photograph shows the Knobbly Knees Competition being held within the Princes Ballroom at Skegness in 1962. One Redcoat tries to get a better look from floor level. In the background, the Butlin's 'Go Dancing Contest' is advertised.

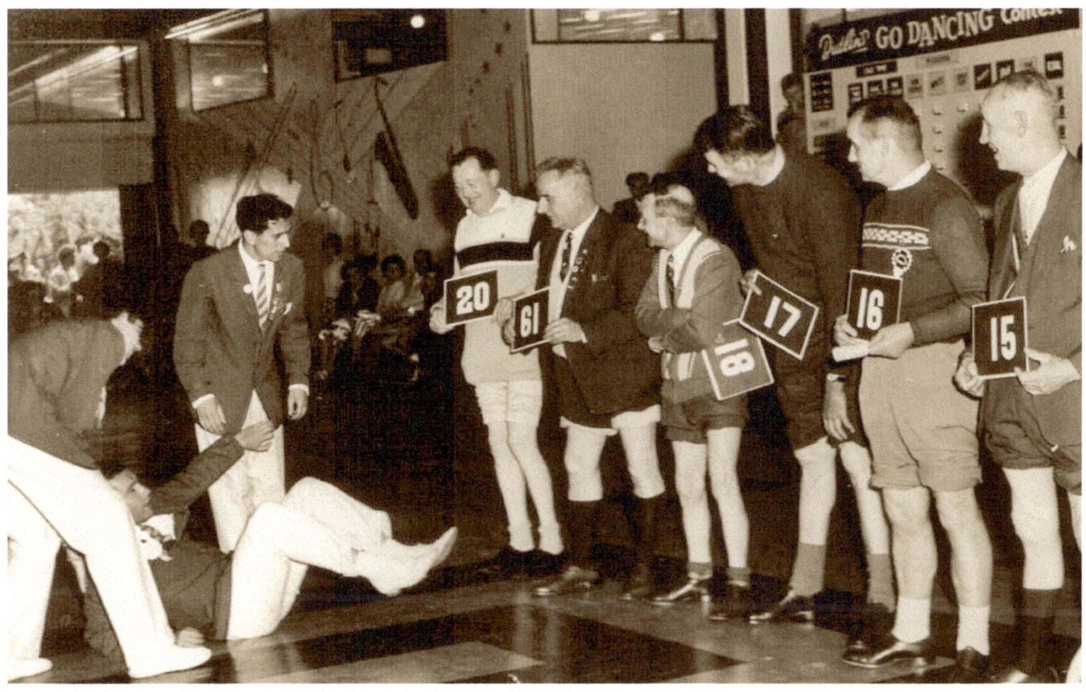

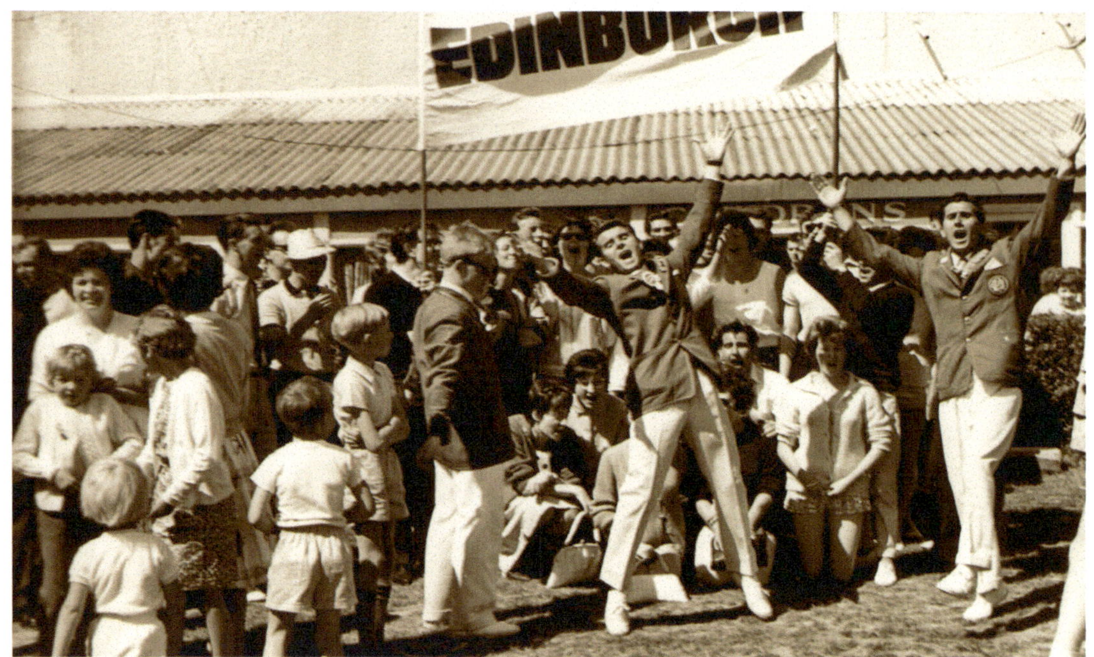

Cheers go up as Edinburgh House wins some points. In the early days, approximately 100 Redcoats were employed on camp and they organised and ran all the inter-house contests and competitions. By 1984, there were far fewer Redcoats employed in each camp and the numbers were down to about thirty. The second photograph shows Norman, one of the camp comics, and Redcoat Billy taking part in a football game with a female camper.

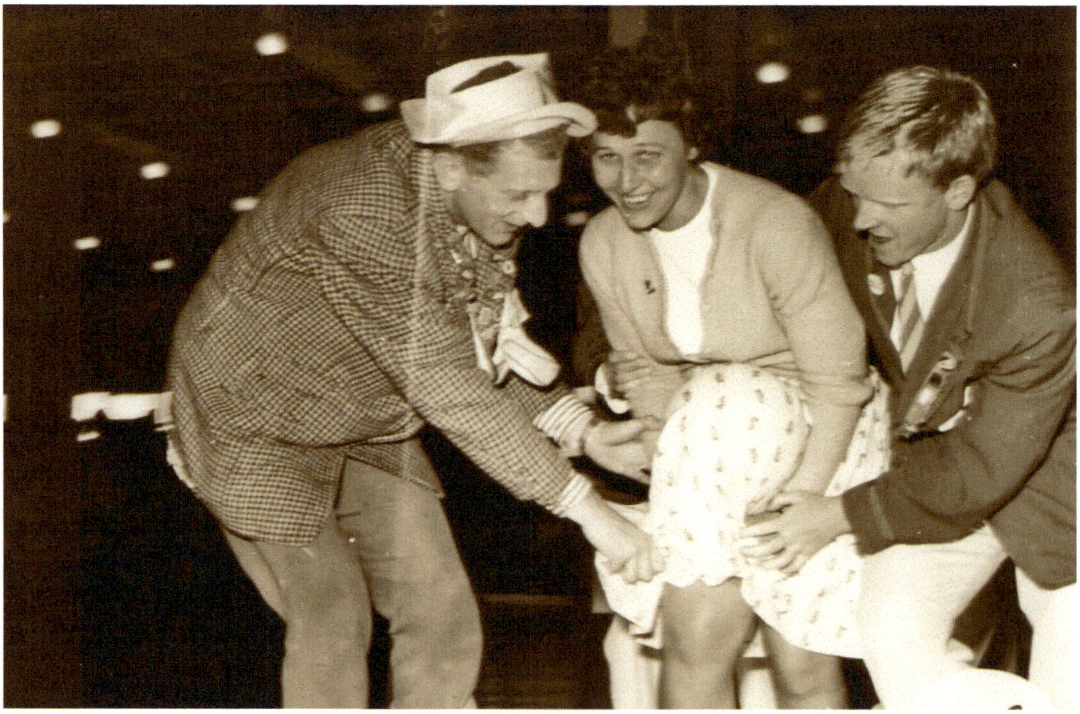

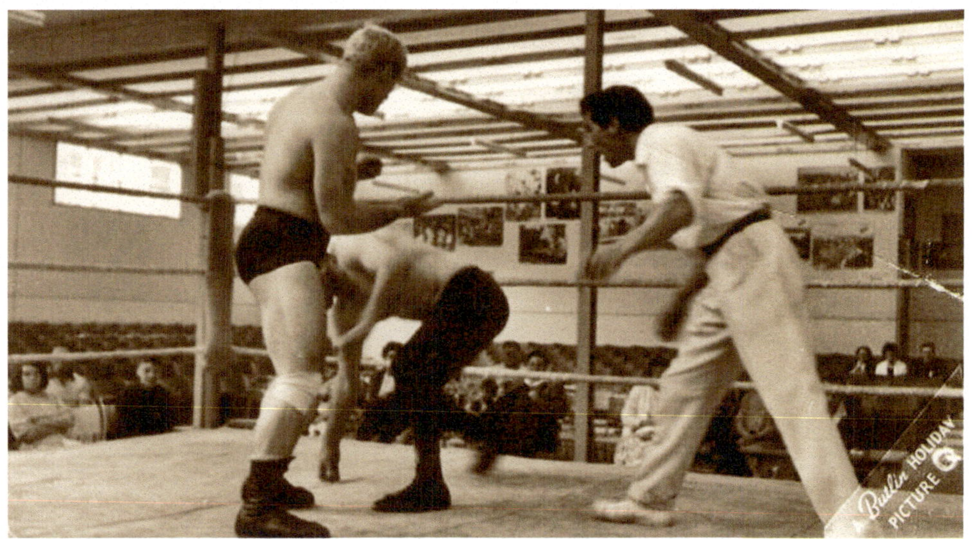

In the 1960s and 1970s, wrestling was hugely popular. Streets and shops would clear on Saturdays as 4 p.m. approached and the wrestling was broadcast on ITV's *World of Sport*. At the time, many bouts were well-rehearsed and some wrestlers were more actors than fighters. There were regular wrestling bouts at Butlin's and everyone would cheer the 'goodie' and boo the 'baddie' while others chanted and shouted, 'Public Warning'. Some campers would get irate and older women would bang their handbags at the side of the ring if there was any foul play. At Bognor, the wrestling was held in the Regency Ballroom on a Wednesday and was extremely popular.

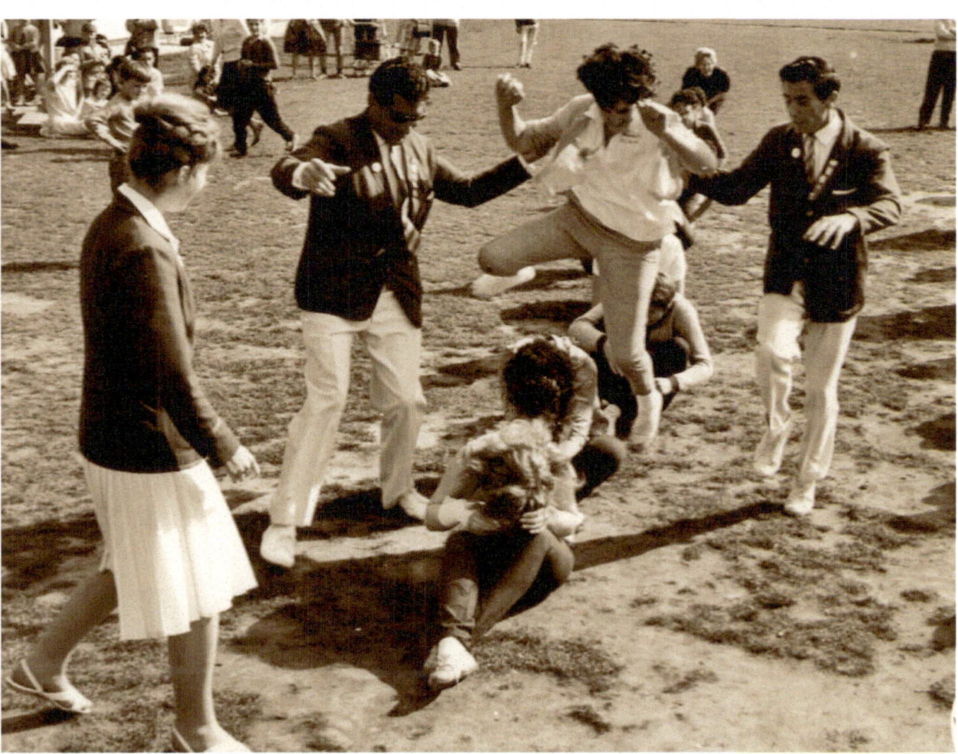

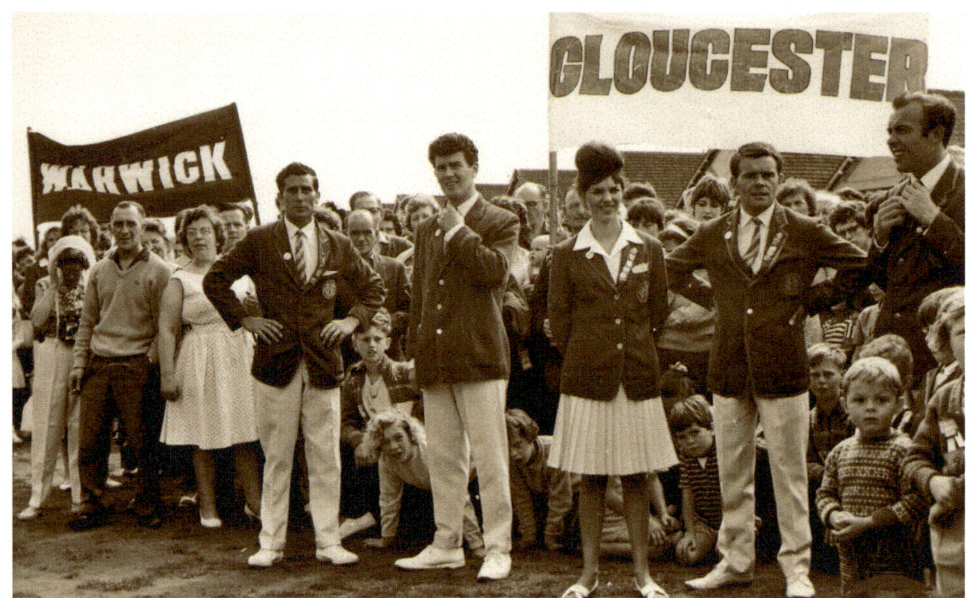

Gloucester and Warwick House compete at Skegness. Redcoat Andy King can be seen in the top photograph as part of Warwick House together with Redcoats Wayne, Brenda, Joe and Roger. The photograph was taken at Skegness in 1963. Members of Gloucester House can be seen gathered indoors in the second photograph. Redcoats received no training but were told to smile a lot and always be helpful and happy.

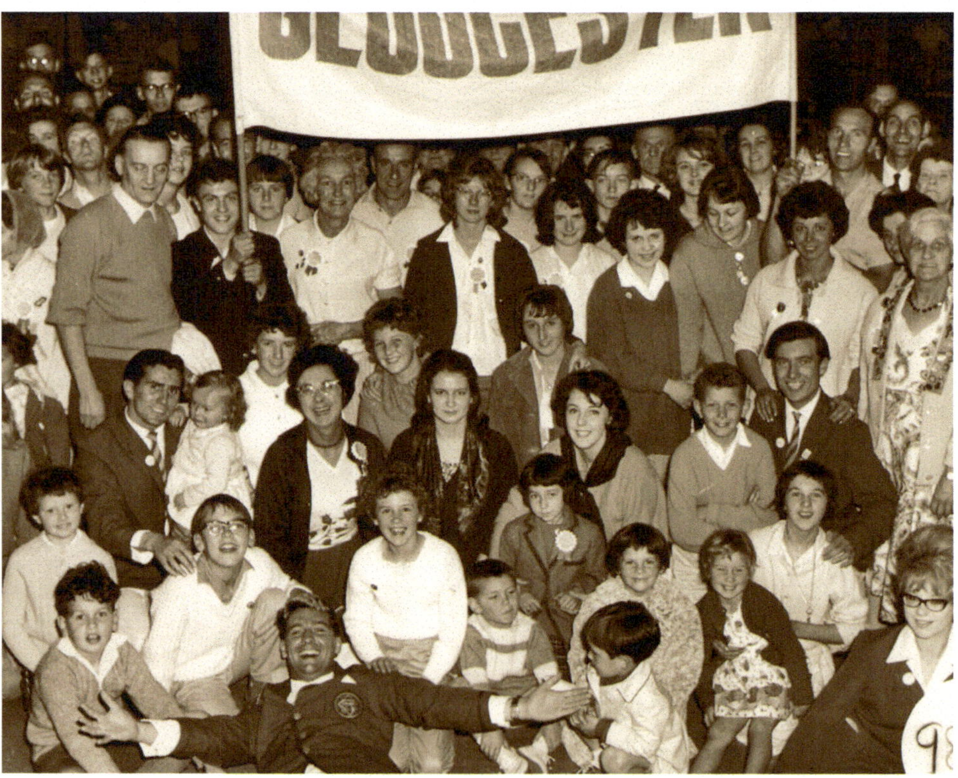

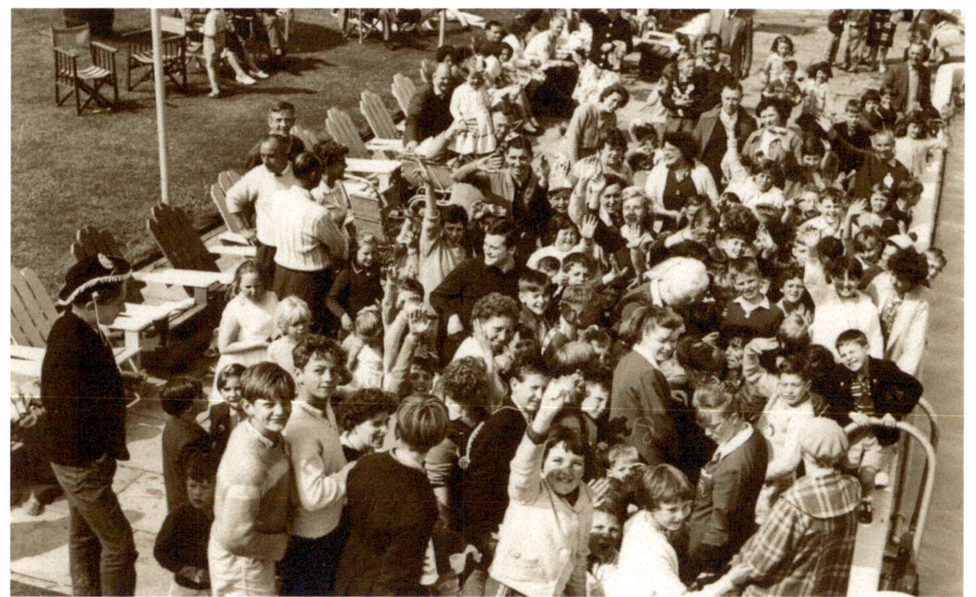

In the top photograph, members of the Beaver Club gather around the pool after searching for Chief Running Bear (Andy King) who they've captured and are eager to throw into the pool. The second photograph shows the Redcoats singing in the Princes Ballroom at Skegness in 1961. Redcoat shows were extremely popular with campers and featured comedy, singing and dancing. Redcoats who went on to find fame on television included Charlie Drake, Terry Scott, Johnny Ball, Colin Crompton (Wheeltappers and Shunters Club), Jimmy Cricket and William G. Stewart (Fifteen to One).

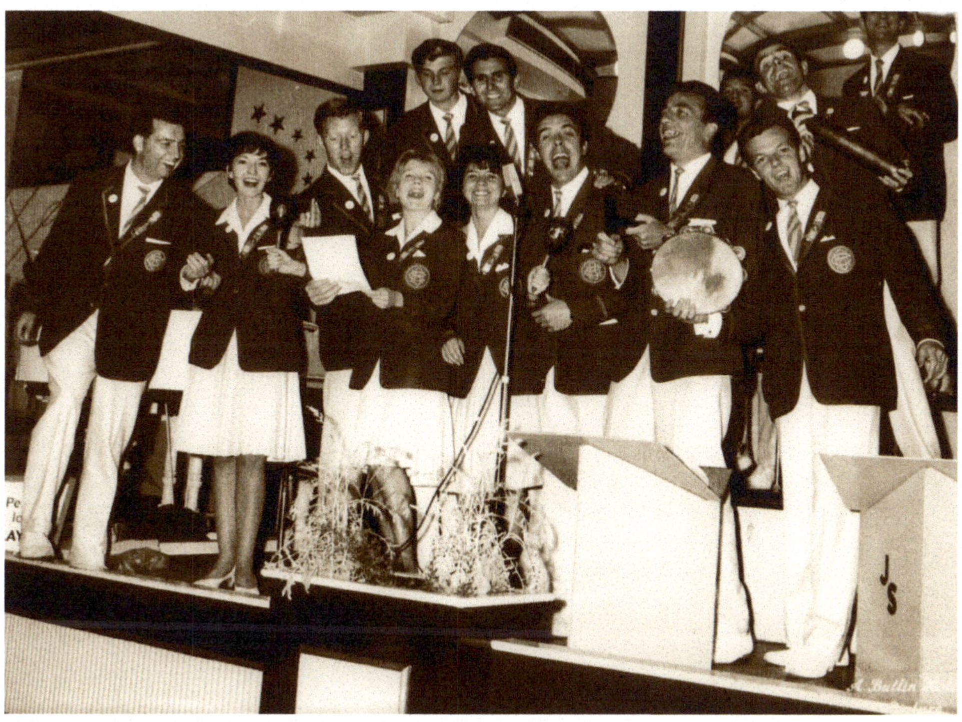

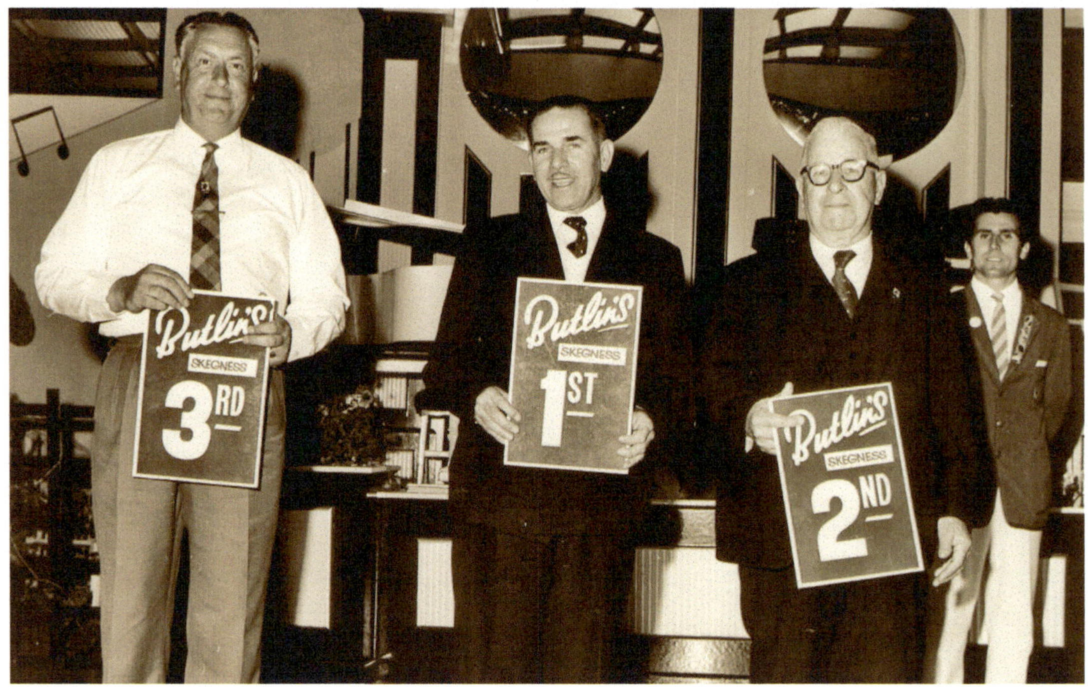

The top photograph shows entrants in the Grandest Grandad Competition at Skegness in the 1960s. Butlin's welcomed campers of all ages and there was a competition for everyone. The contest didn't prove as popular as the Glamorous Grandmother Competition and is little remembered by most.

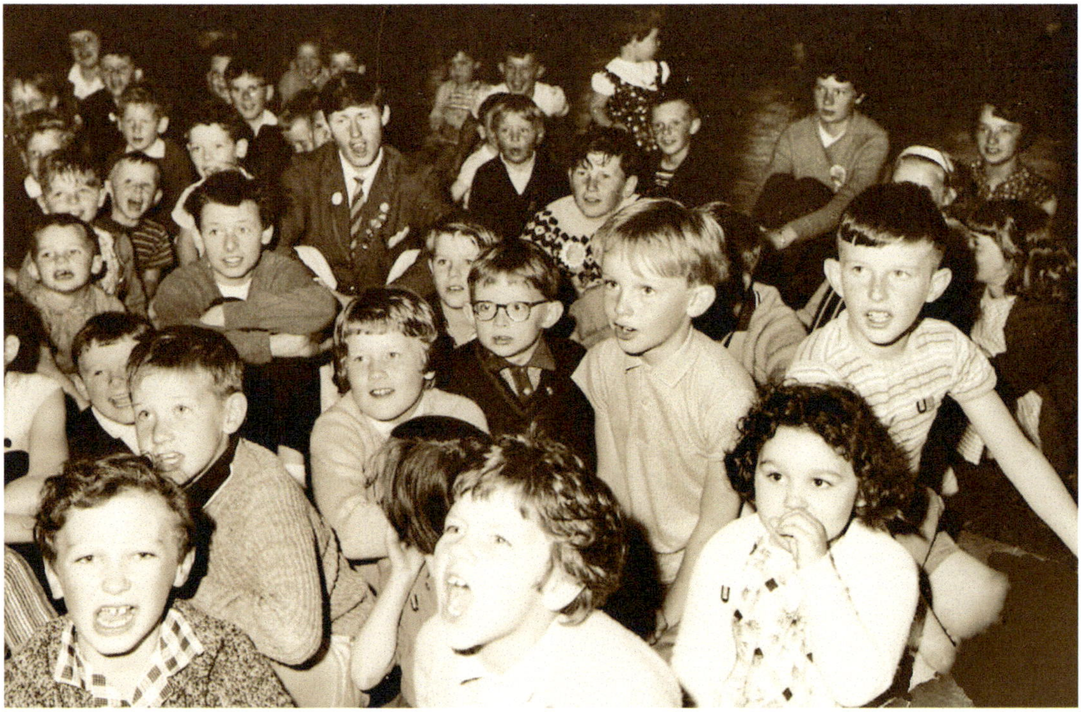

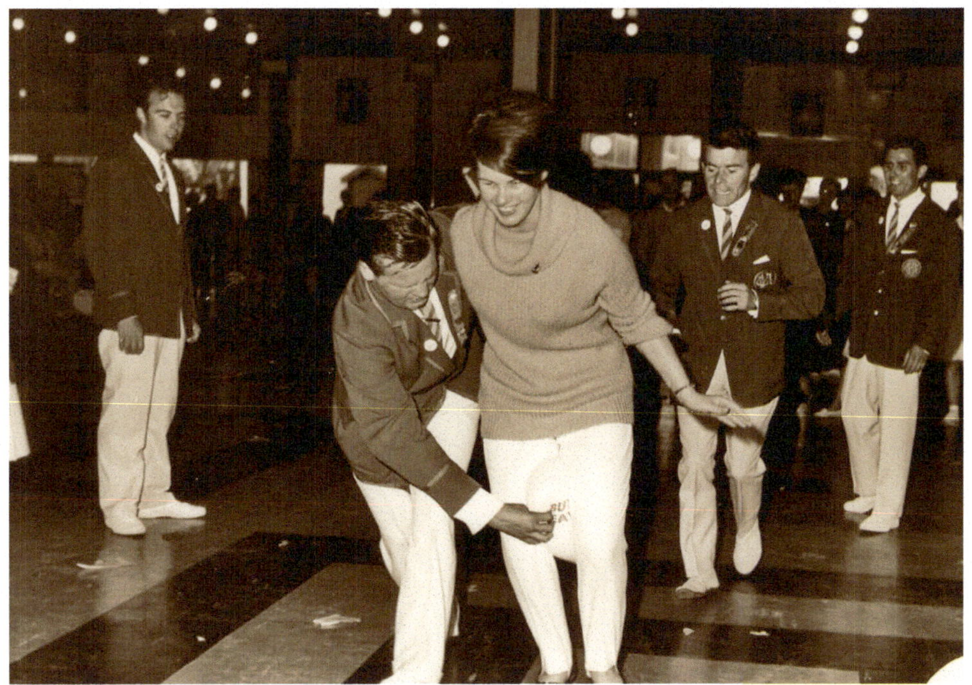

The first photograph shows entertainment in the Princes Ballroom at Skegness. Apart from indoor games and competitions, ballroom dancing proved very popular with campers. After the war, Butlin's held the National Valeta Competition. The heats were judged by the resident dance instructor at each camp. The Royal Albert Hall hosted the finals, which attracted thousands of dancers. Dance competitions over the years have included Ballet, Old Tyme, Highland, Latin and Disco. At the first dance festival at Filey in 1951, Jack and Joyce Briggs, both amateur dancers, won the Old Tyme dance contest. They went on to win many more competitions at Butlin's and turned professional in 1955.

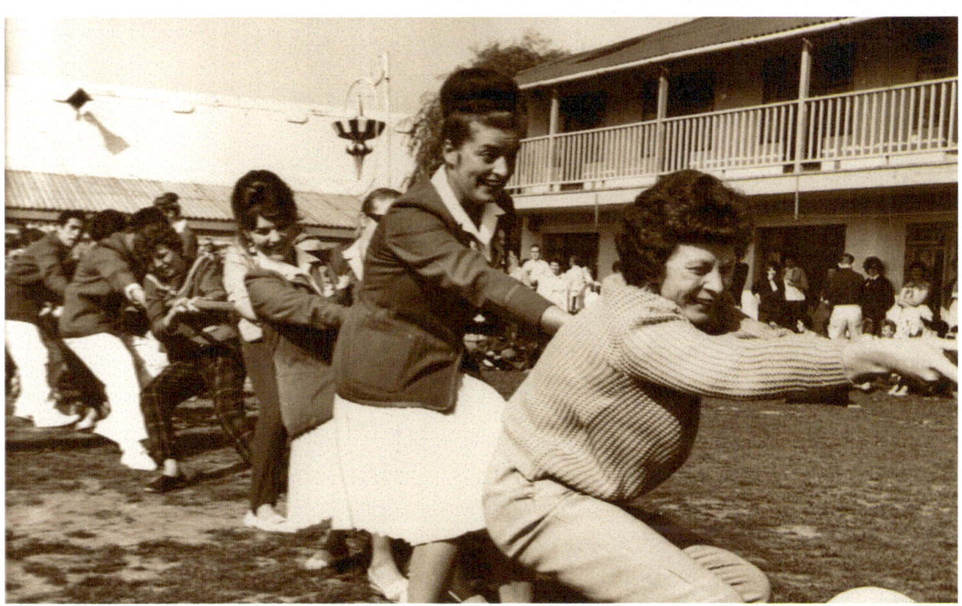

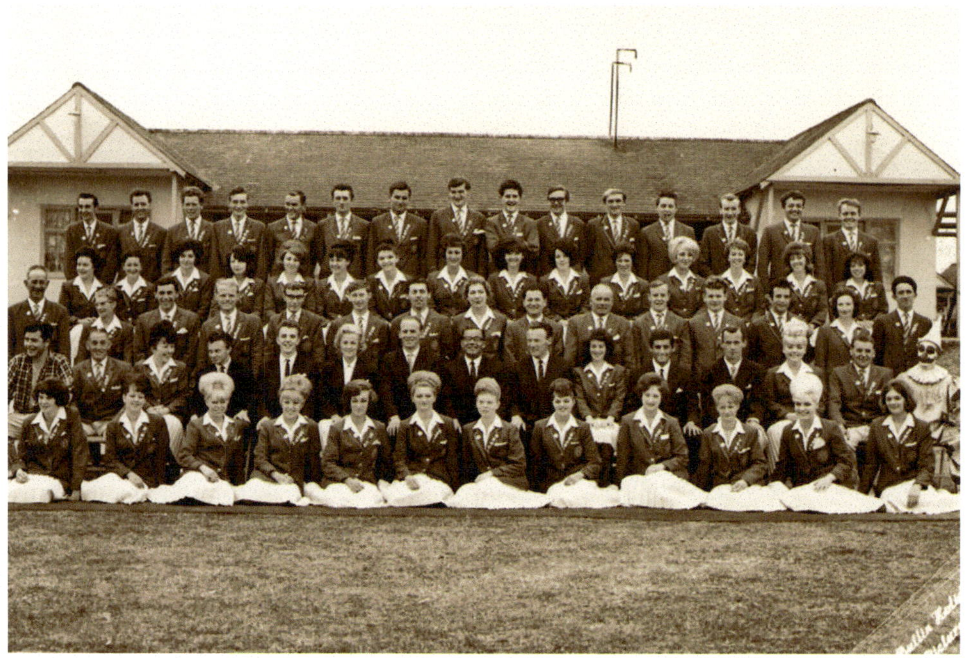

The phrase 'Hi-de-hi' came from a popular American film starring Cab Calloway. Norman Bradford, the first Redcoat, had seen the film, and one day took to the stage and shouted 'Hi-de-hi' to the campers. They had also all seen the film, and instantly shouted back, 'Ho-de-ho!' The catchphrase caught on and Redcoats used it every time they wanted to make an announcement. At other times, Redcoats and campers passing each other would shout, 'Hi-de-hi' to which the other would quickly reply, 'Ho-de-ho'.

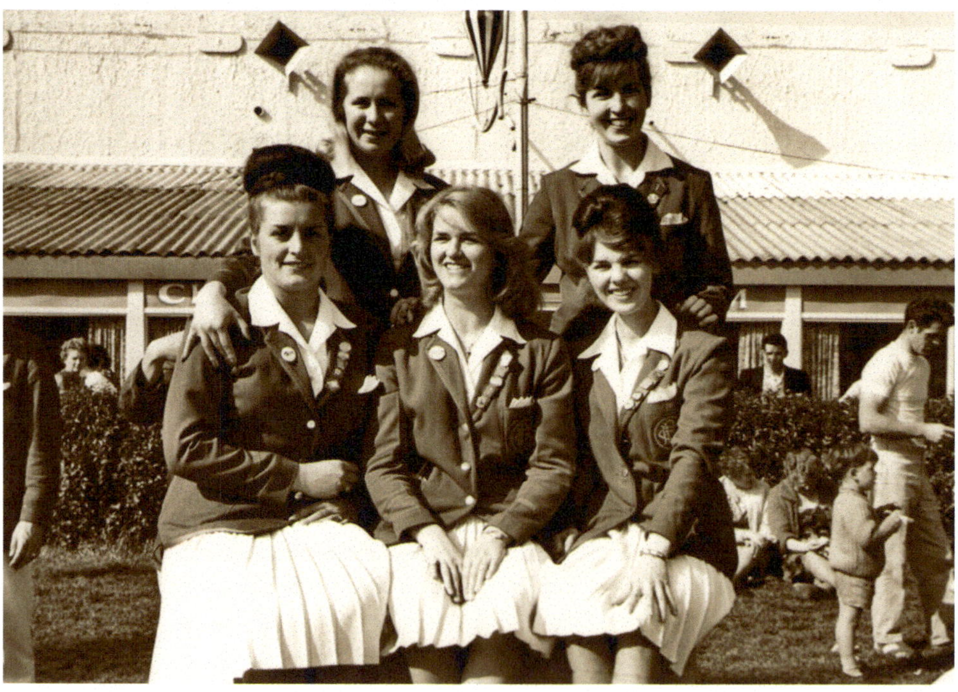

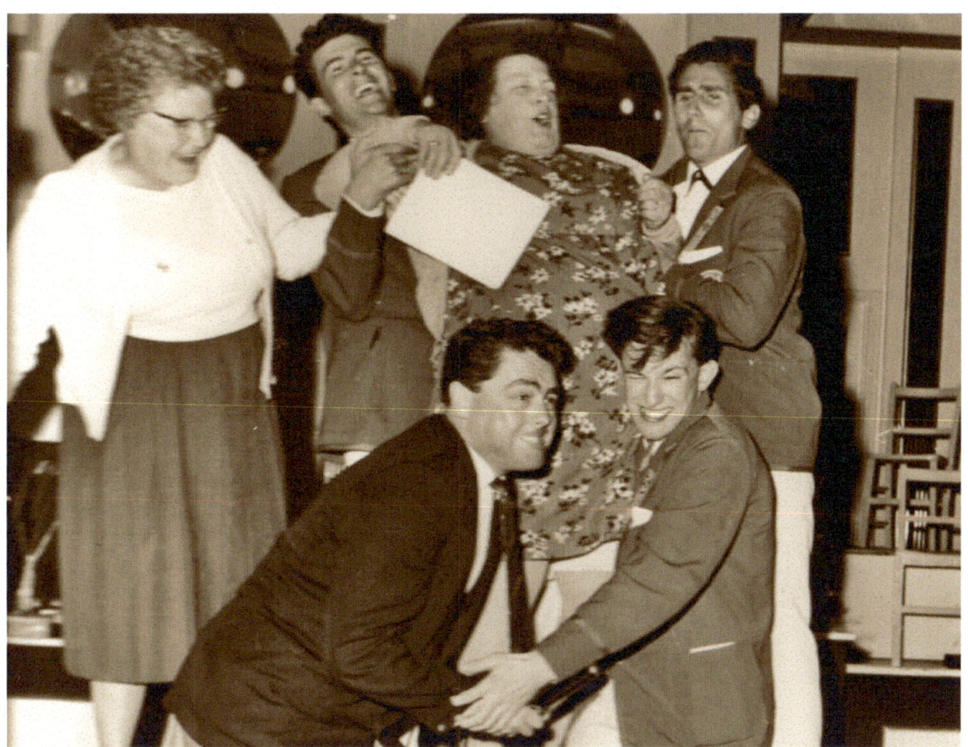

Both photographs show entrants for the Cheerful, Charming and Chubby Competition in 1962. Evening entertainment came from a host of well-known names in the 1950s including Arthur English who topped the bill after appearing on Radio Band Box. Tommy Trinder also entertained, as did Hughie Green who hosted the quiz show, 'Double Your Money' on camp. The quiz was sponsored by Lucozade and also became a very popular television show. Other major entertainers included Benny Hill, Bruce Forsythe, Frankie Howerd, Hugh Lloyd and Norman Vaughan. The Bachelors appeared regularly at Mosney and other singers who appeared at the camps included Helen Shapiro, Dusty Springfield, the Beverley Sisters and Georgie Fame.

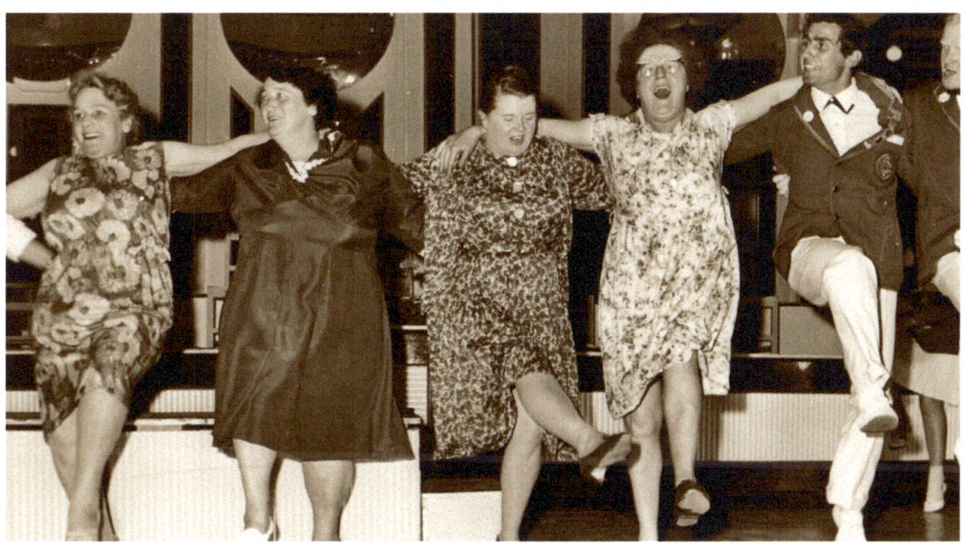

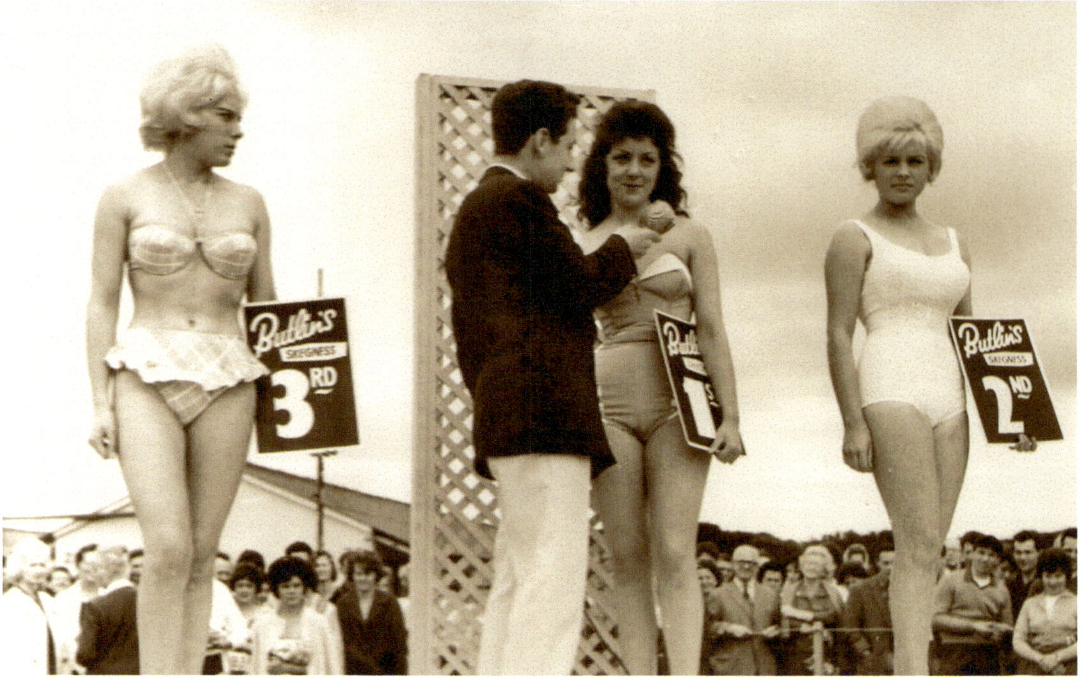

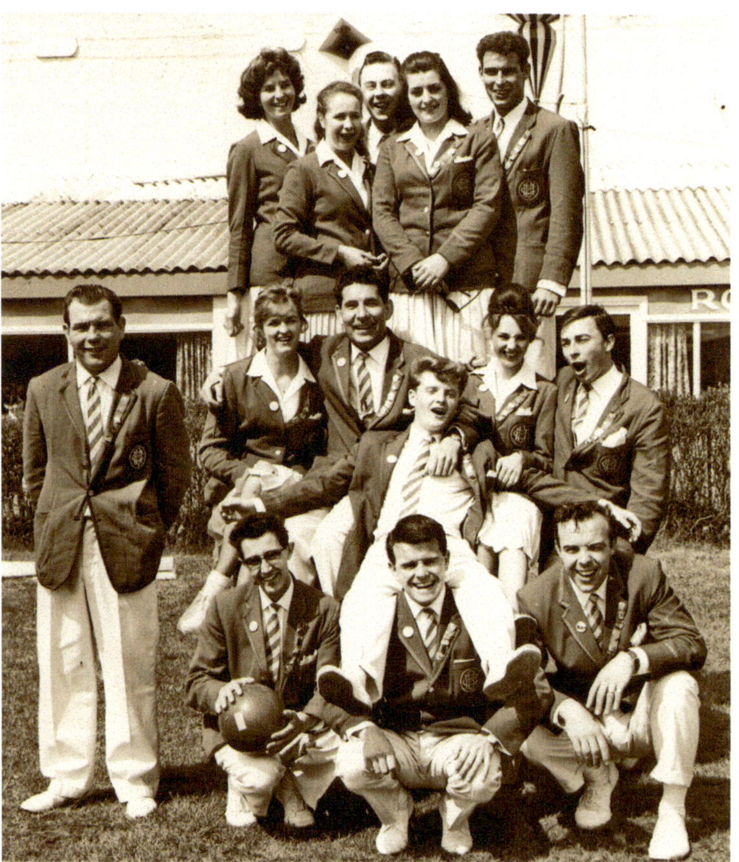

Freddie Davies comperes the Holiday Princess Competition at Skegness in 1962. After turning professional in 1964, Freddie appeared on many television programmes including *Opportunity Knocks, Sunday Night at the London Palladium,* the *Des O'Connor Show,* the *Tom Jones Show,* the *Bachelors Show* and *Blackpool Night Out.* He became popularly known as Freddie 'Parrotface' Davies and even had his own comic strip in the comic, *Buster,* which ran between 1968 and 1971. The second photograph shows the Redcoats at Skegness in 1963.

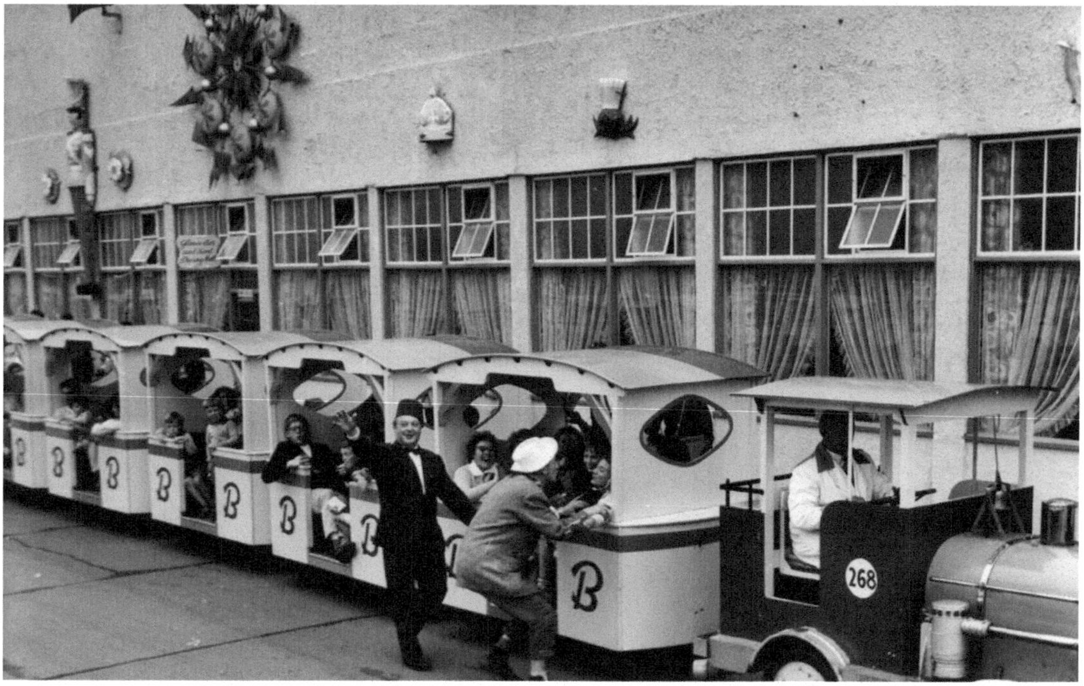

Uncle Boko started at Butlin's in Skegness soon after the war and continued to entertain children until his death, in his chalet, in the 1960s. Uncle Boko wore a fez and performed magic tricks for the children long before Tommy Cooper. He can be seen in the top photograph at Skegness together with the Butlin's train.

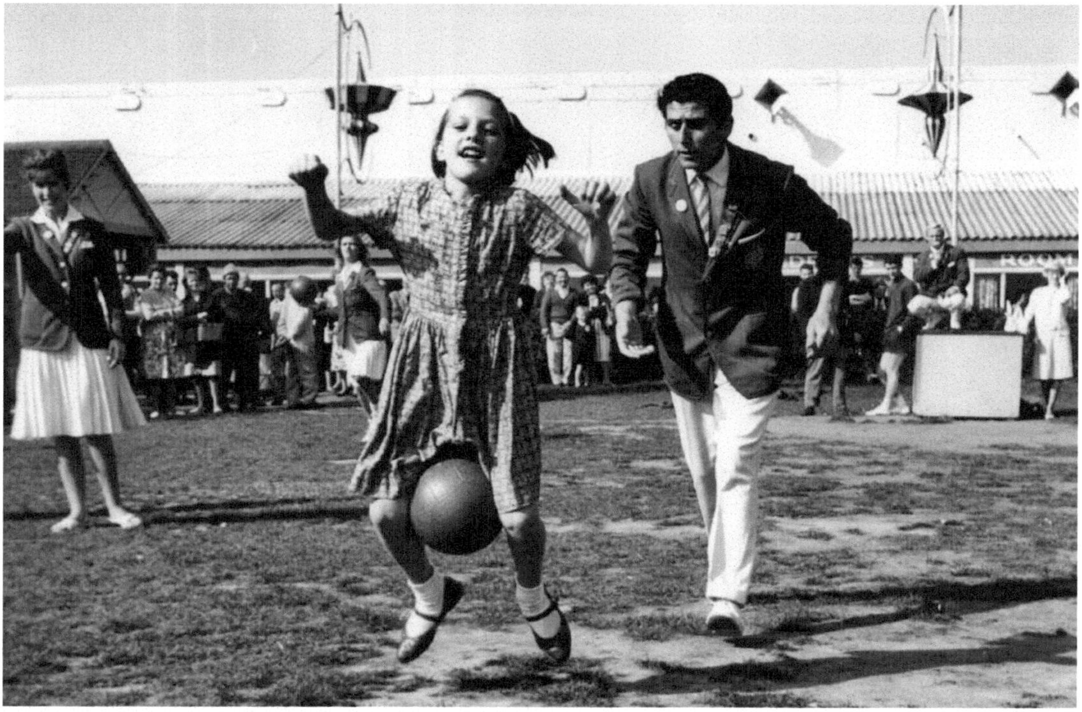

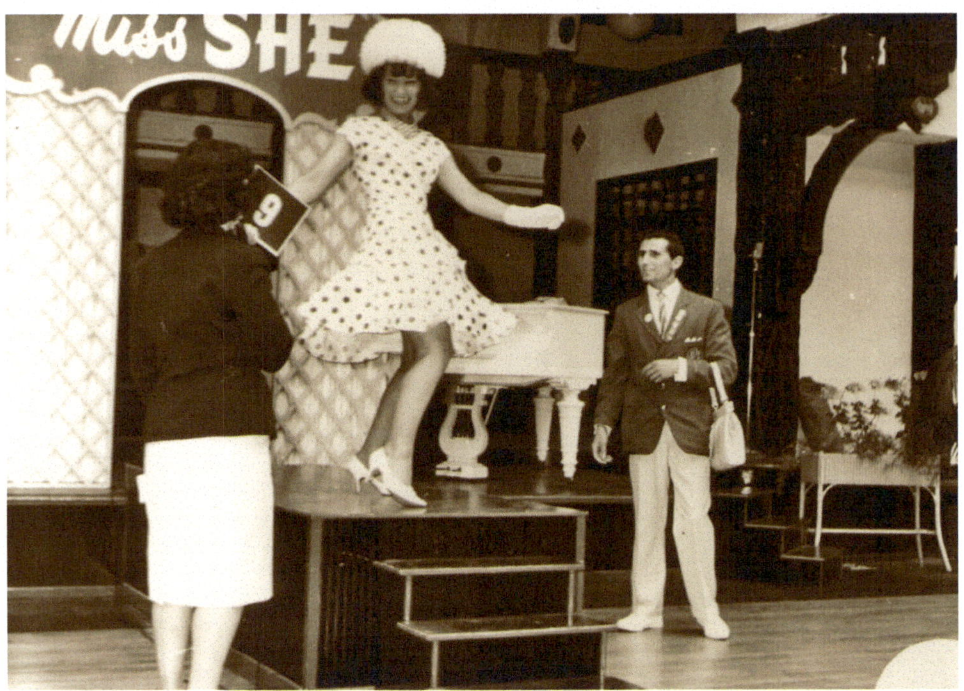

Vanity Fair magazine sponsored a beauty competition at Butlin's in 1954. The following year, *She* magazine took over sponsorship of the competition and it continued for thirty years. Entrants had to be aged between fifteen and fifty to enter and were judged on their fashion sense, charm, personality and confidence. The contests were held weekly and the semi-finals took place at a Butlin's hotel. The finals were held at the Royal Albert Hall. The first contest was won by Sheila Manners in 1956 and her prize was £50 together with a new outfit. The contest was taken over by *Ultra Glow* in the 1980s.

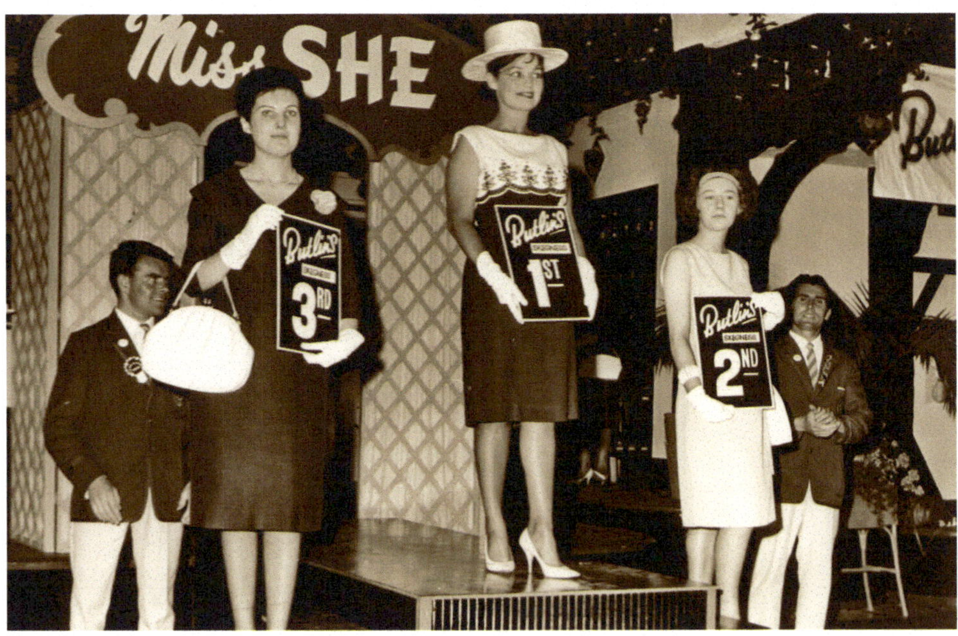

Redcoats Doreen and Pat are pictured at Skegness by the Senior Service cigarette machine. Many competitions were sponsored by tobacco companies including the Players No. 6 Show and the Cigarette Rolling Competition. A Redcoat was expected to be a good mixer, friendly, helpful, sporty and tolerant and always ready with a smile. Their duties included being a sing-song leader, a children's uncle or auntie, a bingo caller, a dancer and a swimmer.

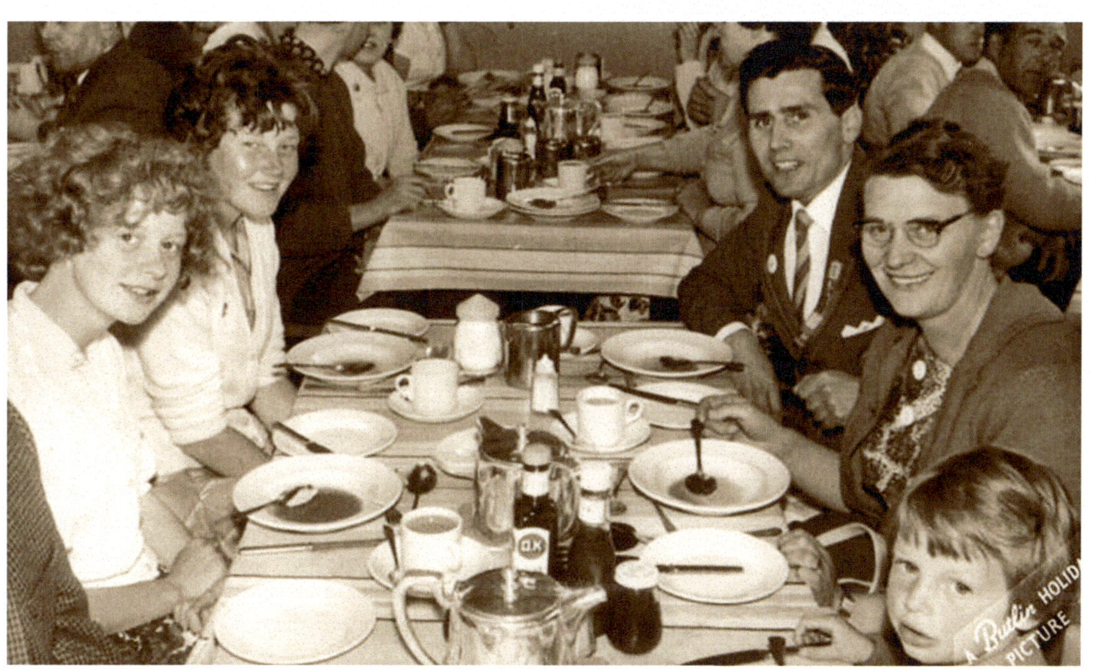

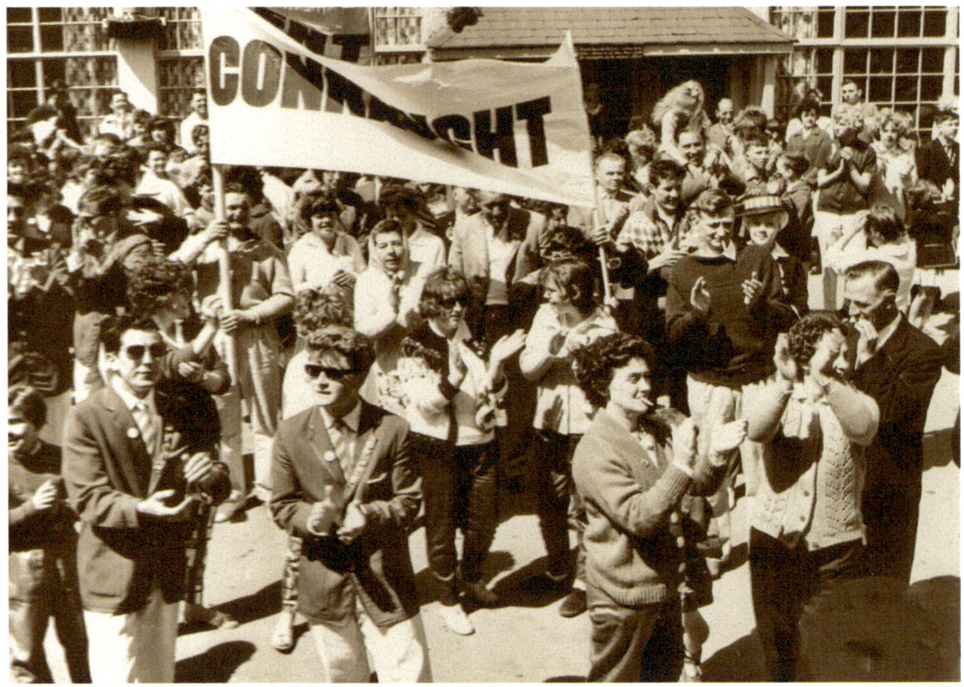

Both photographs show the flying of house flags at Skegness in the 1960s as holidaymakers parade through the camp. In the background of the second photograph can be seen the dining hall of Gloucester and Kent houses. A Redcoat, with a very ripped jacket, gives a friendly 'cock a snook' gesture towards campers and some are returning it.

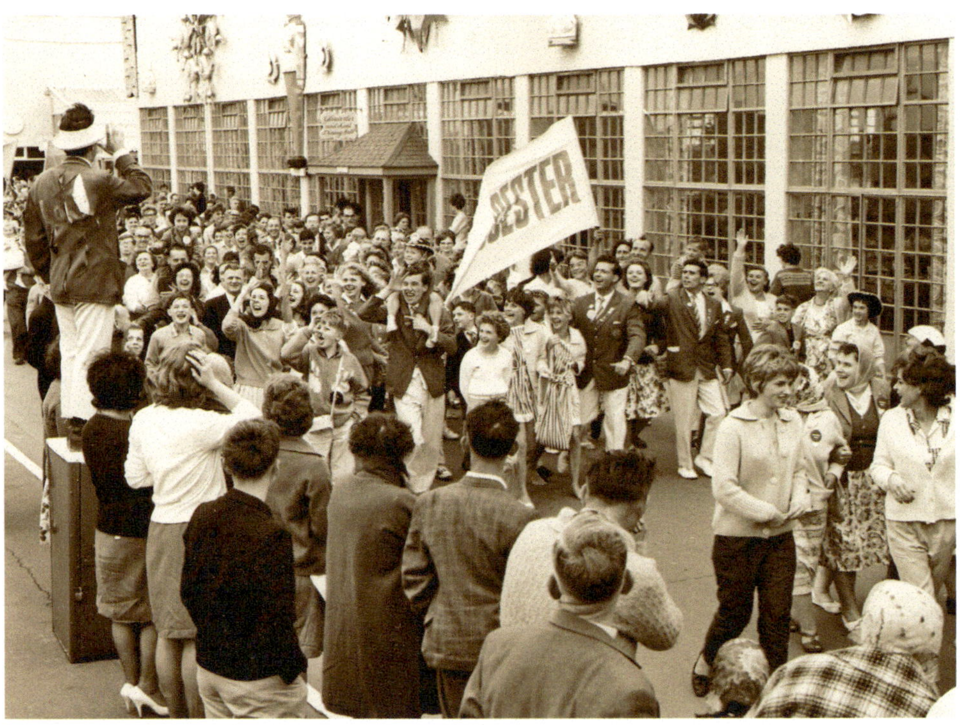

Every year, Butlin's would hold dance festivals for campers of all ages. Contestants ranged from four years old to over eighty. The World Ballet, Tap and Modern Dance Championships were held by Butlin's every year with contestants ranging from ten to seventeen years old. The Highland Dance Festival included a special section for under-fives and the youngest competitor was just 3-and-a-half years old. The Disco Championships became very popular in the 1970s.

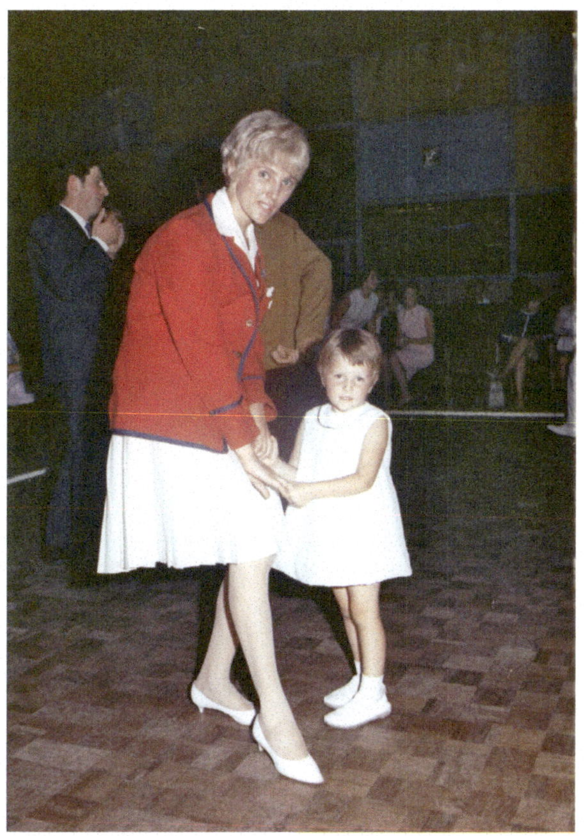

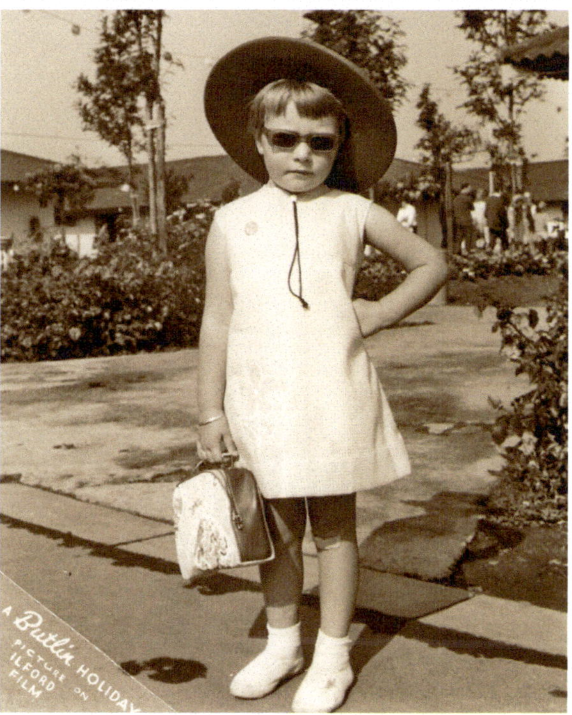

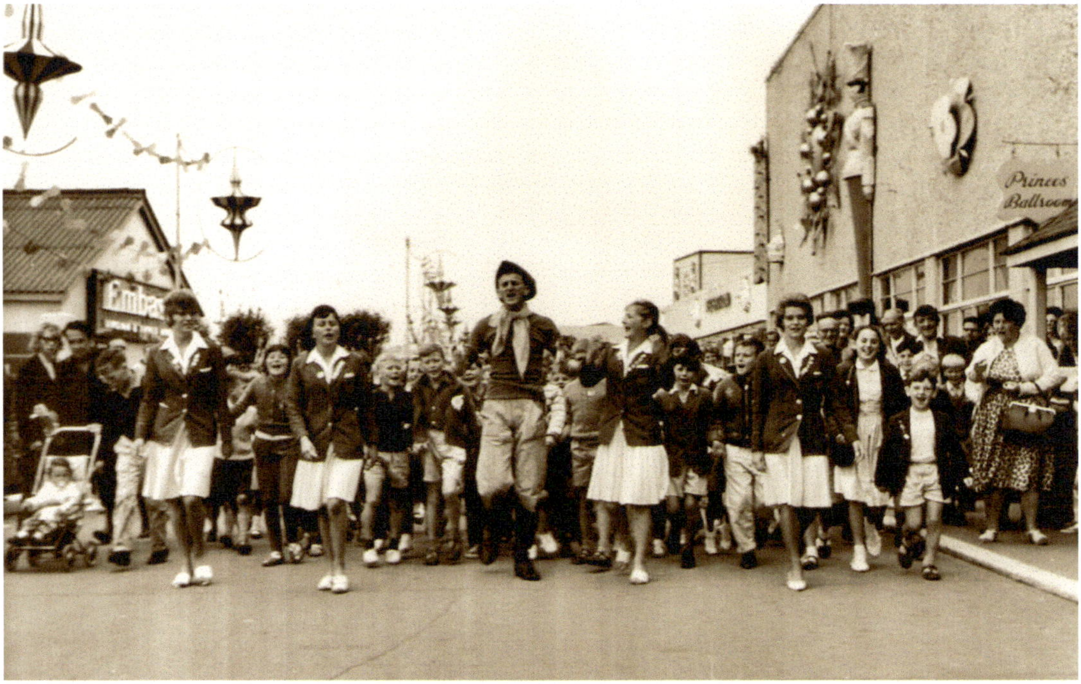

The sheriff and posse, made up of members of the Beaver Club, search for Chief Running Bear at Skegness in 1963. It's not long before Chief Running Bear, Andy King, is found and thrown into the pool as all the kids holler in the background. On the right of the first photograph can be seen the Princes Ballroom festooned with the Christmas decorations bought by Billy Butlin mentioned earlier. The Embassy Theatre can be seen on the left.

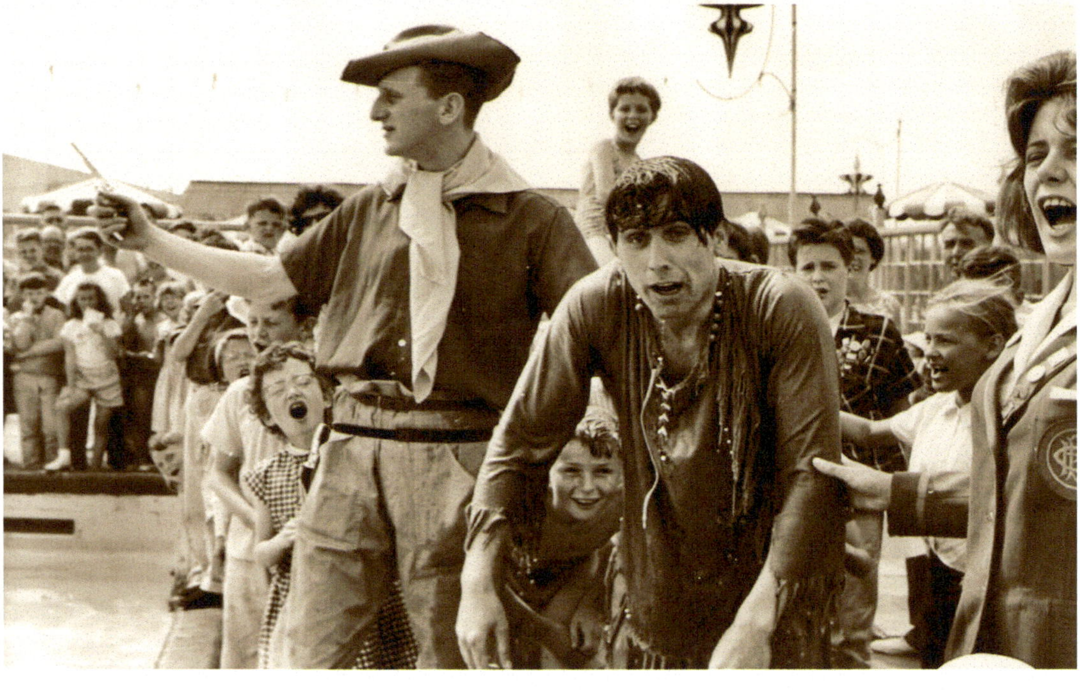

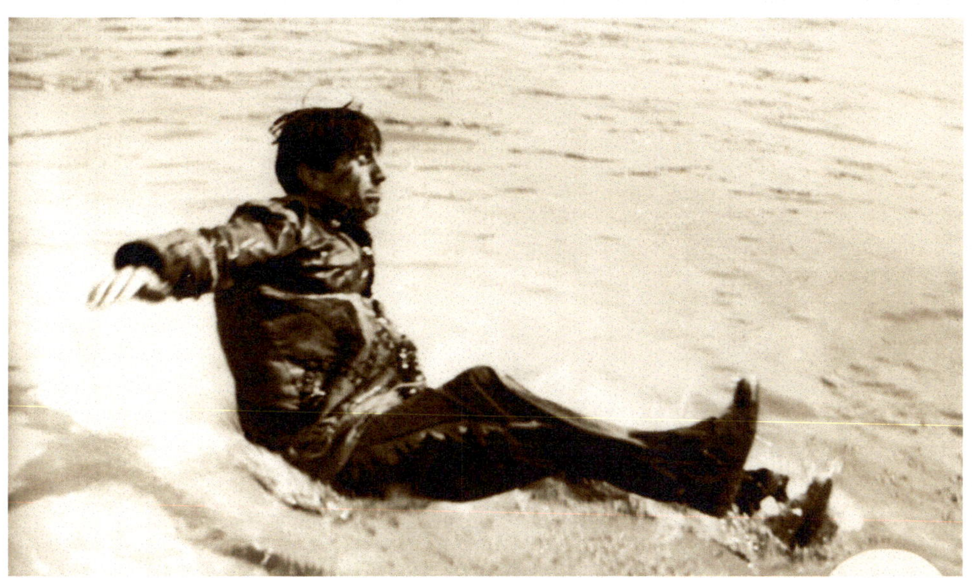

Andy King is thrown back into the pool in the top photograph. Not all Redcoats were pleased to be thrown into the pool by the Beavers. Kerry Conroy remembers a pool incident at Bognor in 1978: 'Over 100 kids went in search of Captain Blood and Redcoats Debbie, Puddles and myself marched the kids around the camp until we caught up with him at a pre-arranged place on the sports field. It was my job to take Captain Blood up to the high board above the pool while the girls kept the kids safely on the ground. "What shall I do with him? Should he walk the plank?" I shouted. The kids cheered but one Beaver had decided that he couldn't wait any longer and climbed up the board and pushed me off. I went straight in the deep end and, being a non-swimmer, sank to the bottom. Luckily, Lifeguard Banana jumped in and rescued me. He said that he would have dived in sooner but thought that I was messing about!'

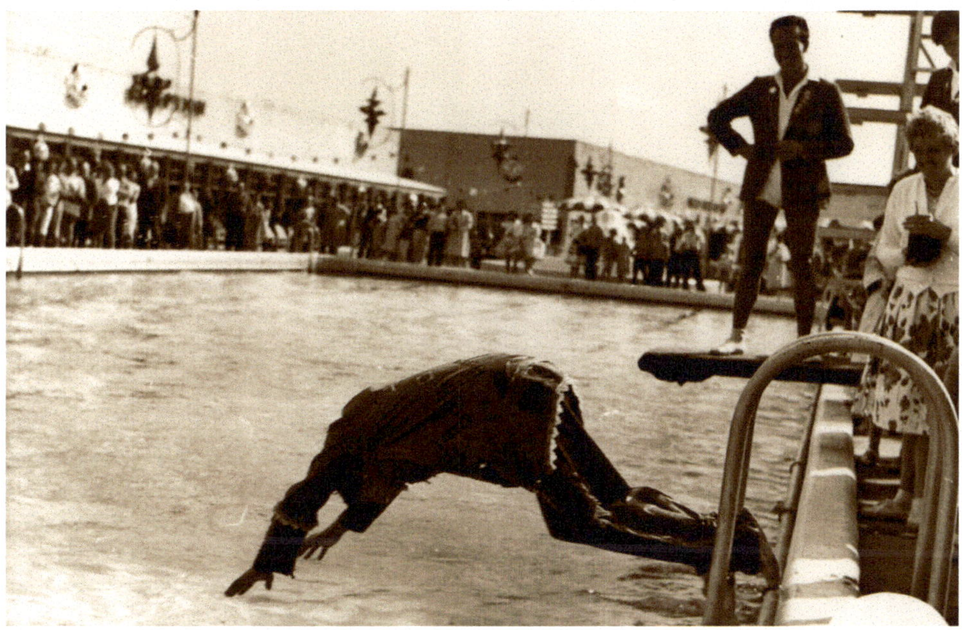

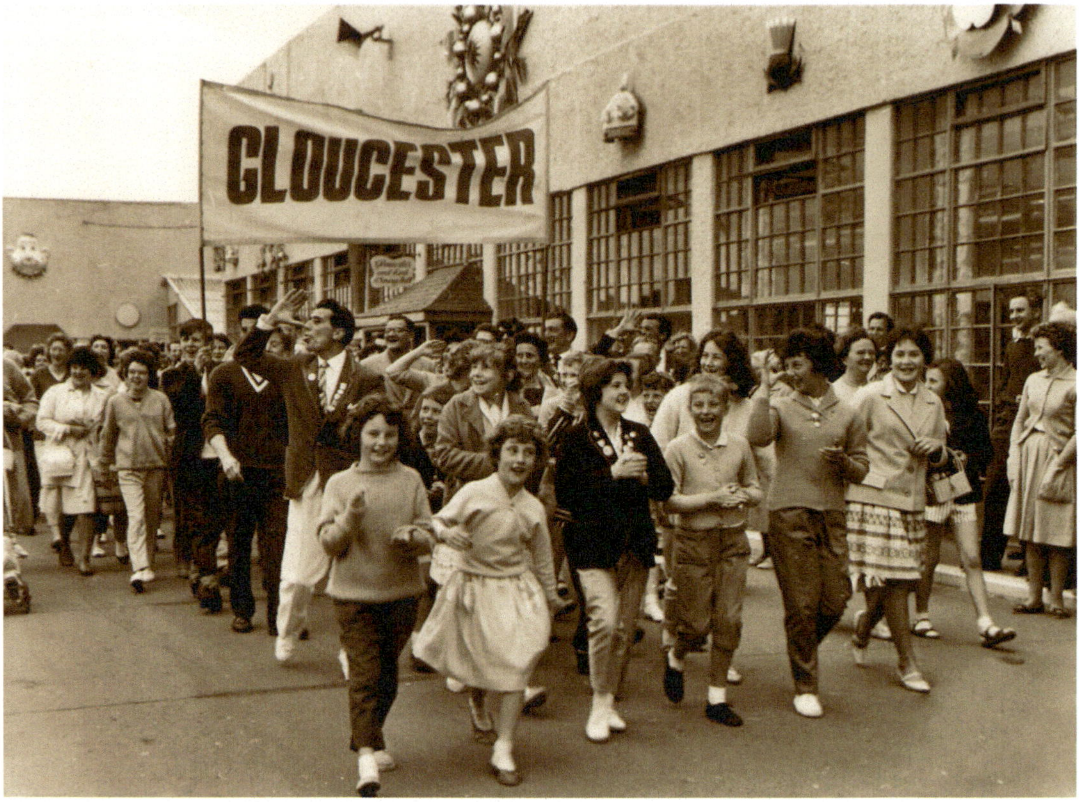

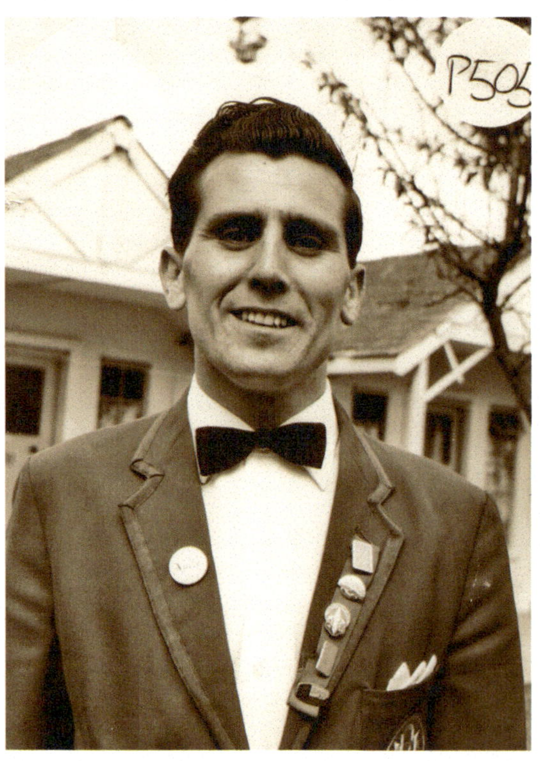

The first photograph shows Gloucester House on a Sunday Morning Parade at Skegness in 1963. Redcoat Andy King can be seen, together with other members of the crowd, giving the 'cock a snook' gesture towards their rivals. The second photograph again shows Andy King who was a Redcoat at Skegness for six seasons between 1954 and 1963. He was a Redcoat alongside television comedians Dave Allen and Freddie 'Parrotface' Davies, as well as working alongside Richard Starkey, who was the drummer with Rory Storm and The Hurricanes and later became Ringo Starr.

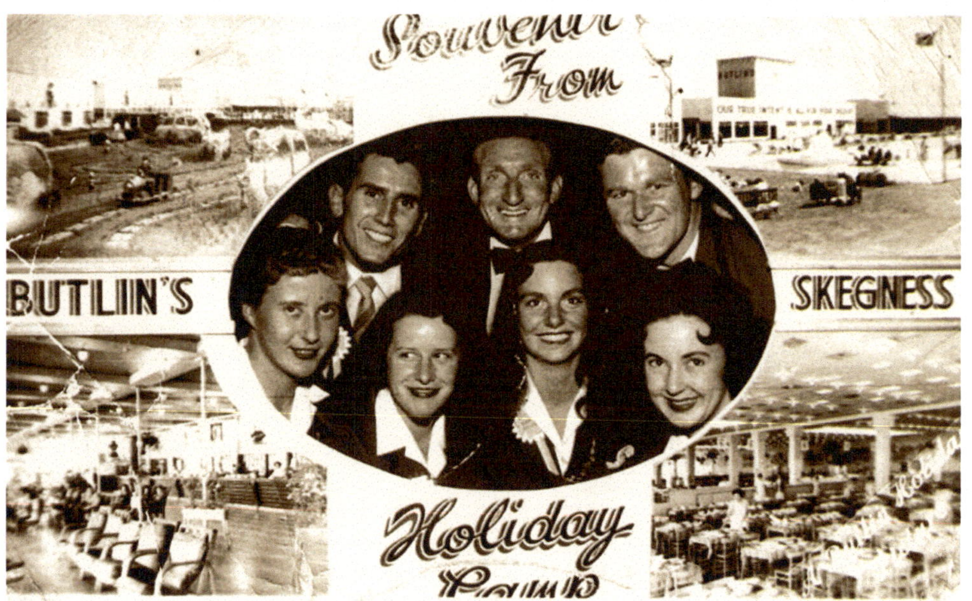

The top photograph shows a souvenir postcard featuring Redcoats from Skegness in the 1960s. There were many souvenirs available from the camps. Photographs could be bought from the foyer and, later on, transparencies were taken and supplied in hold-to-the-light key chains. Other souvenirs included enamel badges, which were given to every camper on their arrival. These were used to prove that the owner was a genuine member of the camp and entitled to food, drink and entertainment. There were also badges for members of the Beaver Club and other clubs and events. They were discontinued in 1967 because of the cost of producing them. Other souvenirs at Butlin's included plates, money boxes, playing cards, aprons and pencils.

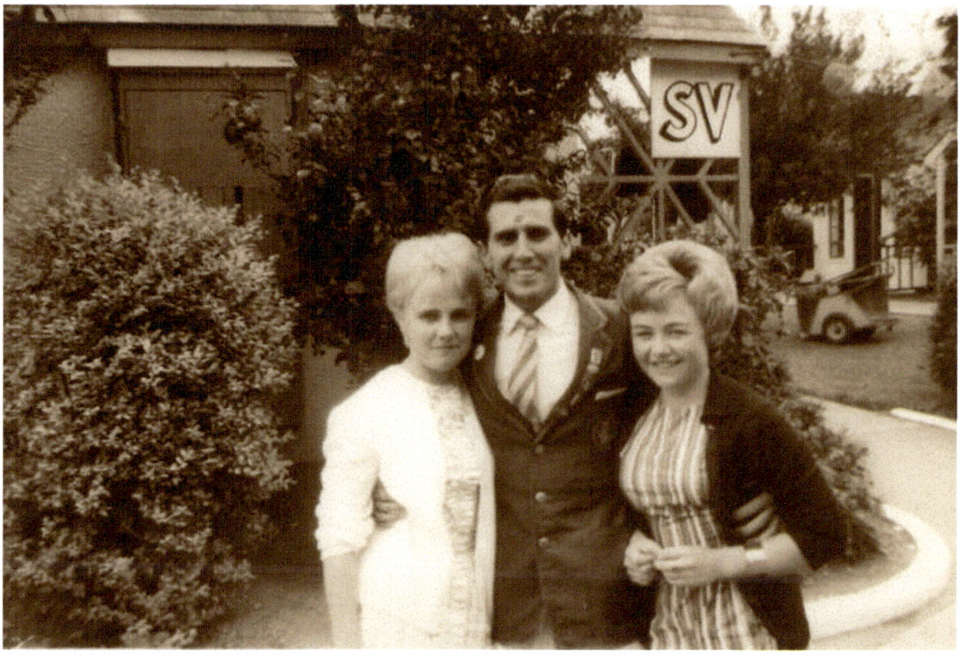

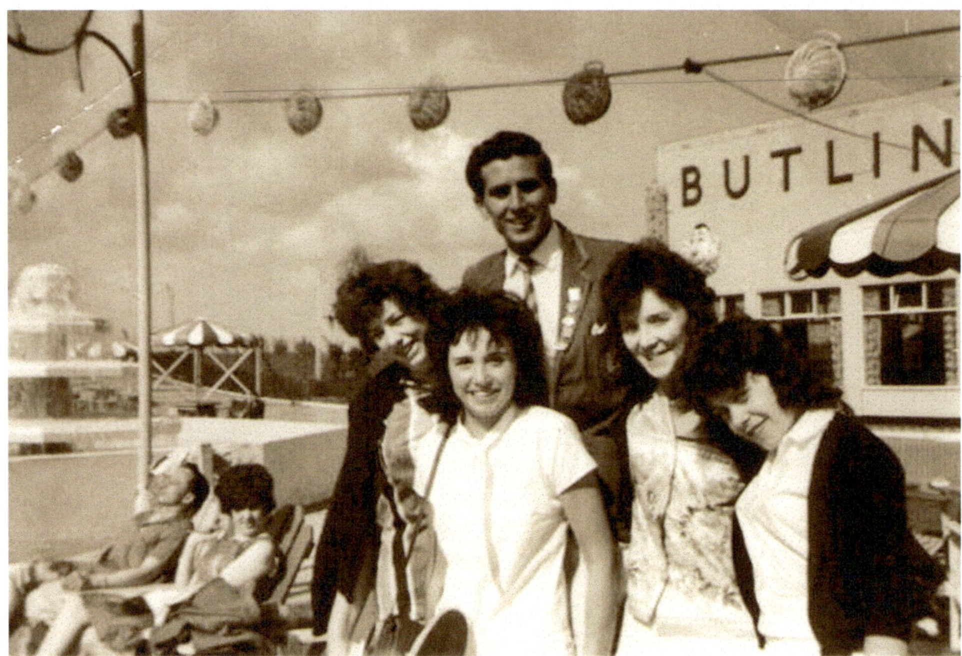

The top photograph shows Andy King with campers at Skegness in 1963. The pool on the left is the one in which Gertrude the elephant drowned in. Billy Butlin had a menagerie of animals on site. In the early days during the 1930s, regular pig, cheetah and greyhound racing was held on camp. The cheetahs were said to be quite tame. There was also 'Mushie', the toothless lion, who appeared at Butlin's amusement site. His trainer was happy to place her head in his mouth during her act without fear of being bitten. Other animals at the Butlin's zoo included bears, monkeys, a leopard, seals and kangaroos.

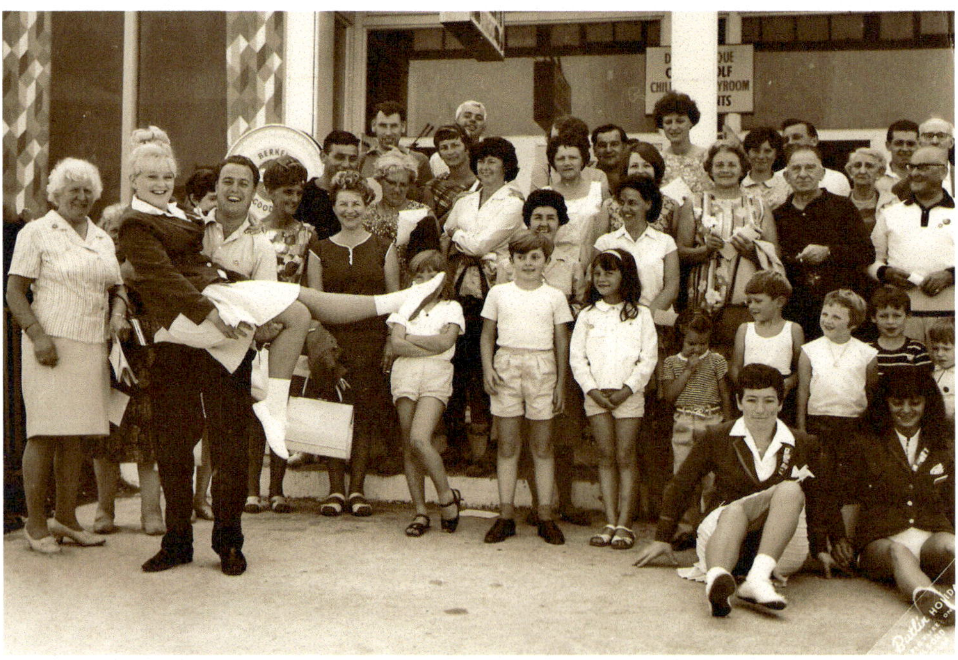

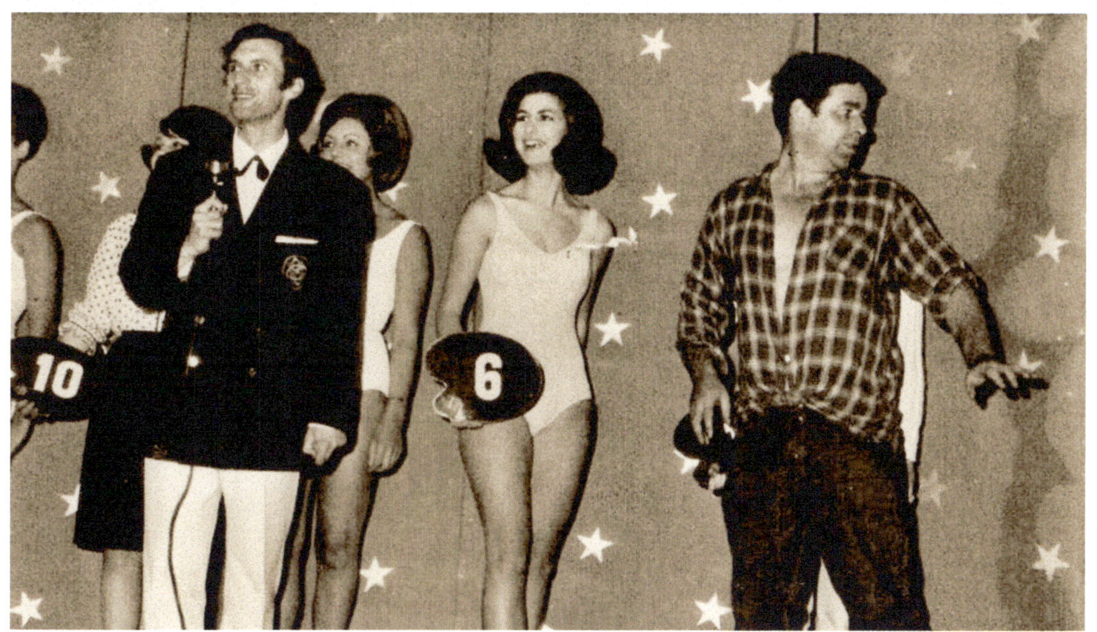

The first photograph shows Mike Onions with the camp comic Johnny O'Mahoney presenting the Holiday Princess Competition at Bognor in 1966. Johnny O'Mahoney was the brother of television comedian Dave Allen who was himself also a Redcoat. By 1975, the top prize for the overall winner of the Holiday Princess Competition was £1,000 and a Hillman *Avenger*. There was also another £1,900 in prizes given away. The second photograph shows Andy King's wife and daughter, who were both called Anne, winning the Mother and Daughter Competition at Skegness in 1973.

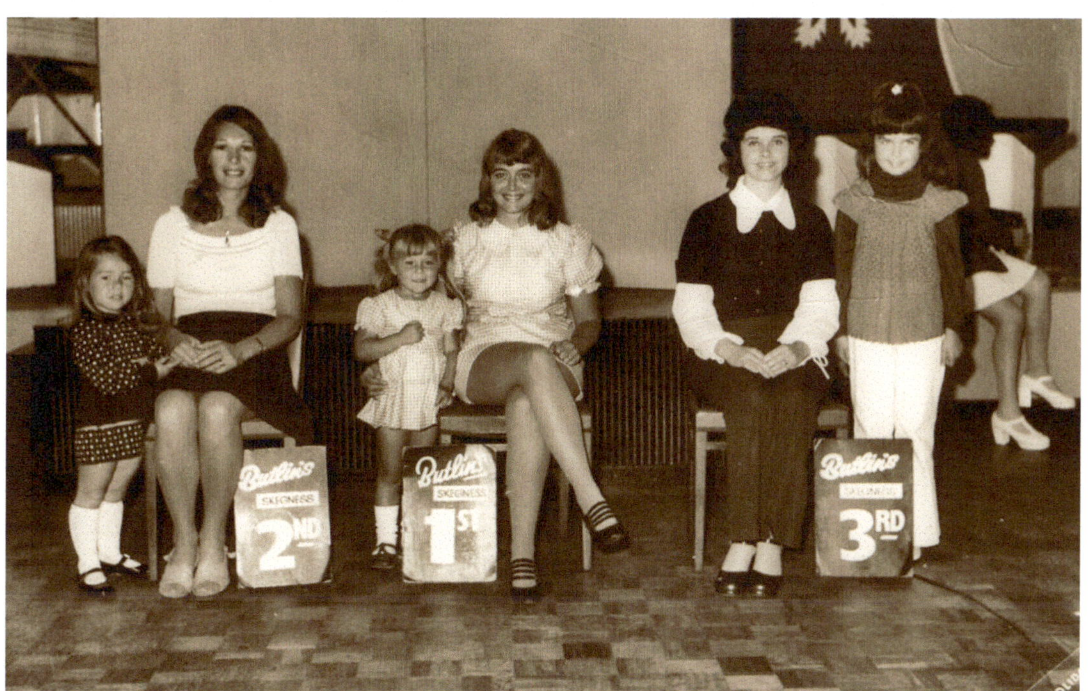

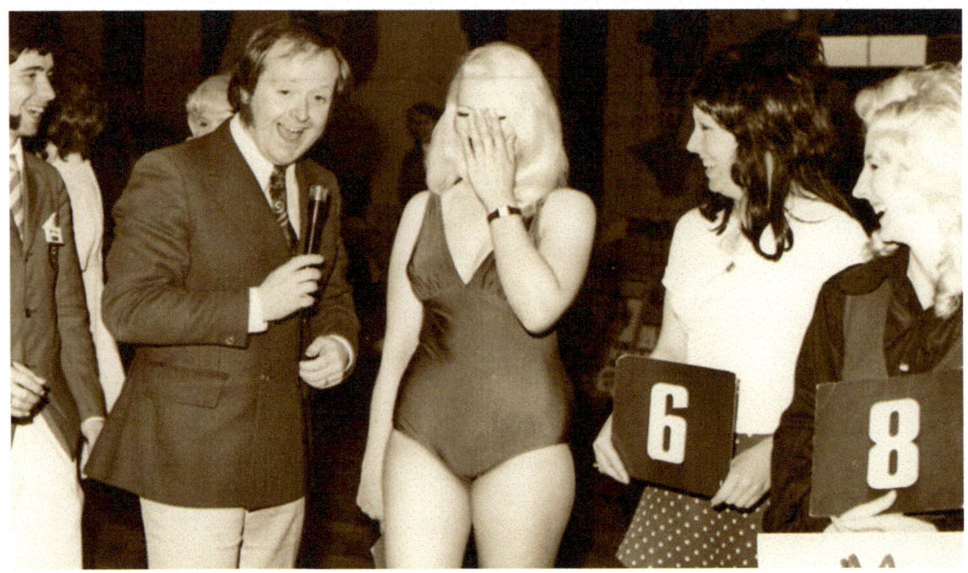

Late-night cabaret in the Regency Cabaret Lounge at Skegness featured a host of star acts during 1975. These included Roy Castle, Bob Monkhouse, Frank Carson, The Bachelors, Frankie Howerd, Ted Rogers, Les Dennis, Mike Newman and Jack Douglas. The Star Trail Talent Contest in the 1970s produced some well-known household names. Mike Reid was runner up to the popular Liverpool comic Joey Kaye. Stan Boardman won the competition in 1976. Junior Star Trail was just as popular, and winners included Les Dennis and Catherine Zeta Jones.

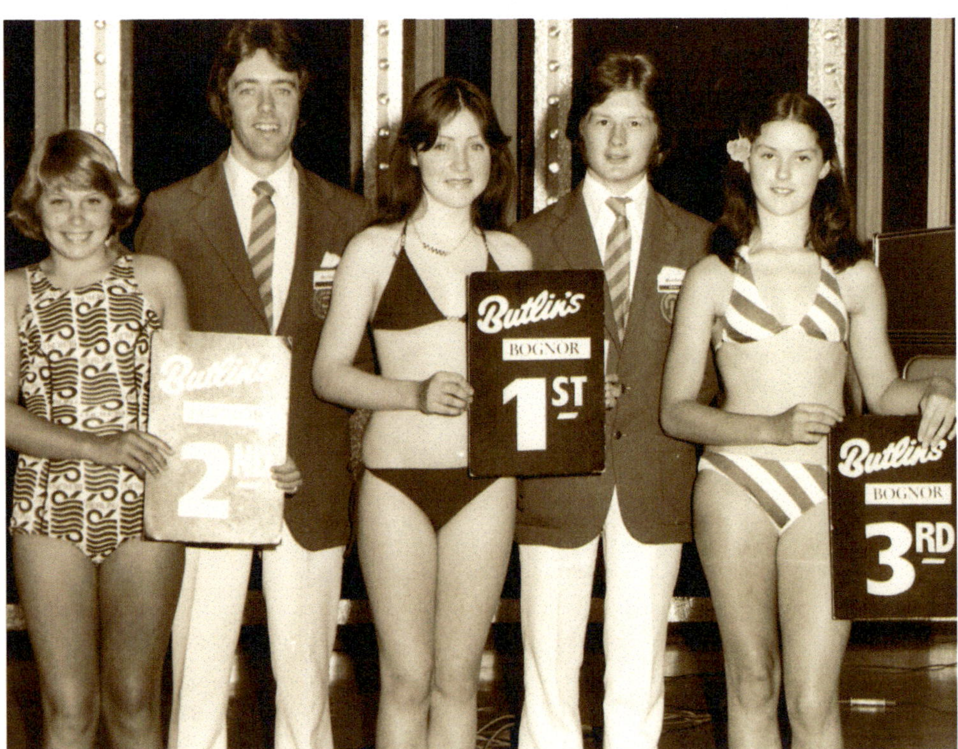

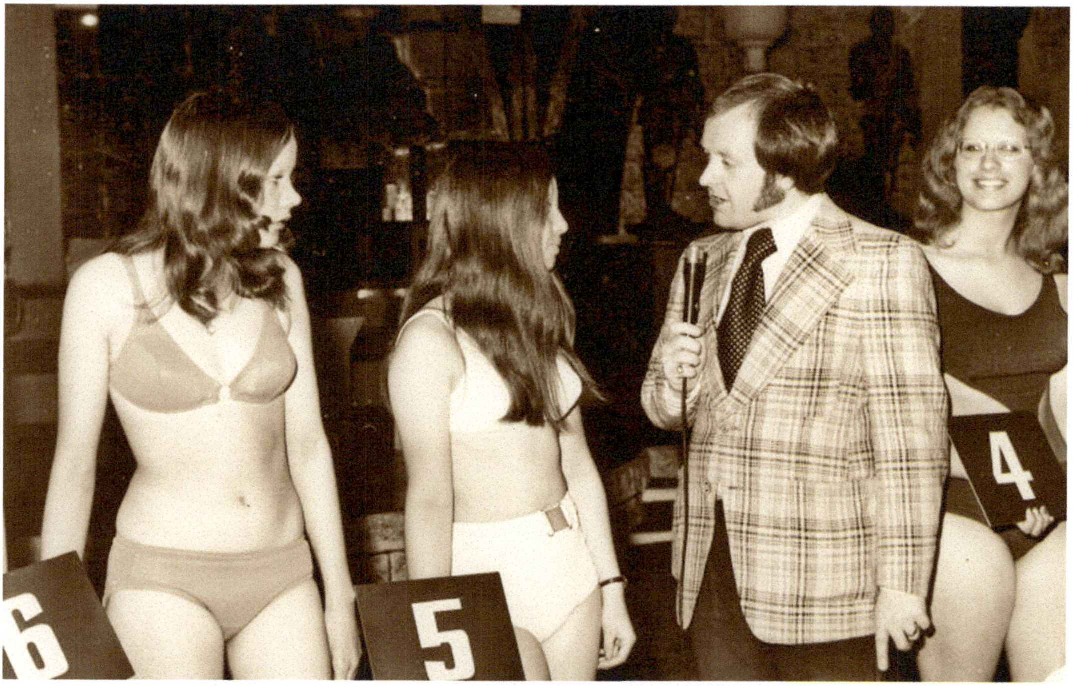

Beauty pageants became very popular right from the early days of Butlin's. The first photograph shows Tony Peers hosting a beauty contest during the 1970s. Tony was a Redcoat compere at Minehead and, in 1972, he moved to Butlin's in Ayr, before working at Butlin's in Filey in 1973. He has appeared in many television programmes since, including *Coronation Street*, *All Creatures Great and Small* and *Last of the Summer Wine*.

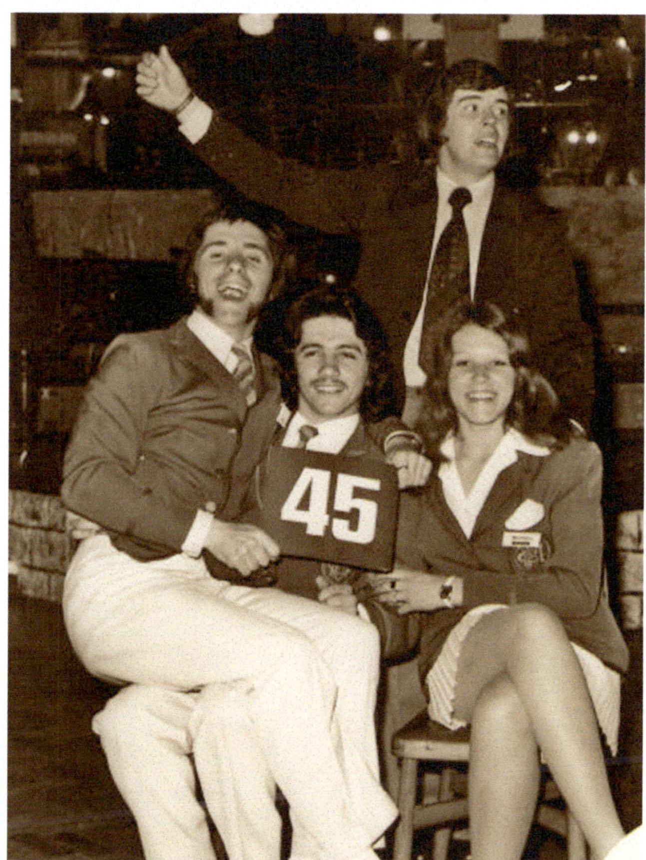

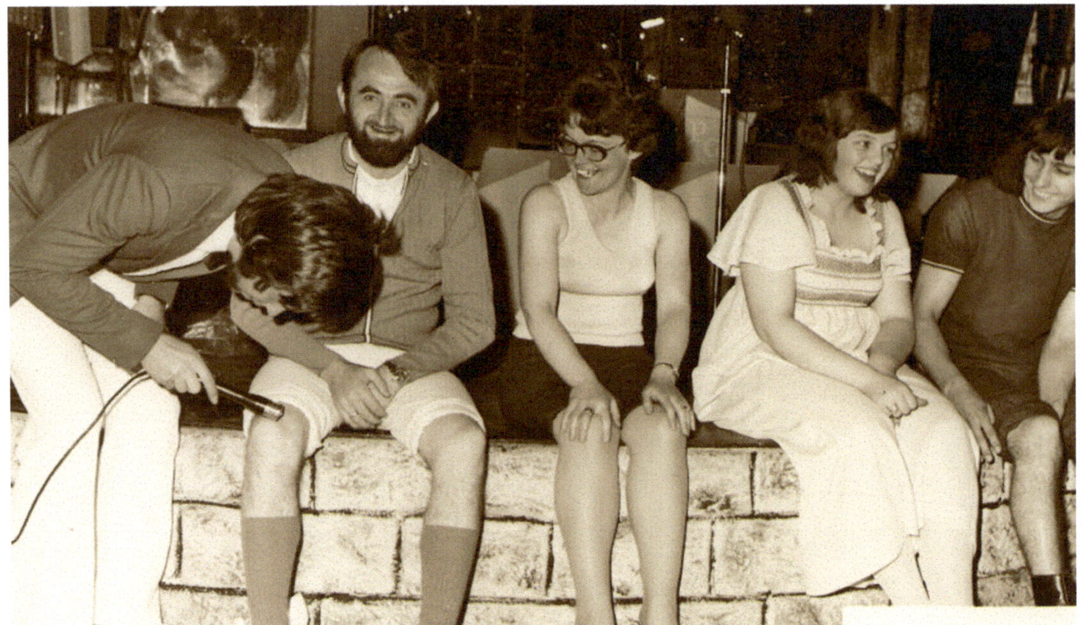

The Knobbly Knees Competition started in the 1930s. In 1947, the prize for the knobbliest knees was awarded by Laurel and Hardy at the Skegness camp. Laurel and Hardy had been touring the UK and played at Skegness during the week commencing the 23 June 1947. In the Empress Ballroom at Butlin's, they judged the 'Holiday Lovelies Competition' followed by the Knobbly Knees Competition. The following day they judged many of the junior competitions and took part in activities such as roller skating, before meeting Billy Butlin himself.

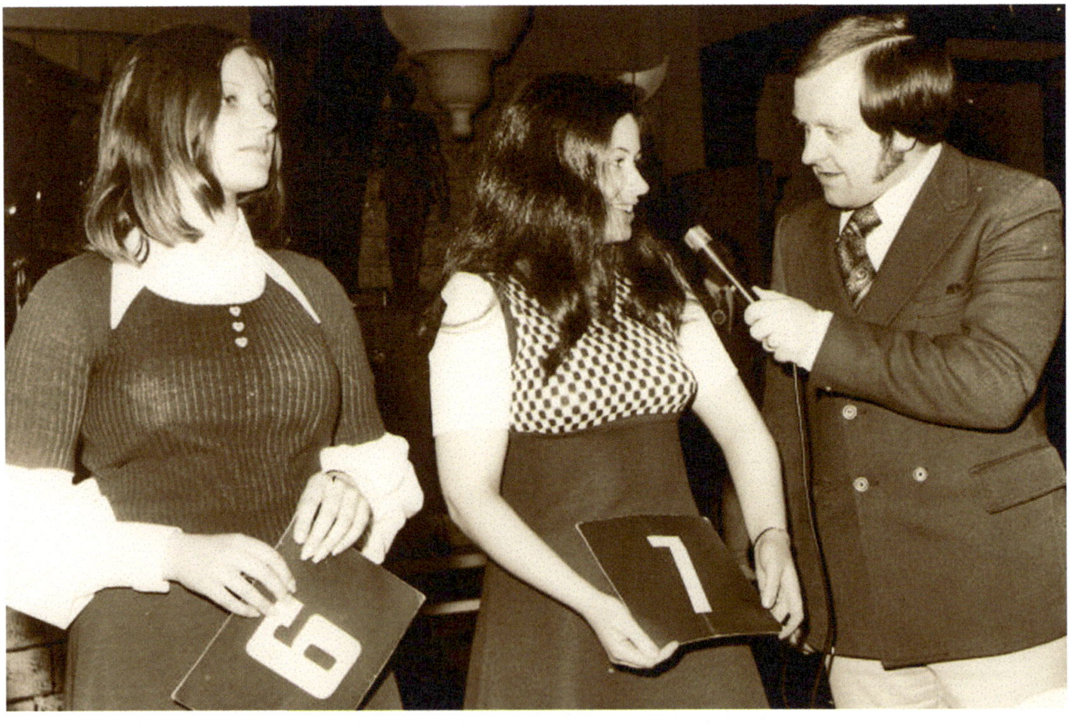

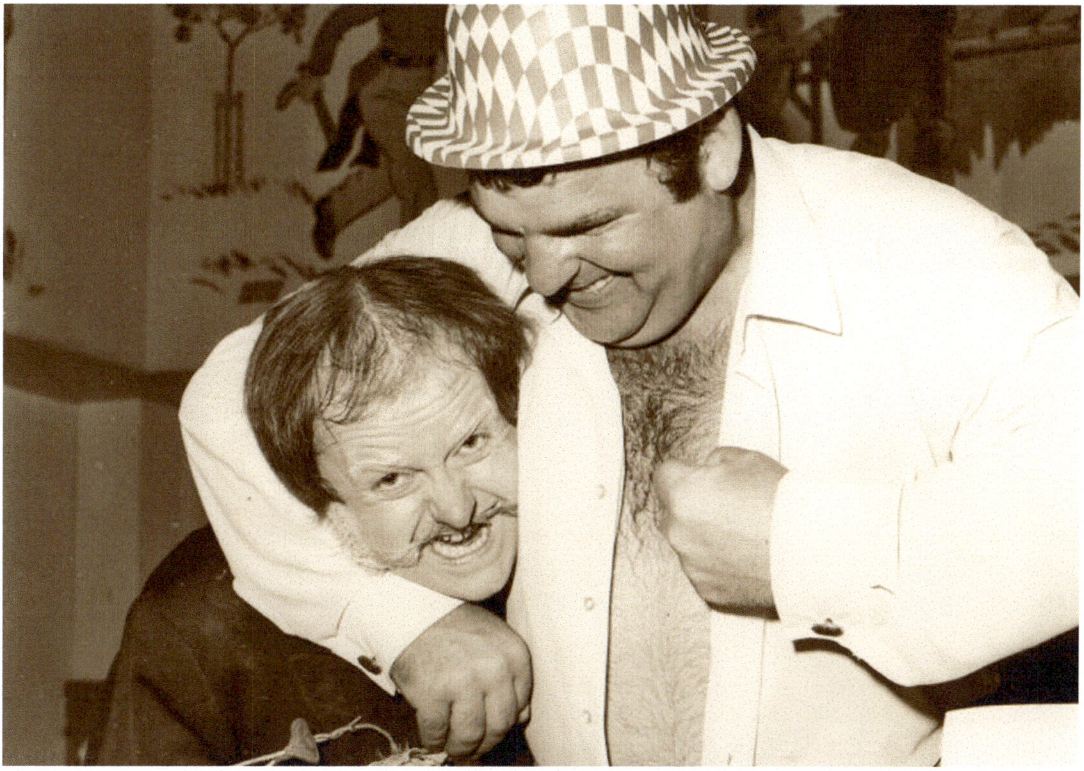

Compere Tony Peers finds himself in a headlock in the first photograph at Filey in 1973. The camp at Filey was being built when the Second World War started in 1939. Immediately, the camps at Clacton and Skegness were requisitioned and turned into military bases. Work on the Filey camp would have remained unfinished but the government requested that Billy Butlin finished the camp so that it could be used by military personnel. Butlin agreed on the agreement that he could buy it back after the war was over. The camp reopened in June 1945 and welcomed thousands of visitors, until it finally closed in 1983.

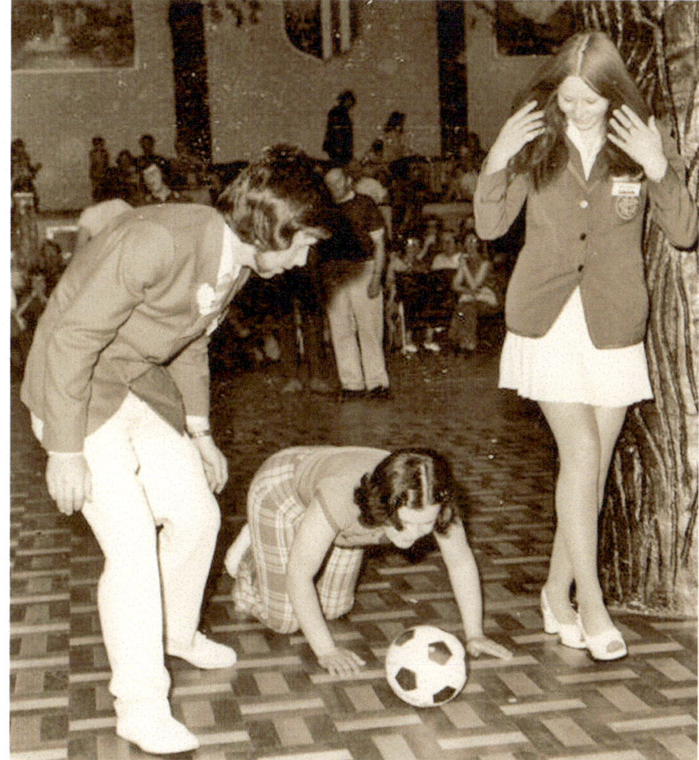

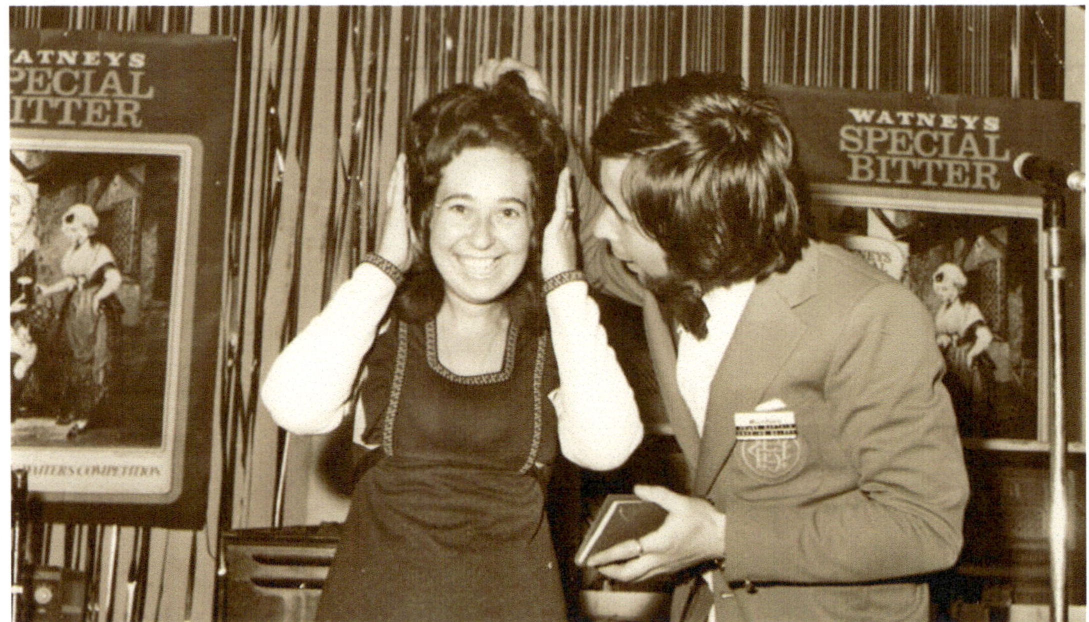

The camps continued to flourish in the 1970s. The top photograph shows the interval between acts taking part in the Watney's Special Bitter Singing Waiters Competition at Filey in 1974. The bottom photograph shows Redcoat Kerry Conroy posing for souvenir photographs with young campers at Bognor in 1978. A contest for younger teenagers proved popular in the late 1970s and was called, 'Miss Elegance and Master Mod', which was a competition to find the smartest fourteen and fifteen year olds.

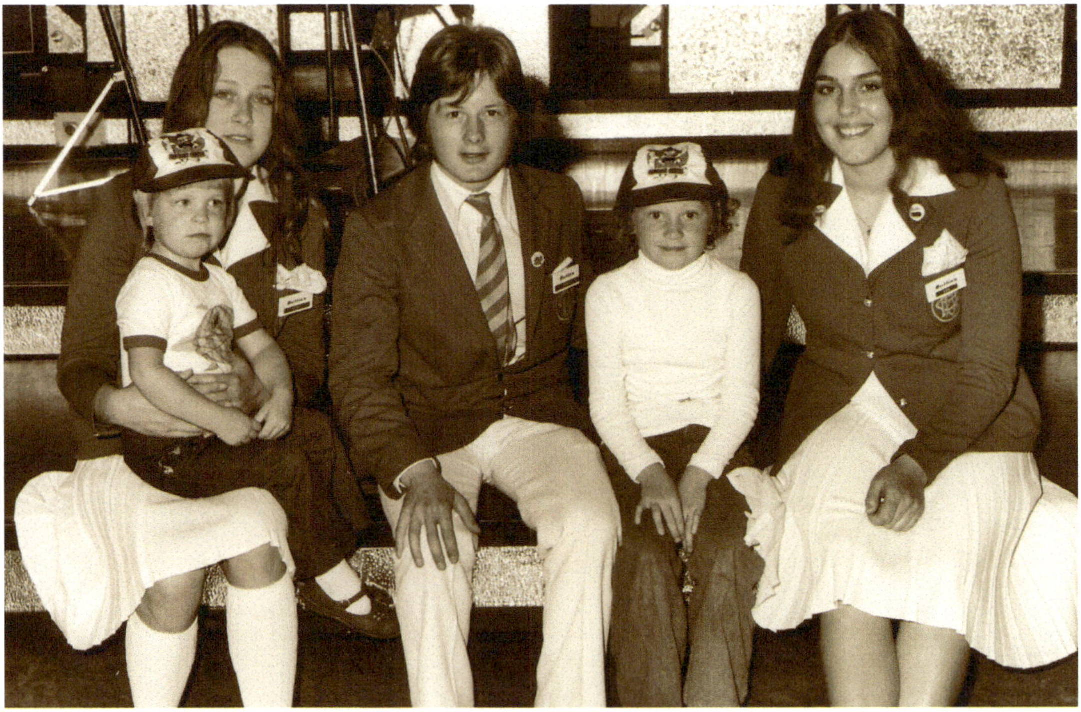

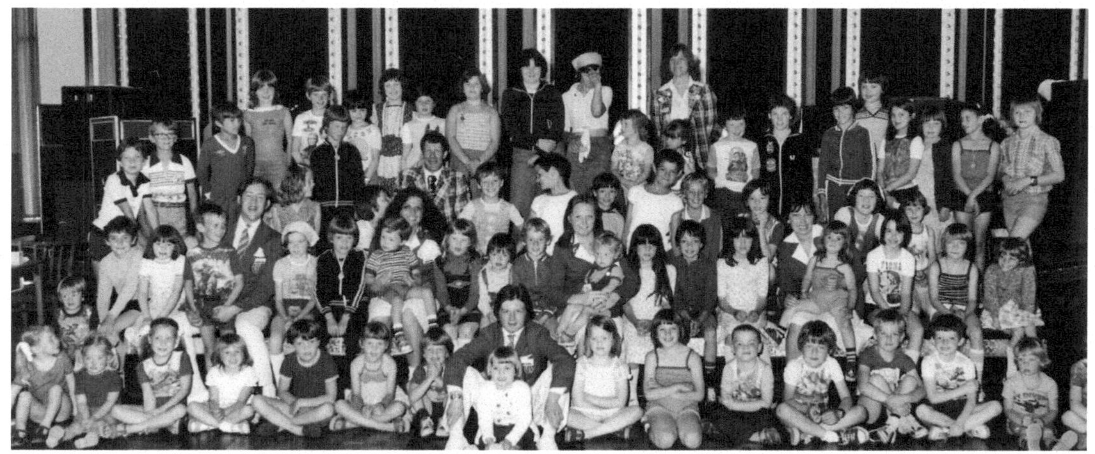

Junior campers enjoy the Donkey Derby at Bognor in 1978 in the first photograph. Their parents, some with rosettes, stand behind them while the photograph is taken. In the background a giant golf ball is visible, which advertises the nearby putting green. The second photograph shows members of the Beaver Club complete with their Redcoat uncles and aunties.

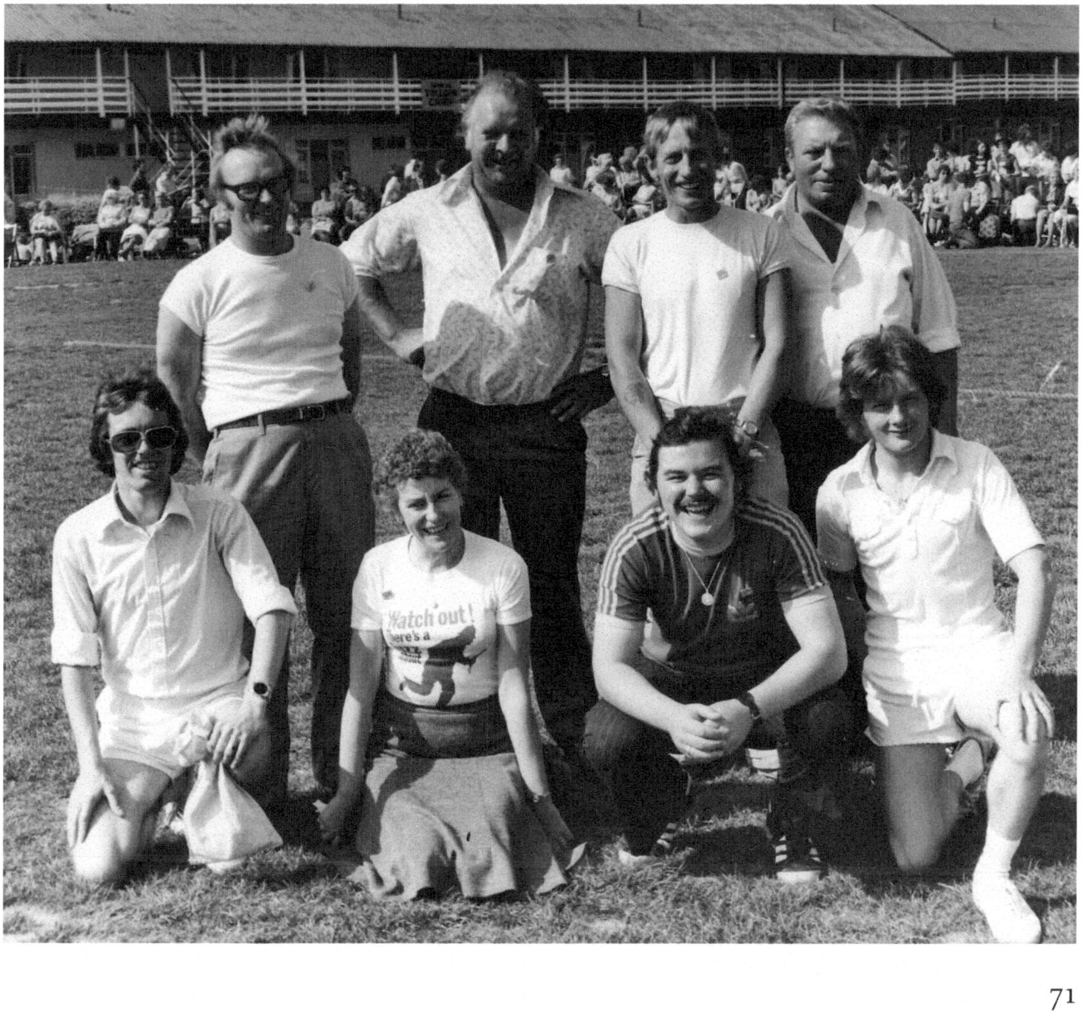

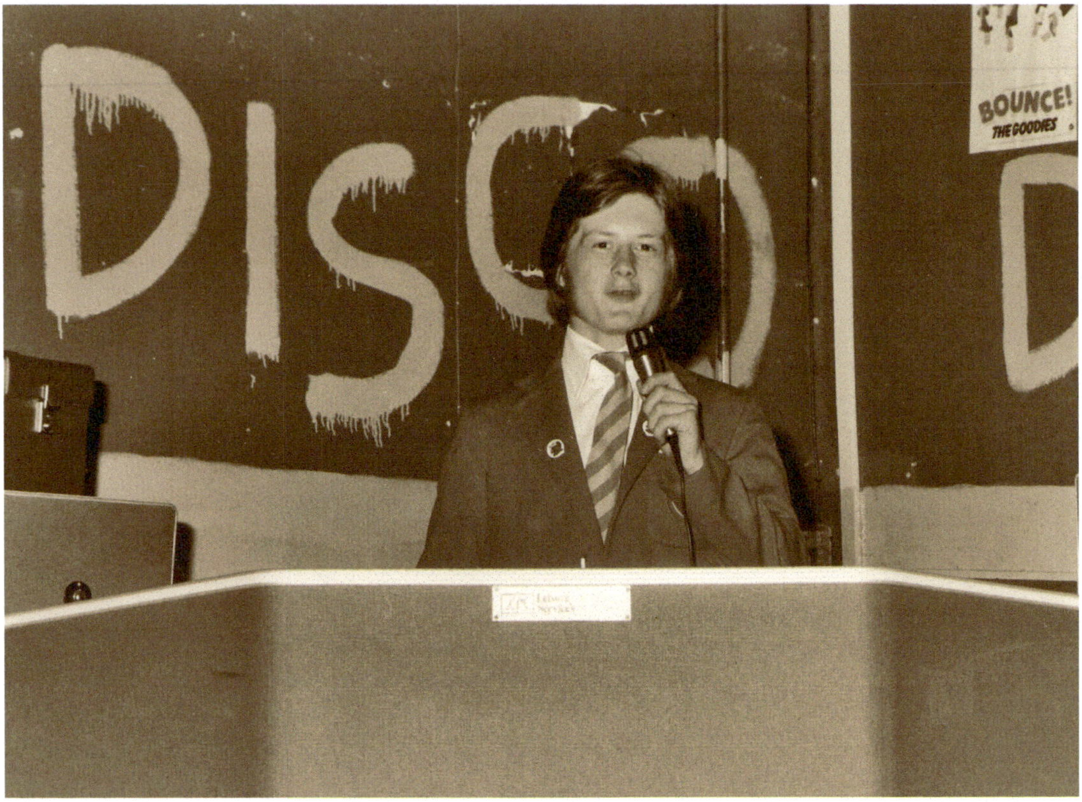

Kerry Conroy hosts the Disco at Bognor in 1978 in the first photograph. Regular children's events included the pirate hunt (in the 1960s, it had been a Red Indian hunt), the egg and spoon race, the balloon race and the sack race. In the 1978 holiday brochure, other entertainment listed for members of the Beaver Club included rounders on the sports field, table tennis and soccer coaching, and roller skating. Events also included the junior swimming gala.

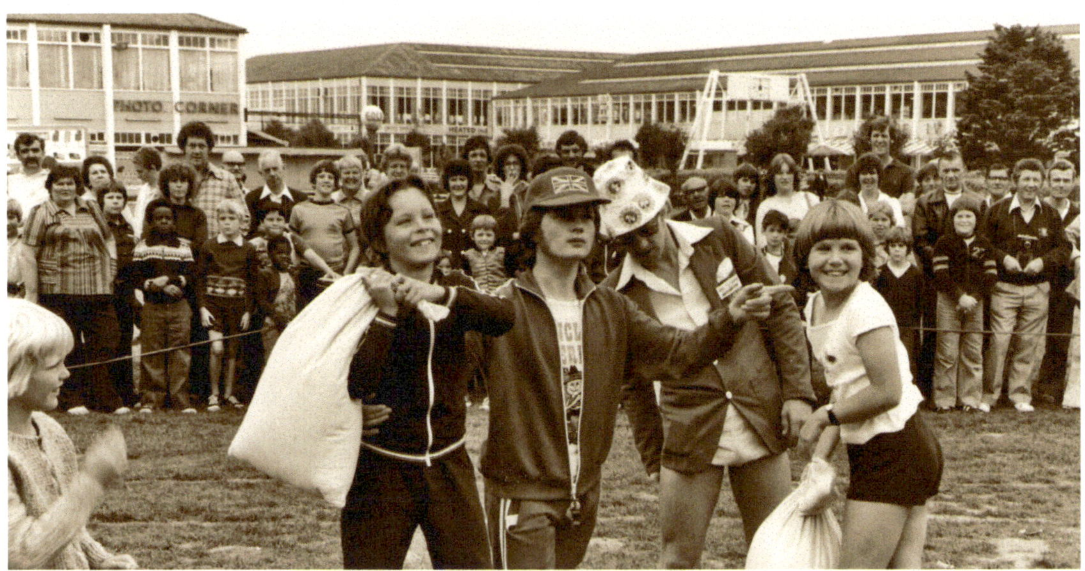

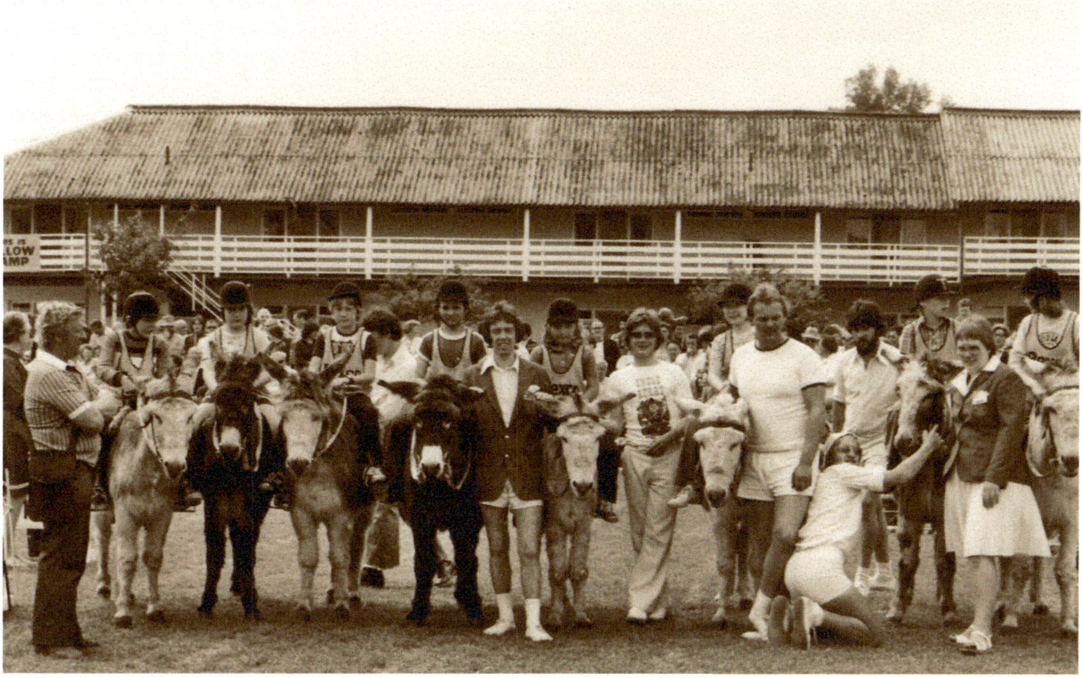

The Donkey Derby prepares to begin in the earlier photograph. Long before the advent of the digital camera and the camera phone, most photographs would be taken by the camp photographer who then had to develop the images the same day so that they would be ready for campers to view the next morning. Ten of thousands of photographs must have been taken in Butlin's heyday and unfortunately, many seem to have been destroyed or lost over the years. Today, in the age of digital photography, it's all a far easier process.

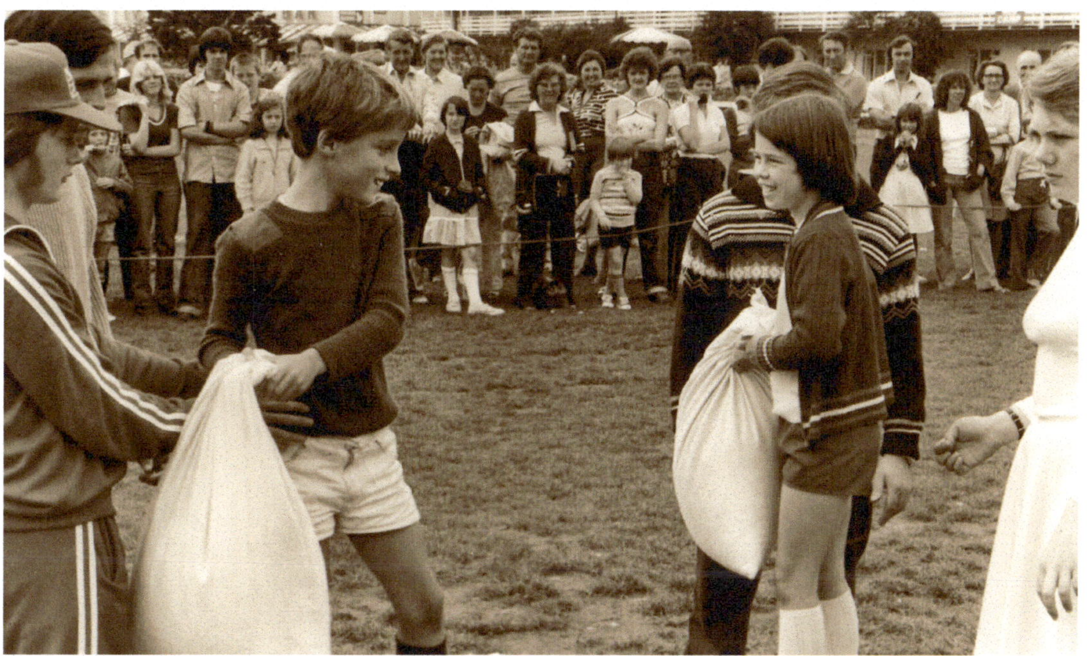

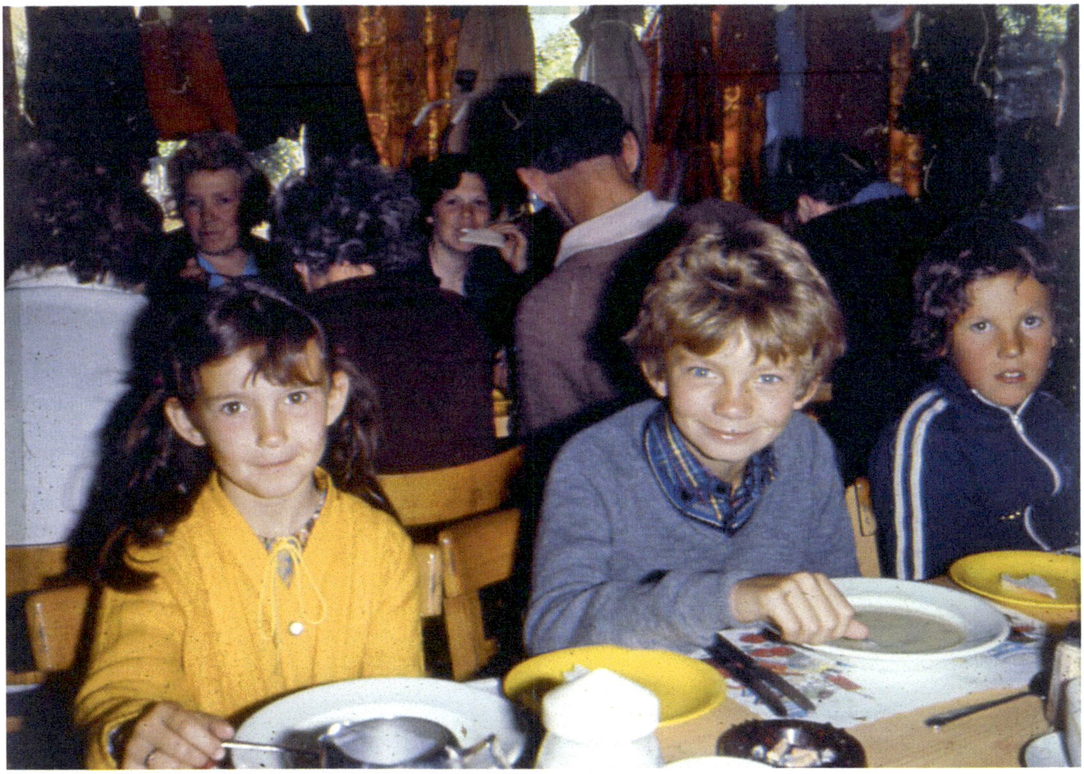

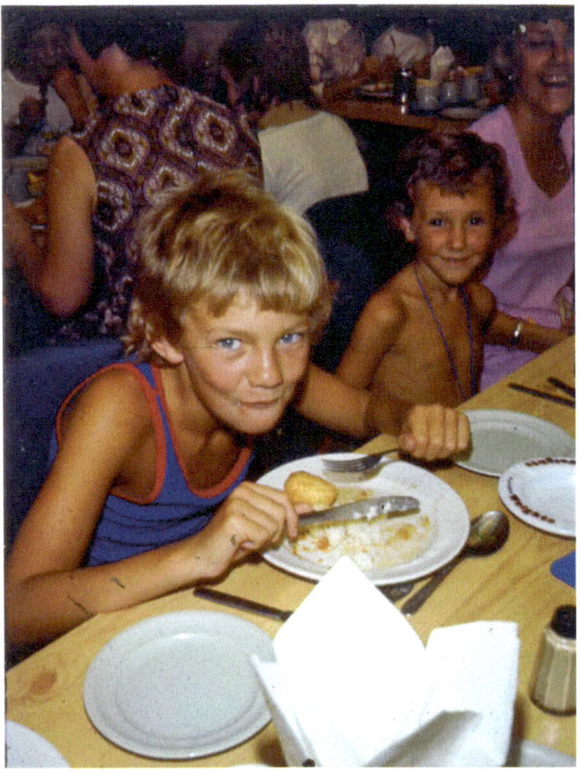

The dining halls would compete with each other in competitions. Several Redcoats would join each dining hall (or house) and encourage campers to enter the various competitions to gain their own house points. The house with the most points would win the inter-house trophy, which would be awarded at the end of the week. Volunteers from each dining hall would also take part as members of the weekly campers committee and would voice any complaints or suggestions from other campers. Billy Butlin didn't like the idea of self-catering and felt being cooked for was a chance for mothers to take it easy and enjoy themselves. However, when Bobby Butlin took over the reins from his father, he decided to introduce self-catering which commenced in the late 1960s. There were also on-site supermarkets although the full-board option still existed.

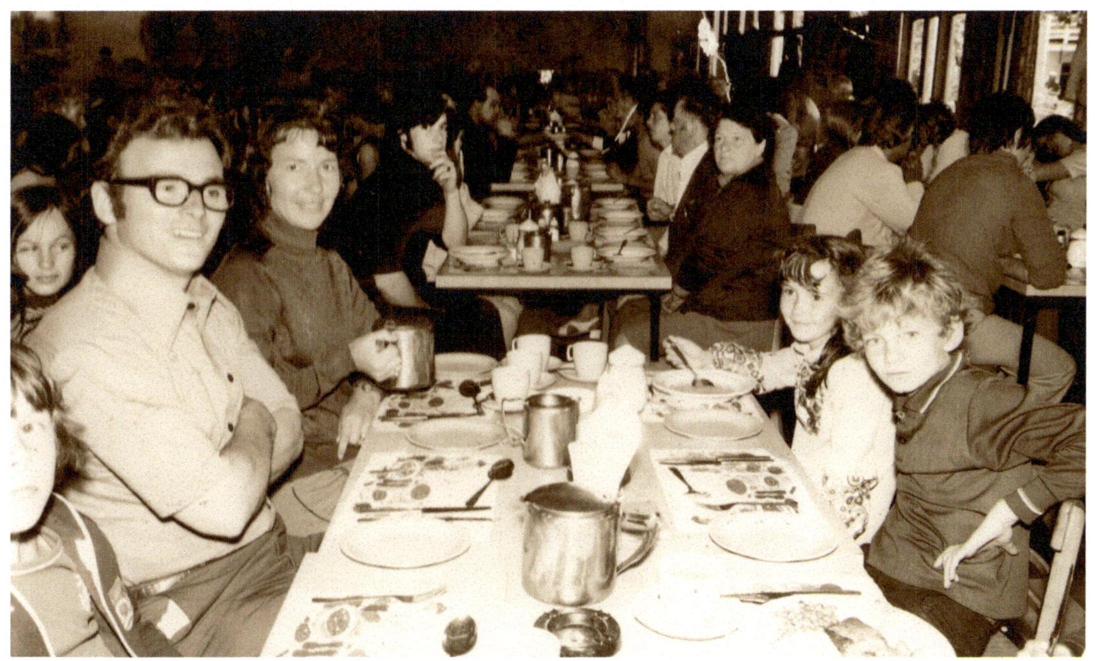

The two photographs show happy campers at Minehead during the 1970s. The Minehead camp opened in 1962. In 1981, £1.2 million was invested in the camp and in the late 1980s, a further £10 million was spent to rejuvenate the camp which included adding flumes, whirlpools and rapids to the indoor pool. In the late 1990s, the camp received new accommodation as well as a new swimming pool and a skyline pavilion. Over £139 million was spent on refurbishing the three camps that remained.

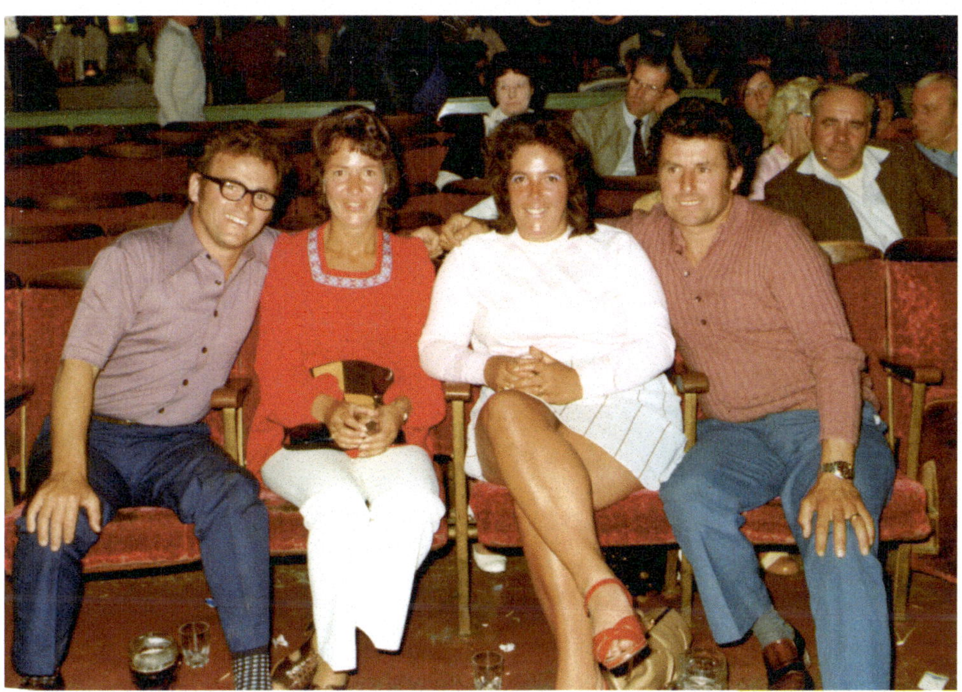

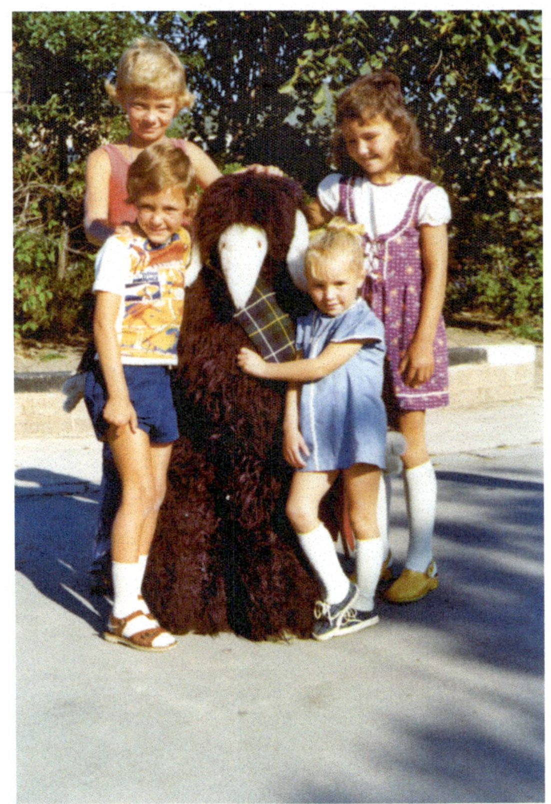

The Wombles were very popular in the early 1970s and the camp at Minehead had its own Womble that children could have their photograph taken with. The camp photographers always had several props with them that campers could use when being photographed. These included sombreros and toy monkeys. The real Wombles appeared themselves in later years at Butlin's, as part of the entertainment.

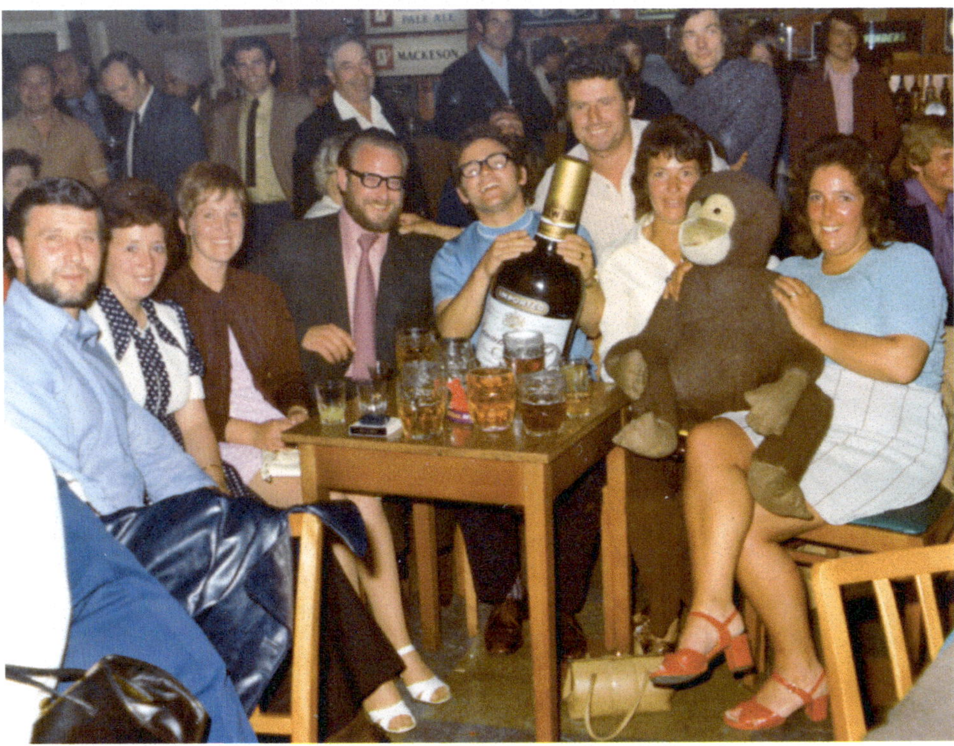

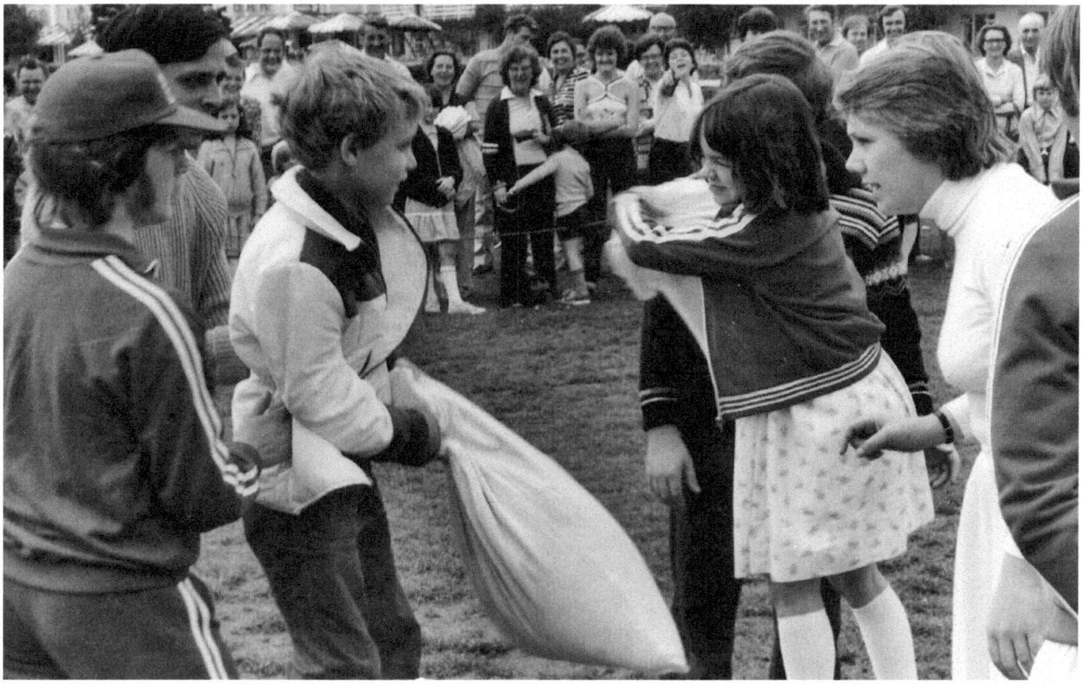

Kerry Conroy supervises the children taking part in a pillow fight on the sports field at Bognor in 1978. They are cheered on by their parents in the background. On 14 November 2008, the Guinness World Record for the largest pillow fight was set at the Butlin's camp at Minehead.

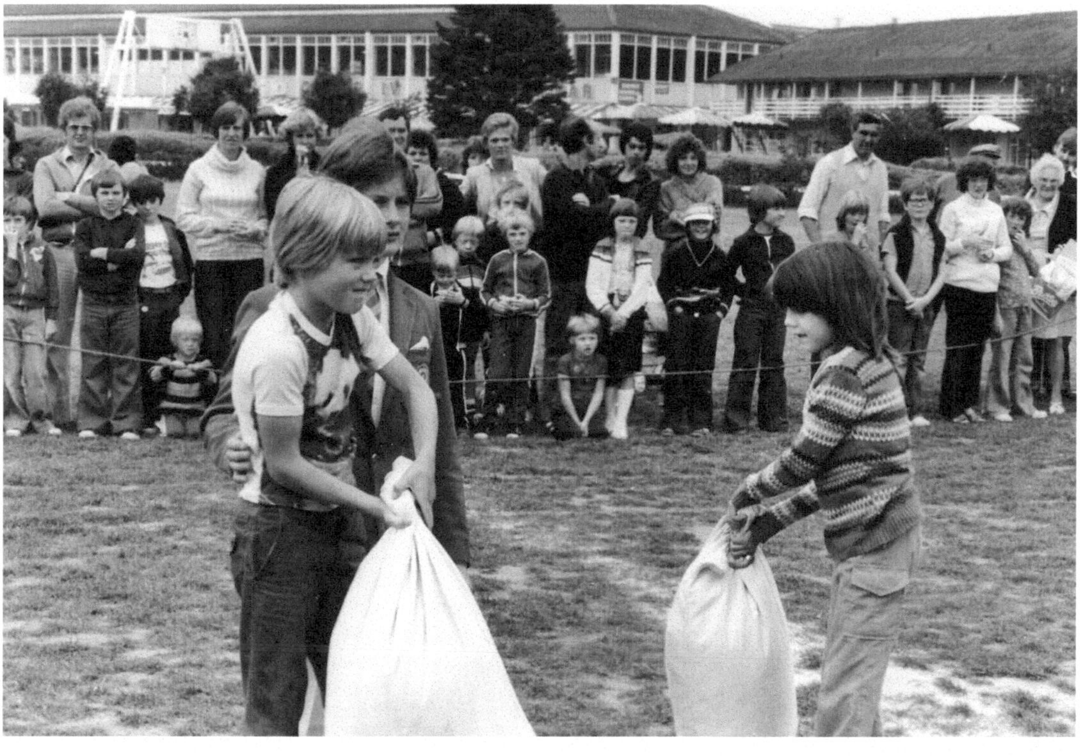

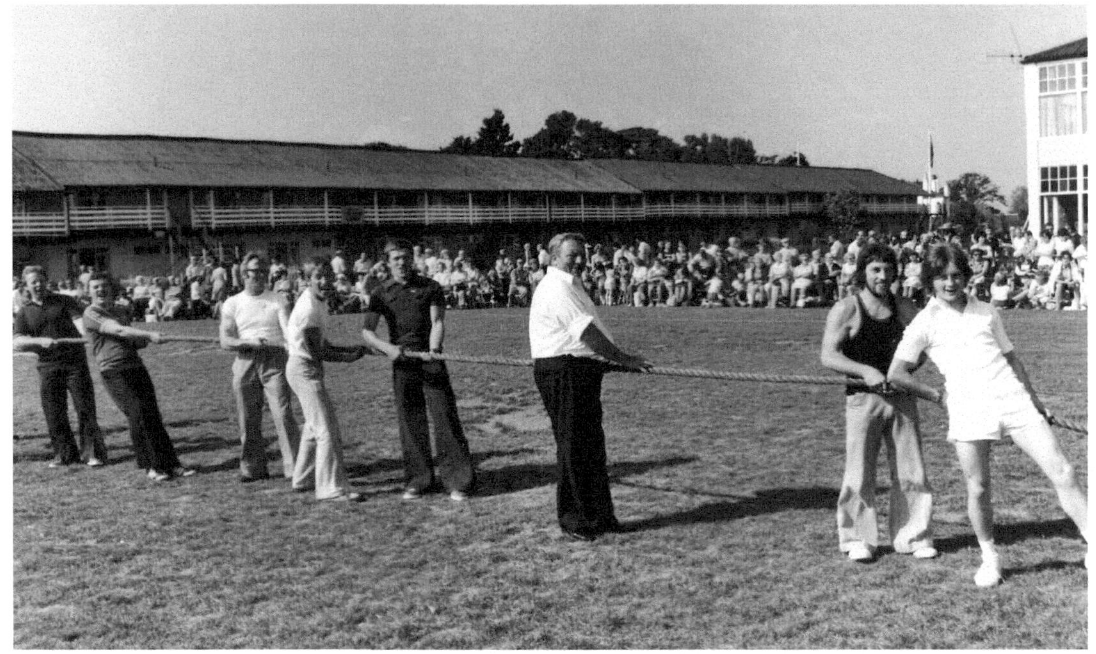

The top photograph shows Kerry Conroy with his team taking part in the Tug of War Competition in 1978 at Bognor. A successful tug of war team consisted of the heaviest and strongest campers from each house. In September 2011, Butlin's at Minehead hosted the European Outdoor Tug of War Championships and both men and women competed for gold in different weight categories. Competitors came from all across the world and eighty-five teams entered the championships. In total, England won one gold medal and three bronze medals in the contest.

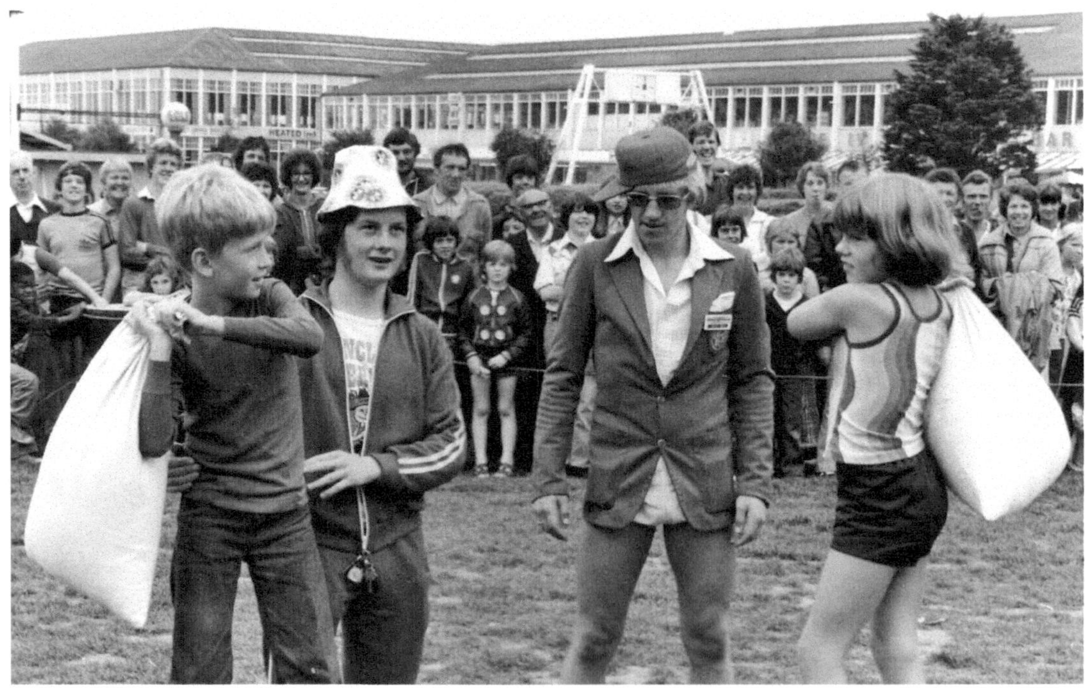

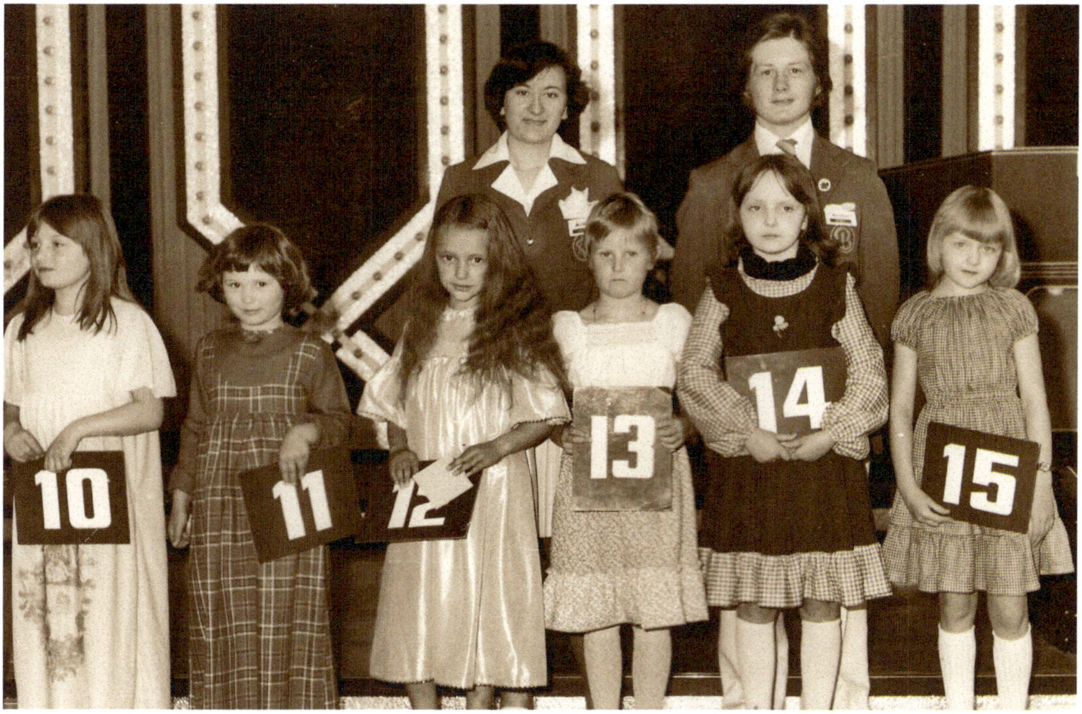

The top photograph shows contestants taking part in the Junior Miss Competition. The bottom photograph shows games taking place on Sunday morning during the 'Meet the Redcoats' event. Besides the Junior Miss Competition, other contests for children included the Kiddies Holiday Lovelies Contest, the young Tarzan Contest and the Fancy Dress Competition.

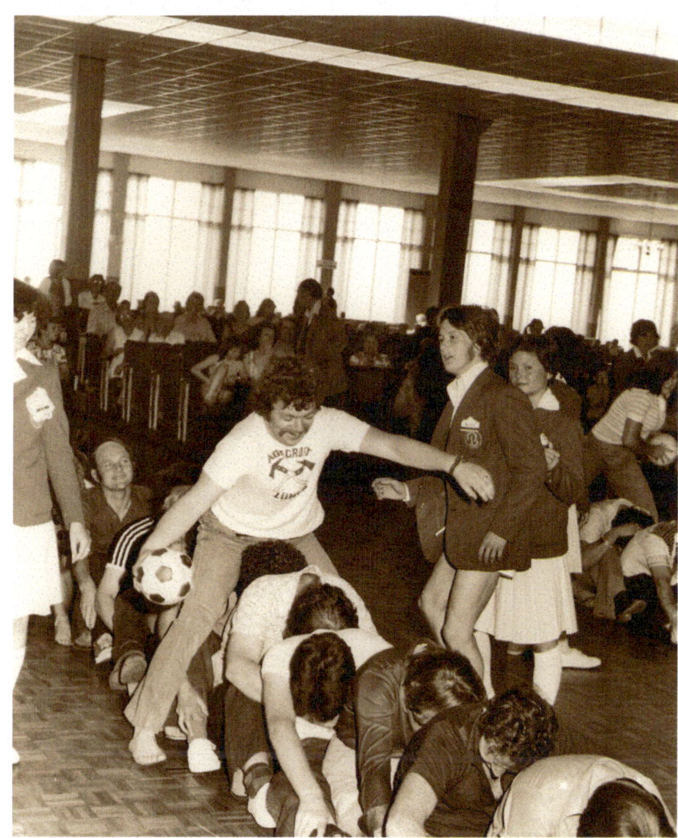

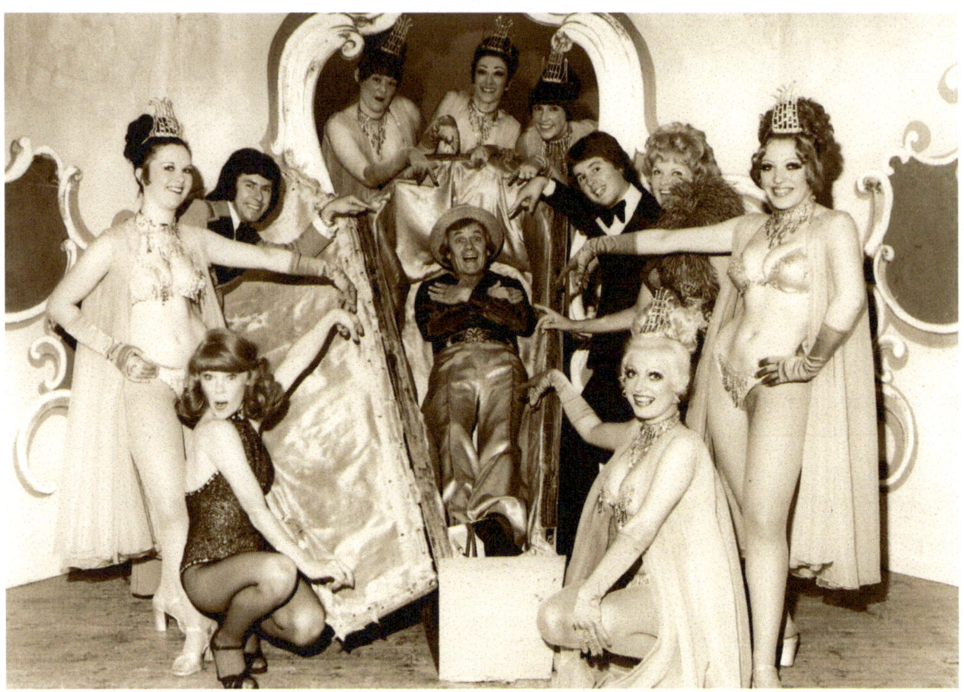

The first photograph shows Vanessa Morgan in the Revue at Barry in 1977. In the early days, Ian Carmichael directed the Butlin's Resident Revue shows. Between 1947 and 1950, he was paid £10 a show and entertainment had to be just over an hour long with no intervals. There were no programmes produced for the early shows and the acts booked were anonymous. The shows improved greatly in the 1950s with a full pit orchestra and a full line-up of chorus girls. Peter Casson performed as a hypnotist and proved to be very popular. Previously, during the Second World War, he had worked for ENSA.

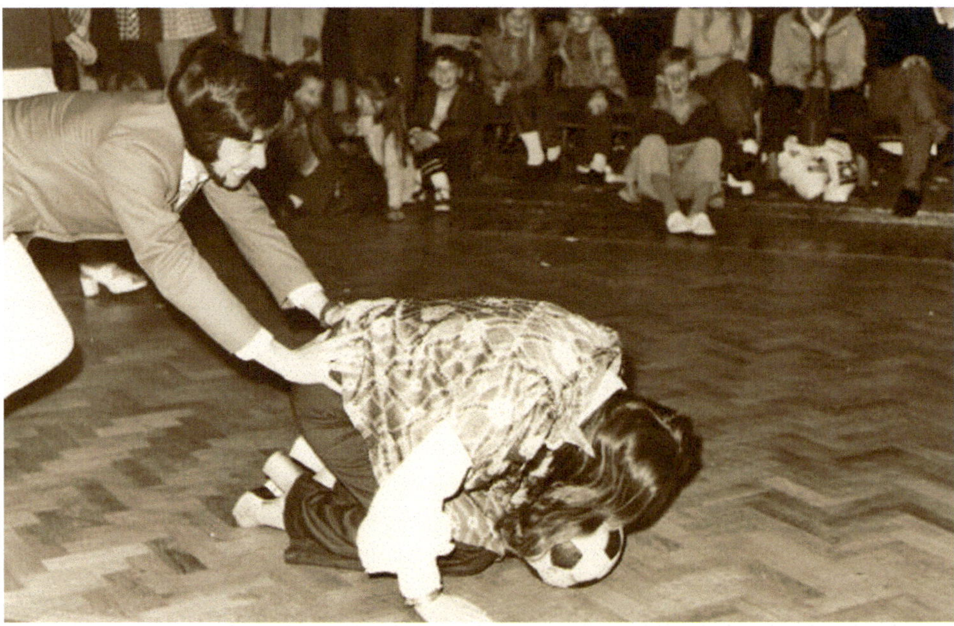

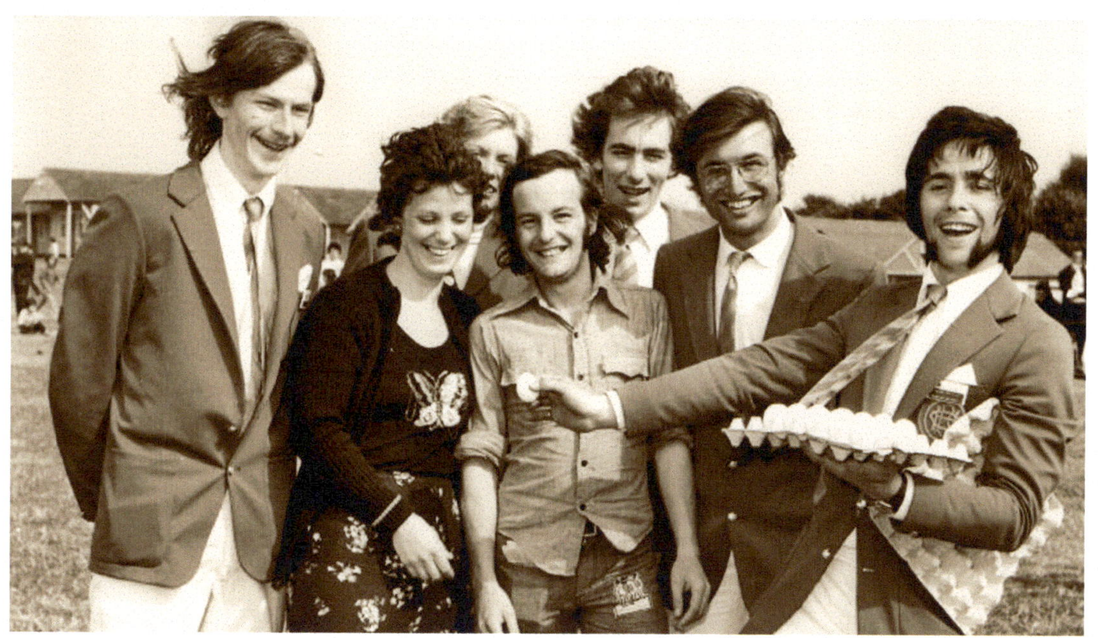

The top photograph shows the Egg Throwing Competition on the sports field in 1974. It was held on Sports Day as part of the inter-house contests. Competitors had to catch the eggs without breaking them. The occasional hard-boiled egg would be slipped in by a Redcoat to ensure that their team won. One contest included couples having to throw eggs to each other while getting further and further apart. When the egg wasn't successfully caught and smashed, the couple were eliminated until only one couple remained. The second photograph shows fun in the ballroom on Sunday morning in 1974.

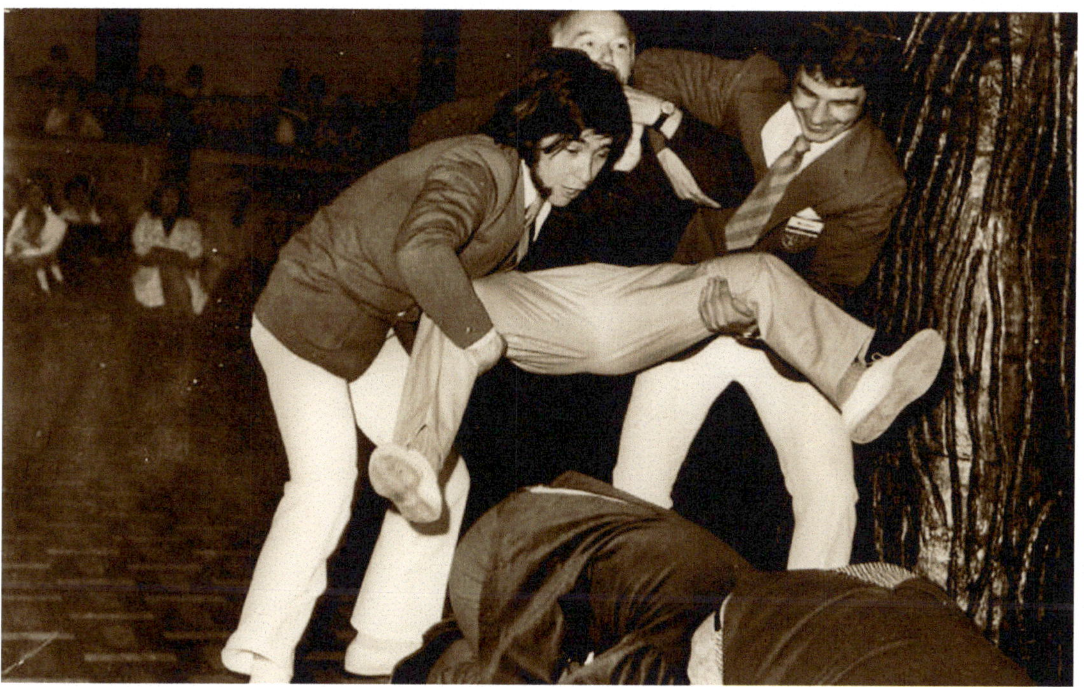

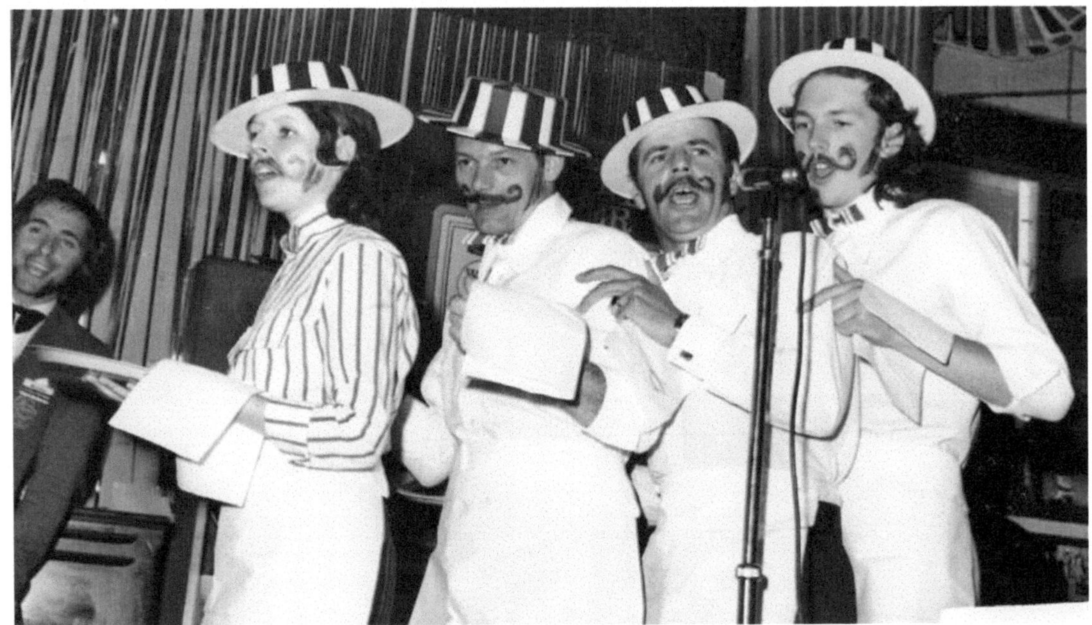

Watney's Special Bitter sponsored the Singing Waiters Competition during 1975. Other entertainment featured in the Skegness programme for that year included the Resident Revue at the Gaiety Theatre, The Albany Players at the Playhouse Theatre, Dancing in the New Empress Ballroom to the Val Merral Orchestra, Saturday Night Variety, Sunday Startime, the Vince Earl Attraction at the Empress, the Philips' Family show featuring audience participation and valuable prizes, Star Trail (Butlin's own Talent Show), the Walter Cosgrove Duo in the New Regency Ballroom, a Discotheque, Cash Bingo, Wrestling, Filmed Horse Racing, It's a Knockout, the Donkey Derby and film shows in the Empire Theatre.

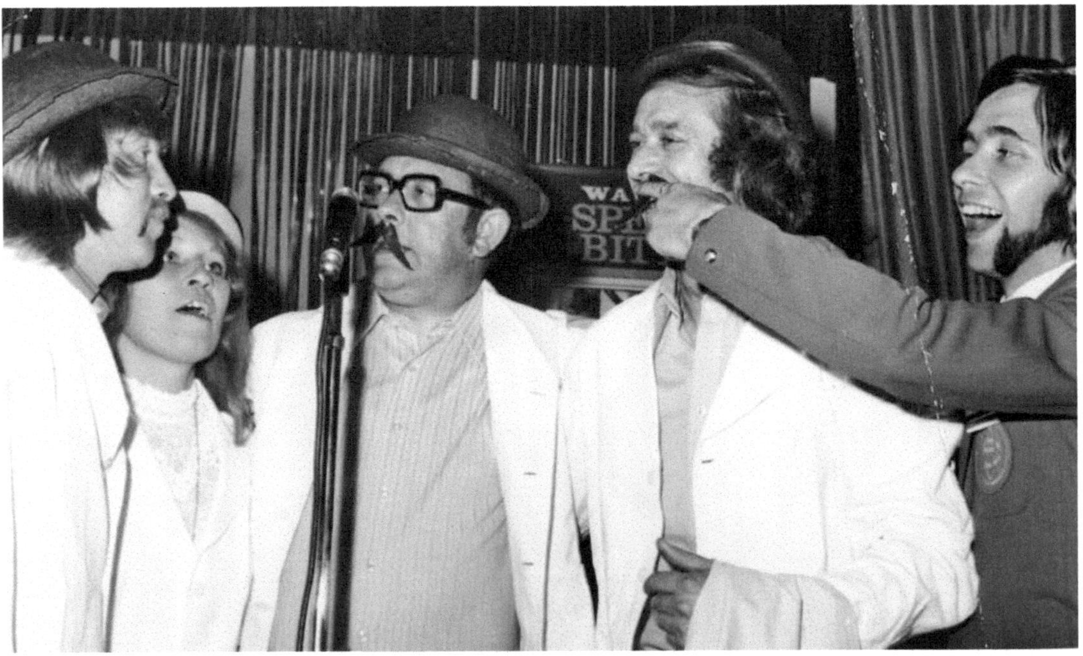

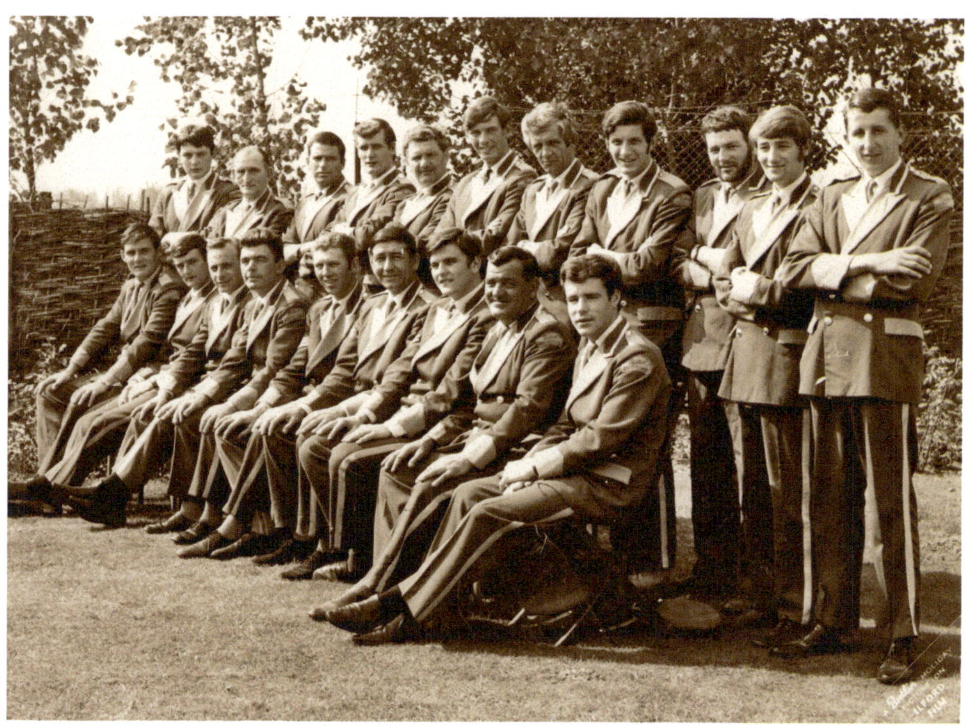

Both photographs show the Security team at Minehead in 1968. Security were responsible for keeping non-paying visitors outside the camp and stopping anyone from wandering around the camp that shouldn't be there. Campers would wear their Butlin's badges or show their keys to prove that they were staying on the site although Butlin's also welcomed day visitors. The camp at Minehead was opened in 1962 and covered 165 acres of land which had previously been marshes used for grazing. In 1964, a miniature railway was added and chairlifts were installed in 1965. The monorail opened in 1967 and covered 800 yards of track.

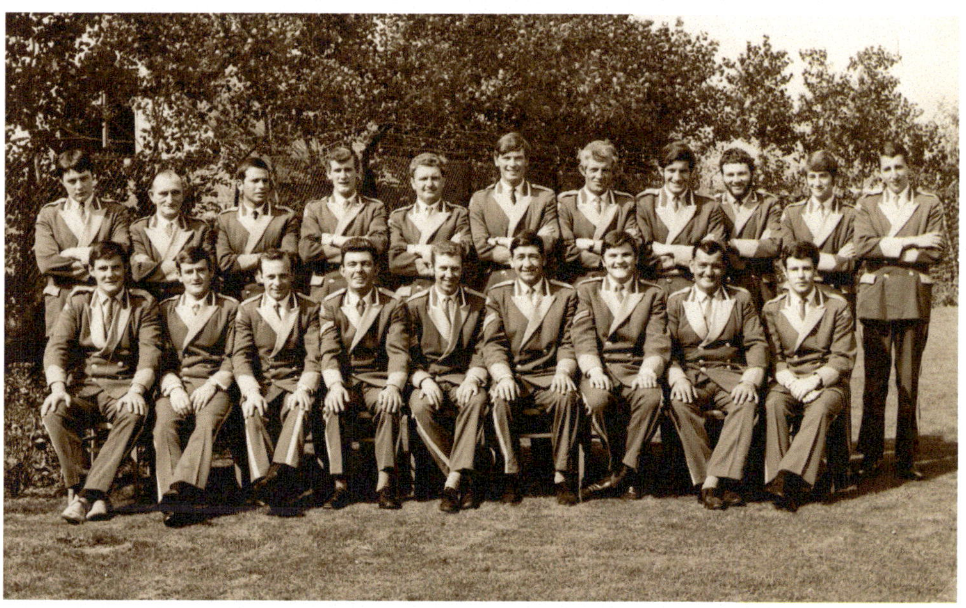

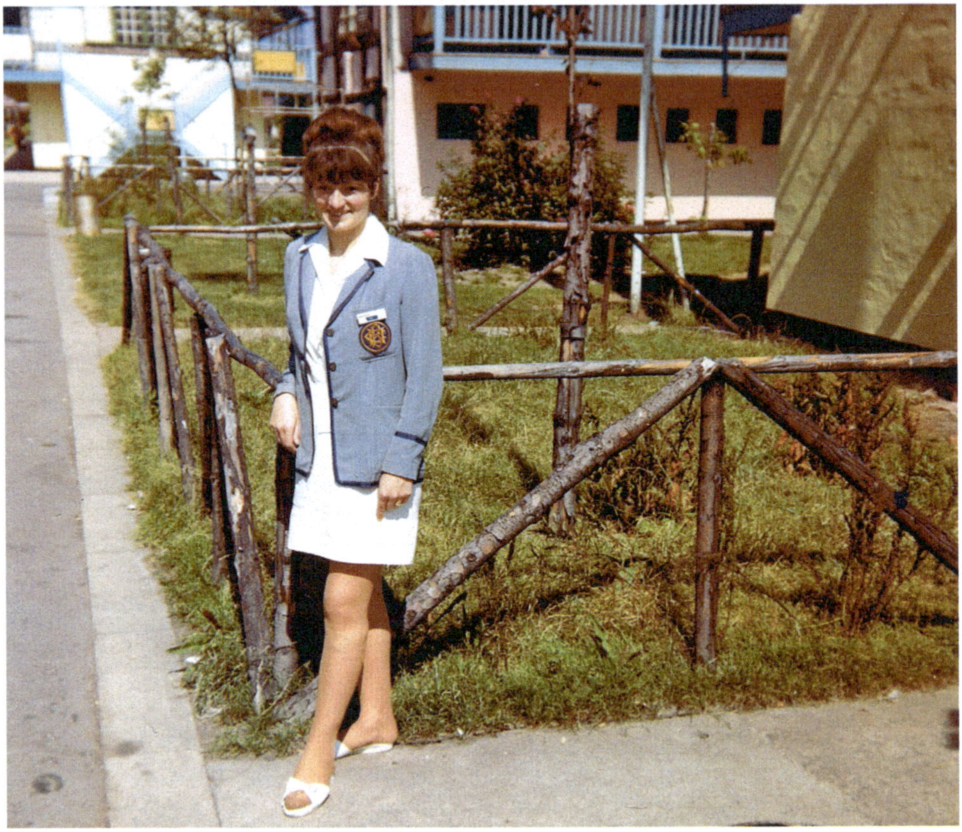

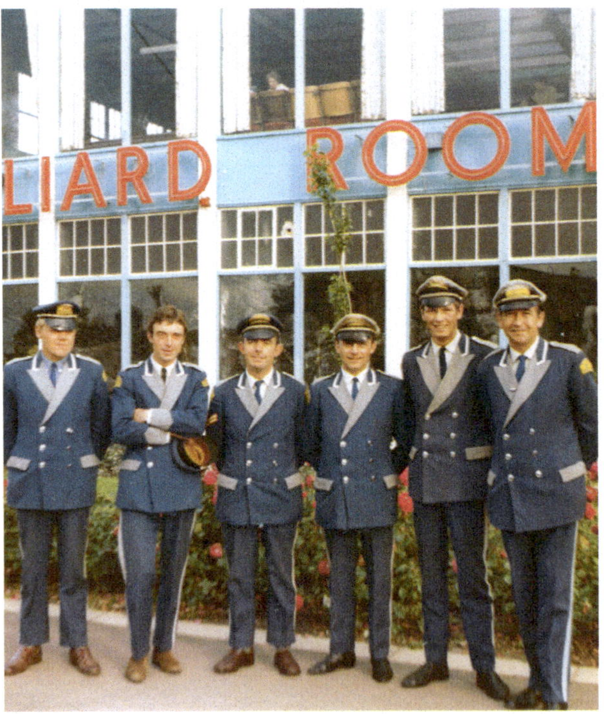

The top photograph shows Mary, the dining hall supervisor, at Minehead in 1968. At Skegness, before war broke out, meals were served four times a day. Breakfast included bread and butter, marmalade, grapefruit, bacon and eggs and tea. Lunch consisted of roast lamb, potatoes, beans, mint sauce, bread and butter followed by fruit tart and custard. Tea included bread and butter and jam and cakes. Dinner started with soup followed by steamed salmon, cucumber and vegetables. Blancmange was served after the meal. Joe Velich was the jolly chef who happily chatted to campers in his white chef's hat and overalls. The bottom photograph shows the security team at Minehead 1968.

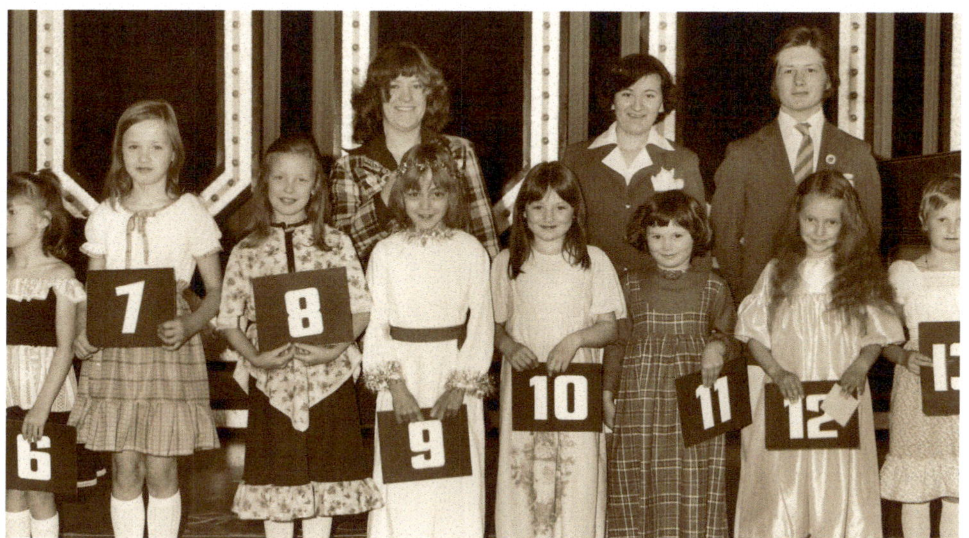

The top photograph shows the Junior Miss Competition. Butlin's competitions, many with cash prizes, were vast and, in 1975, included the Grandest Grandad, the Darby and Joan, the Miss Heineken Contest, Mother and Child Contest, Lucky Dip and Treasure Hunt, Gracious Lady, Man of the Moment, Children's Fancy Dress sponsored by Corona, the Players No 6 Show, the Heinz Baby Show and Junior Star Trail. The equivalent Junior Miss Competition for boys was the Tarzan Contest where children flexed their muscles, beat their chests and did their best to emulate the king of the jungle.

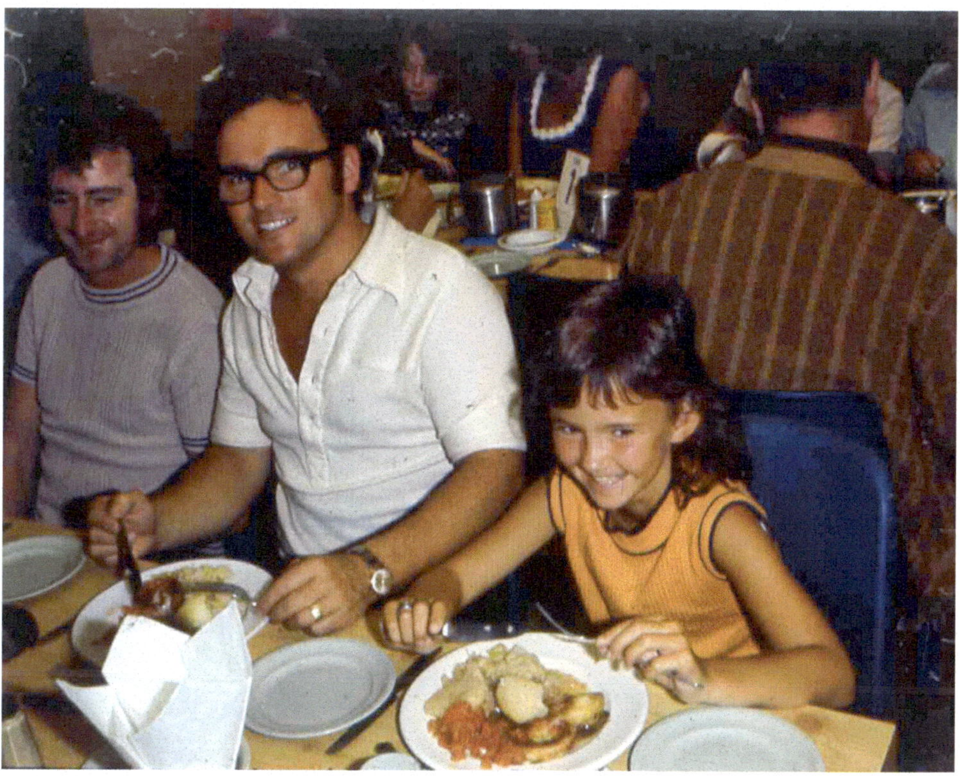

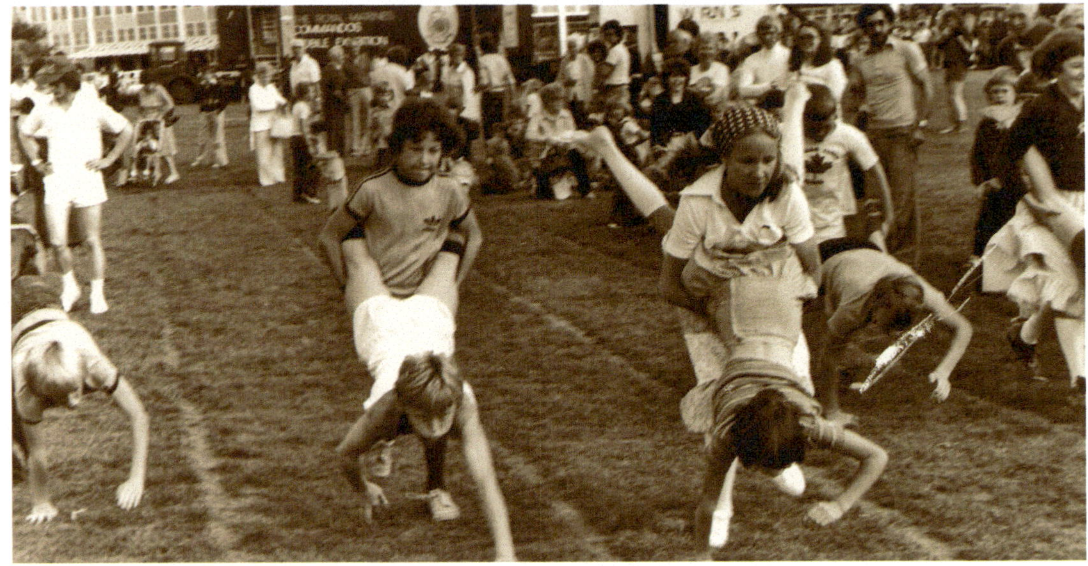

The top photograph shows Sports Day at Bognor in 1978. Children are competing in the wheelbarrow race on the sports field. The Royal Marines Commandos Exhibition can be seen in the background next to the Wrens display. Other sports day events included the Tug of War, the Egg Throwing Competition, Leap Frog and Carpet Racing. More traditional sports played included football and netball. The lower photograph shows a contestant, complete with hairpiece, taking part in the Singing Waiters Contest at Filey in 1974.

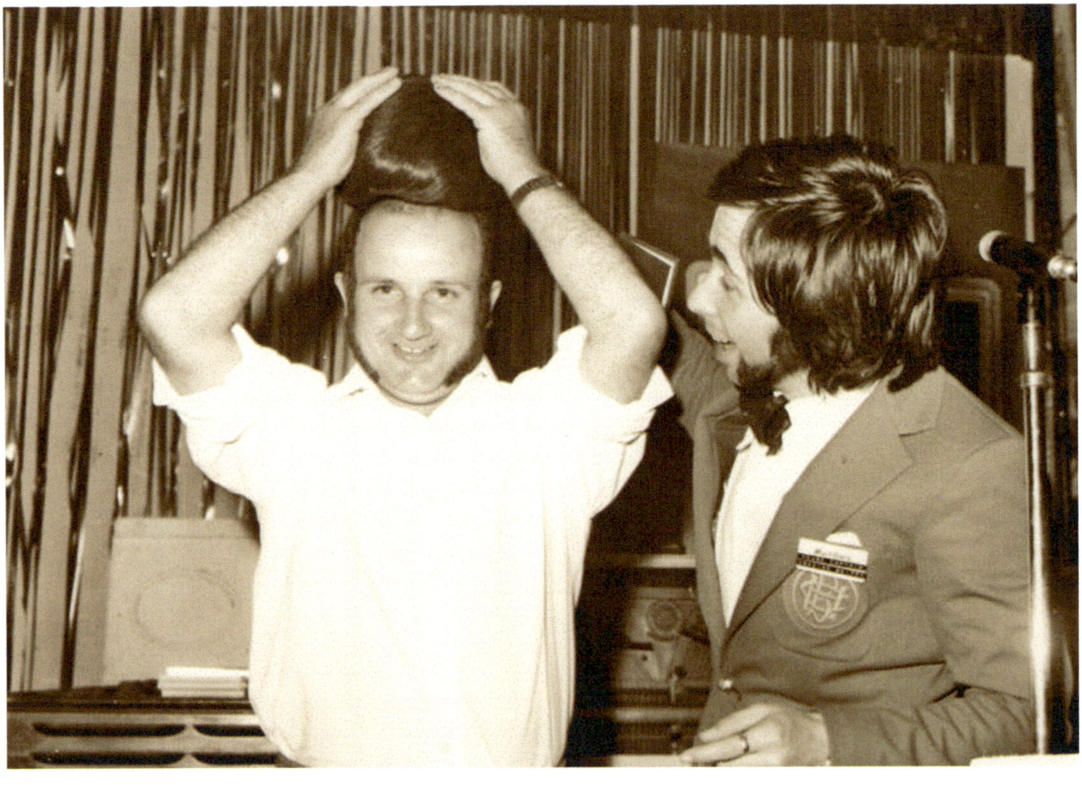

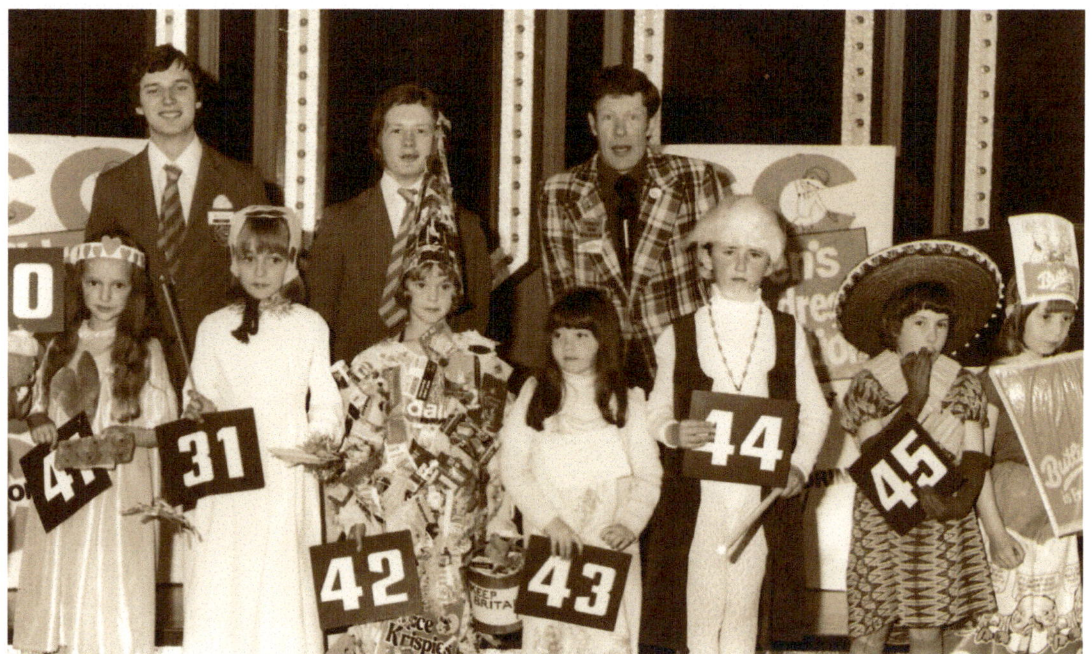

The first photograph shows the Children's Fancy Dress Competition at Bognor in 1978. It features girls dressed in costumes of the world. The Redcoats are John Tait and Kerry Conroy and hosting the show is Bob Malcolm. The second photograph shows the Junior Miss Competition with Annette Malcolm and Kerry Conroy. Both competitions were hugely popular with children and most kids went home with a certificate saying that they had entered or won something. Some children would try and enter as many contests as possible so they could compete with members of other houses.

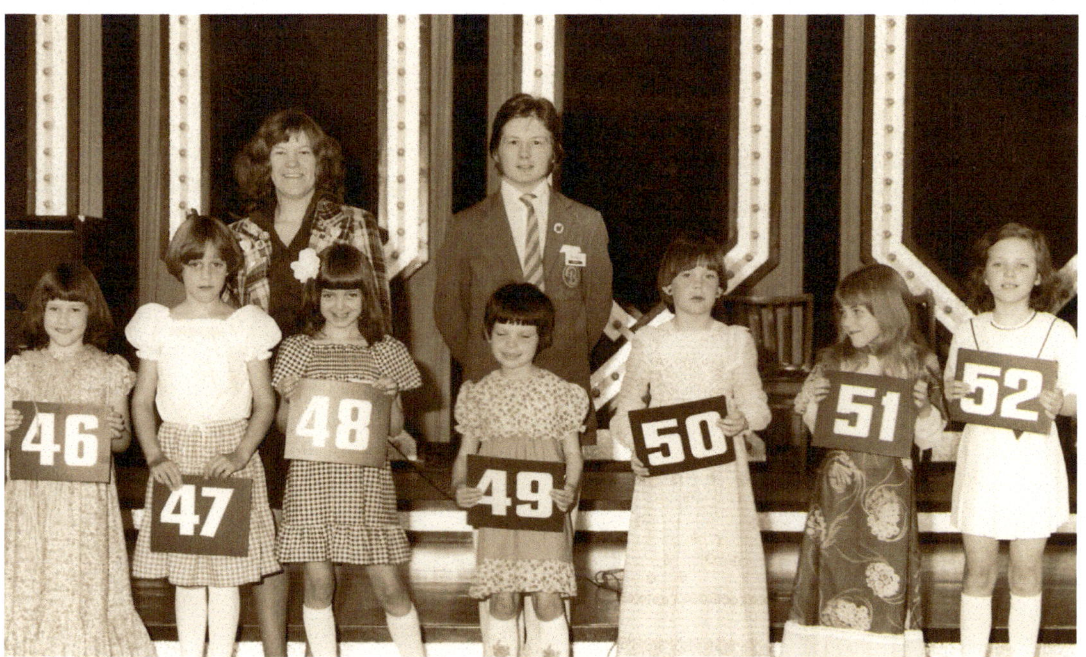

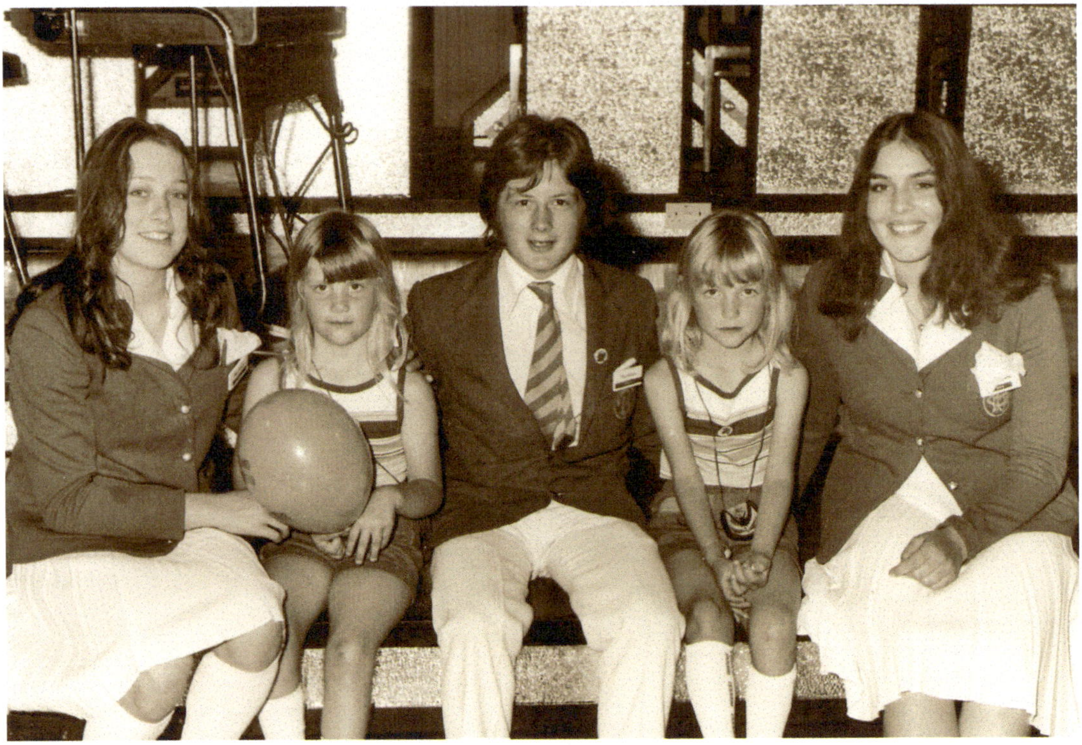

Children get to have their photographs taken with their favourite Redcoat aunties and uncles in the top photograph taken at Bognor in 1978. Kerry Conroy can be seen in the middle of the picture. The bottom photograph shows boys waiting to take part in a running event during sports day as their families look on. Kerry Conroy oversees the event.

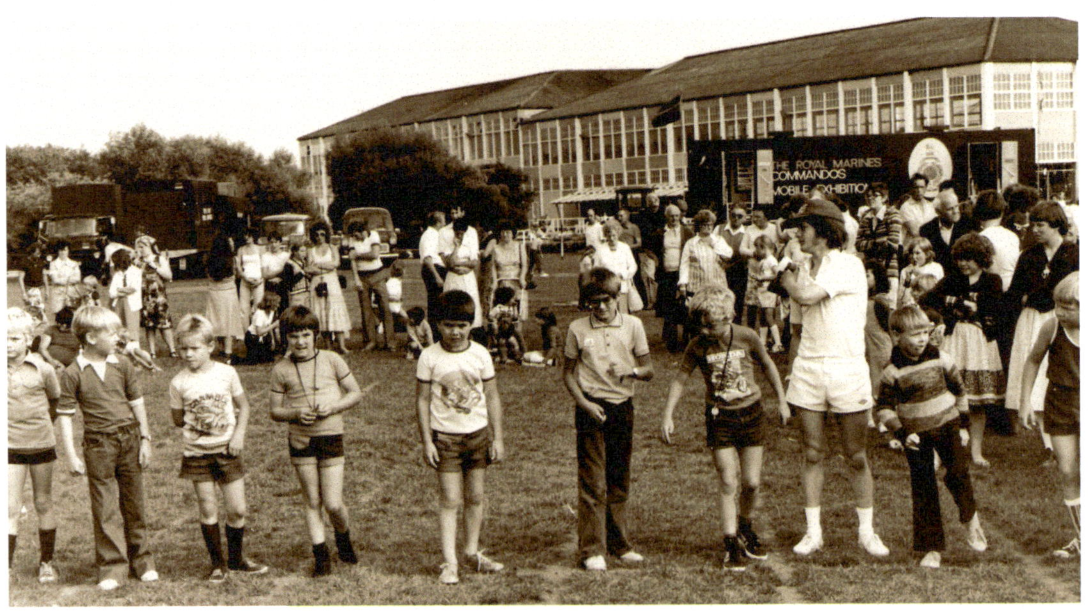

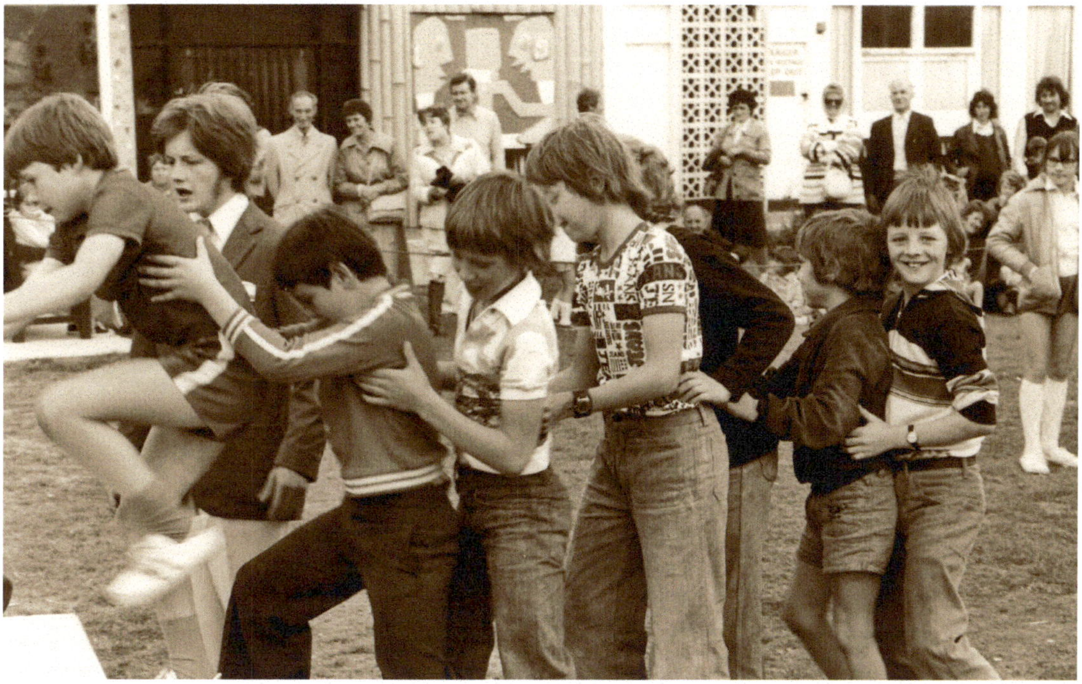

Both photographs show children joining in on Sports Day on the sports field at Bognor in 1978. Space Hopper racing was a popular event, with the challenge finals taking place half way through the week. There were also five-a-side soccer tournaments and family sports on a Thursday afternoon, which included running and novelty races for both children and adults.

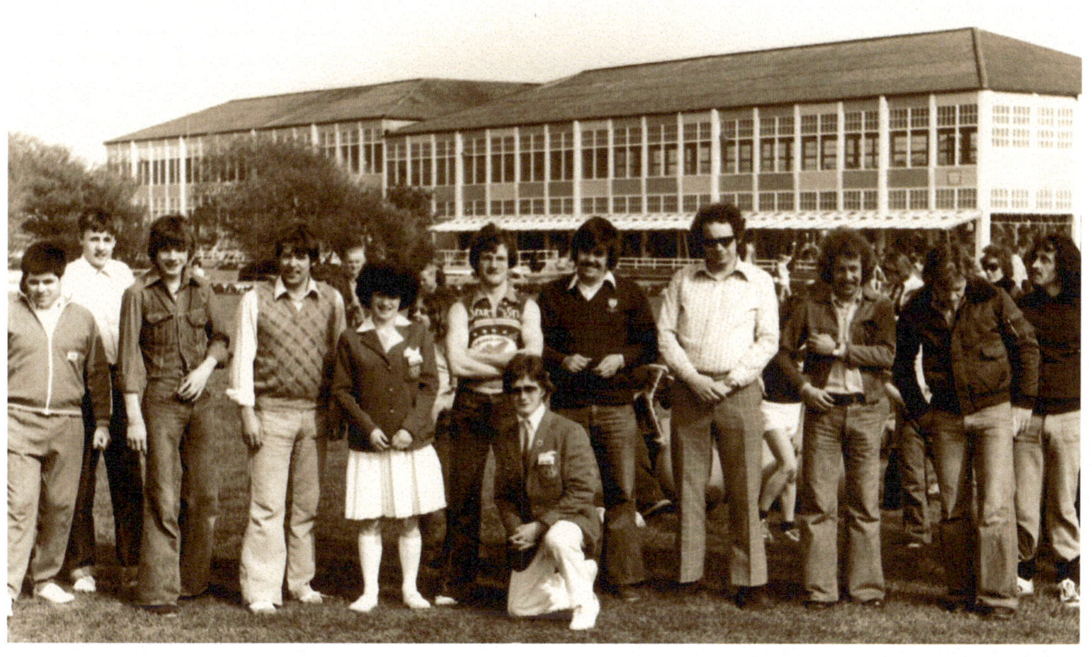

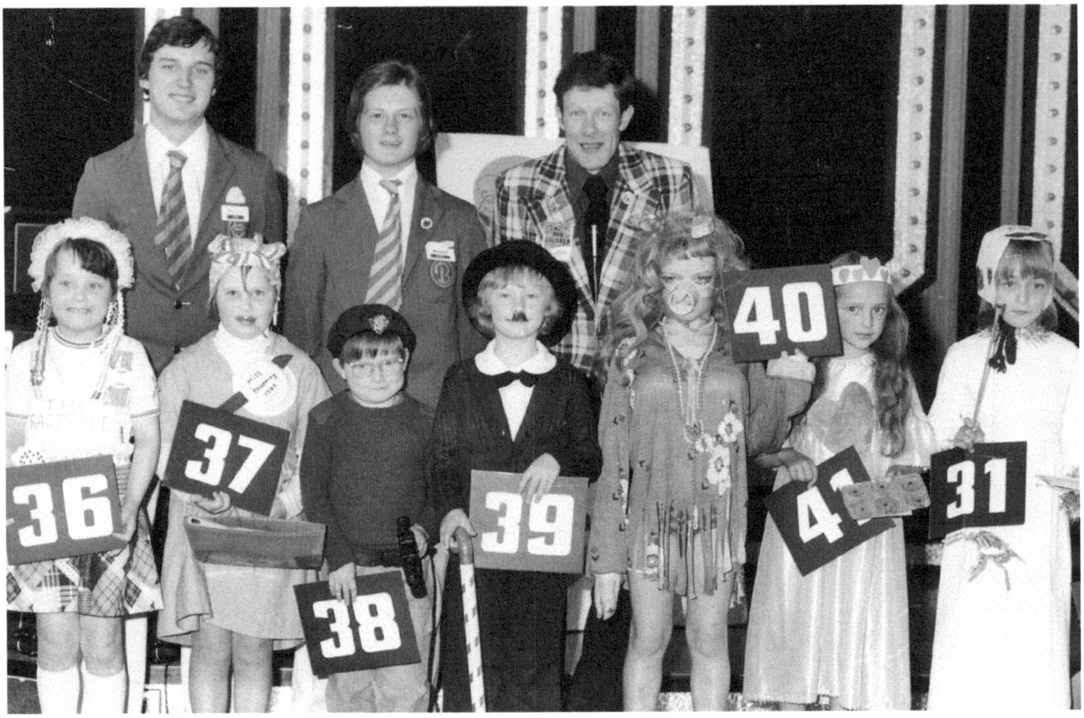

Children gather for the Fancy Dress Competition in the top photograph. In the line-up is a contestant representing the rag trade, another as Miss Charming 1978 (complete with headscarf and cigarette), a soldier, Charlie Chaplin and Miss Piggy (with a nose made out of a plastic drinks cup) together with several other contestants. John Tait, Kerry Conroy and Bob Malcolm supervise the contest. The lower photograph shows a competition taking place in the ballroom.

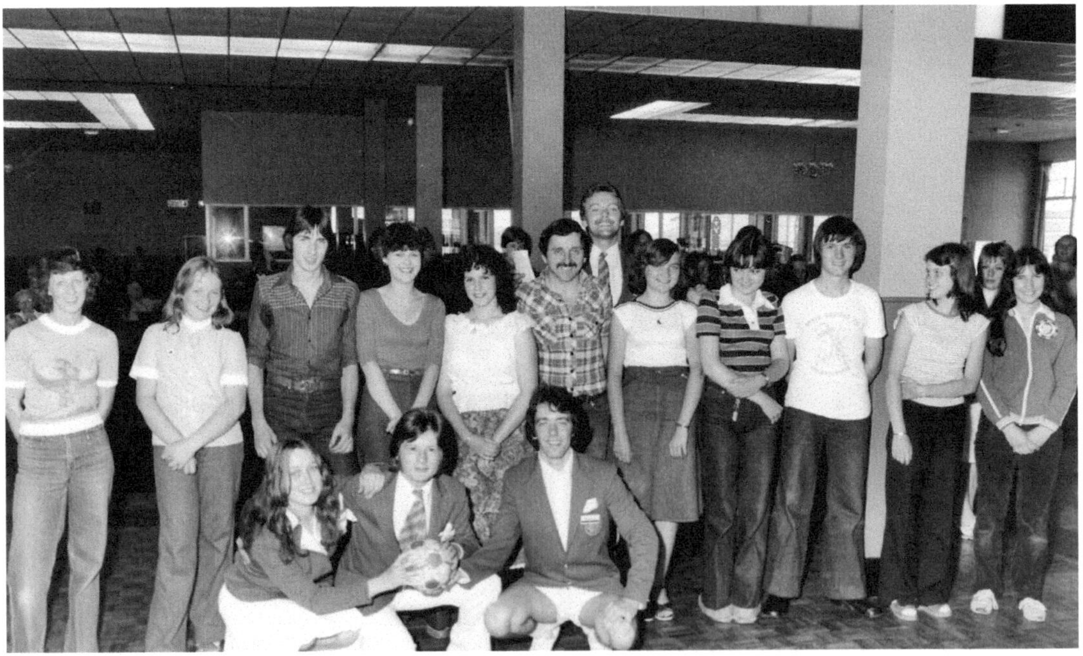

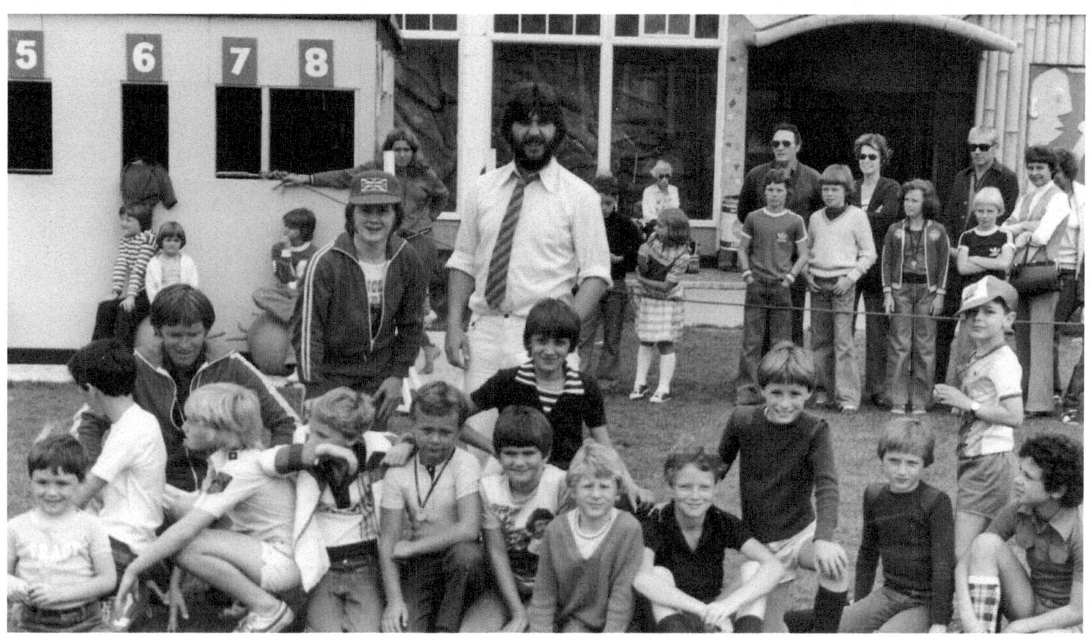

The top photograph shows more fun on the sports field at Bognor in 1978 as children wait to take part in the next event. In the bottom photograph, a piggyback competition takes place indoors at Bognor in 1973. The 'Meet the Redcoats' event took place on Sunday mornings at 11 a.m. and was followed in the afternoon by music and entertainment in one of the bars. Sunday afternoons consisted of the Junior Fancy Dress Contest, cash bingo for the adults, swimming galas and modern and Old Tyme Dancing in the ballroom.

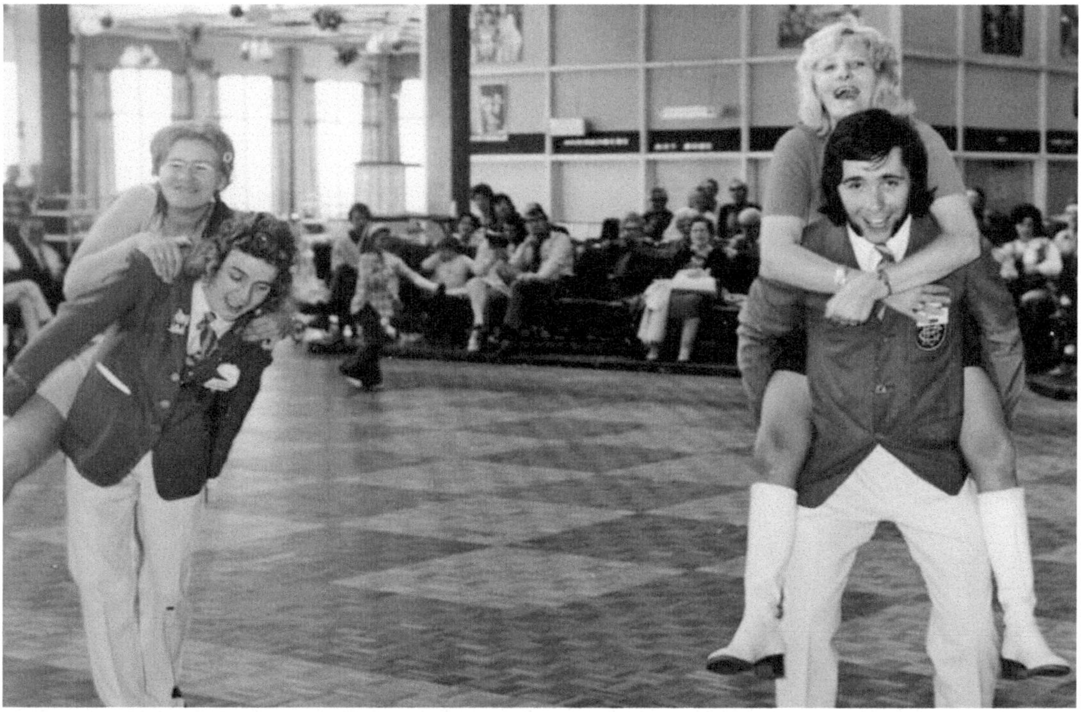

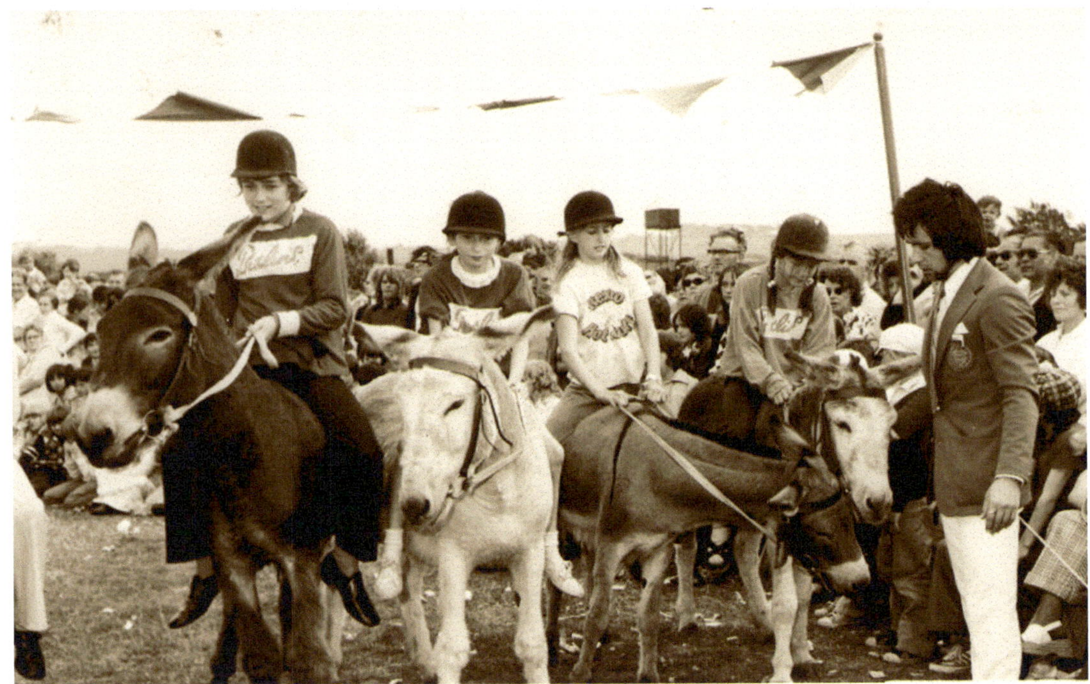

The two photographs show contestants taking part in the Donkey Derby in 1974. The advert in Butlin's programme for 1975 read, 'Donkey Derby. Wednesday at 2.30 p.m. on the Sports field. Why not own a donkey for a race? Price of ownership 75 pence. Nominate your own jockey. Must be under fourteen years and under 7.5 stone. Prizes for owners. Get your programme today. Price 3 pence. Also Big Tote Jackpot. Tickets 10 pence. Sponsored by Bensons Superb Confectionary.'

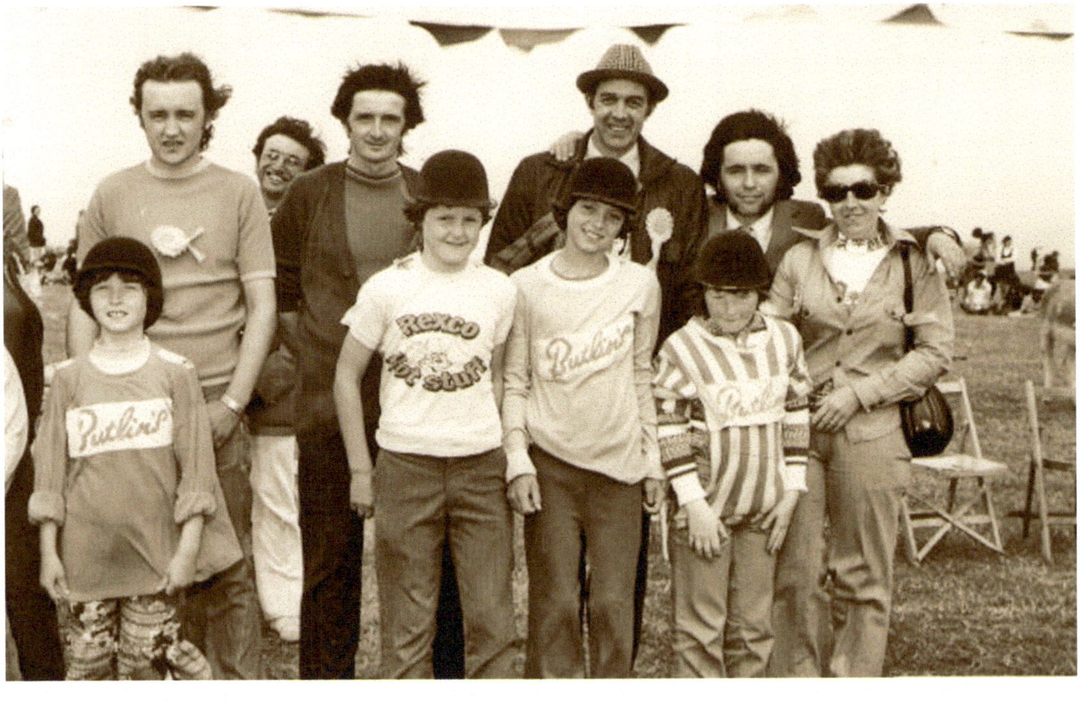

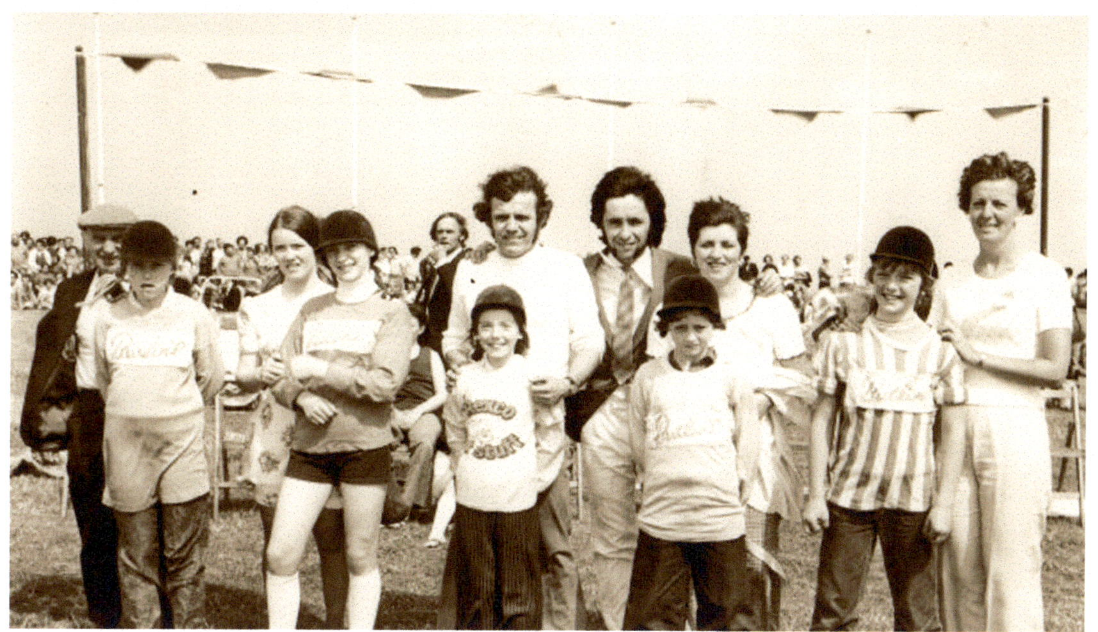

Contestants for the ever popular Donkey Derby line up on the sports field at Filey in 1974 in the first photograph. The second photograph shows the winners at Bognor in 1978 and the donkeys' part-time owners together with their jockeys and winner's rosettes. Kerry Conroy, Joe Cussens and Geoff Donaldson also feature in the photograph. In the background, Don Trapnell's lorry is visible, which was used to transport the donkeys to the event. Don got together his first team of donkeys in 1941 when he was just fourteen. He eventually had over 300 animals and appeared on television programmes with Jimmy Savile, Harry Secombe and Hughie Greene. He died in 2010 aged eighty-three.

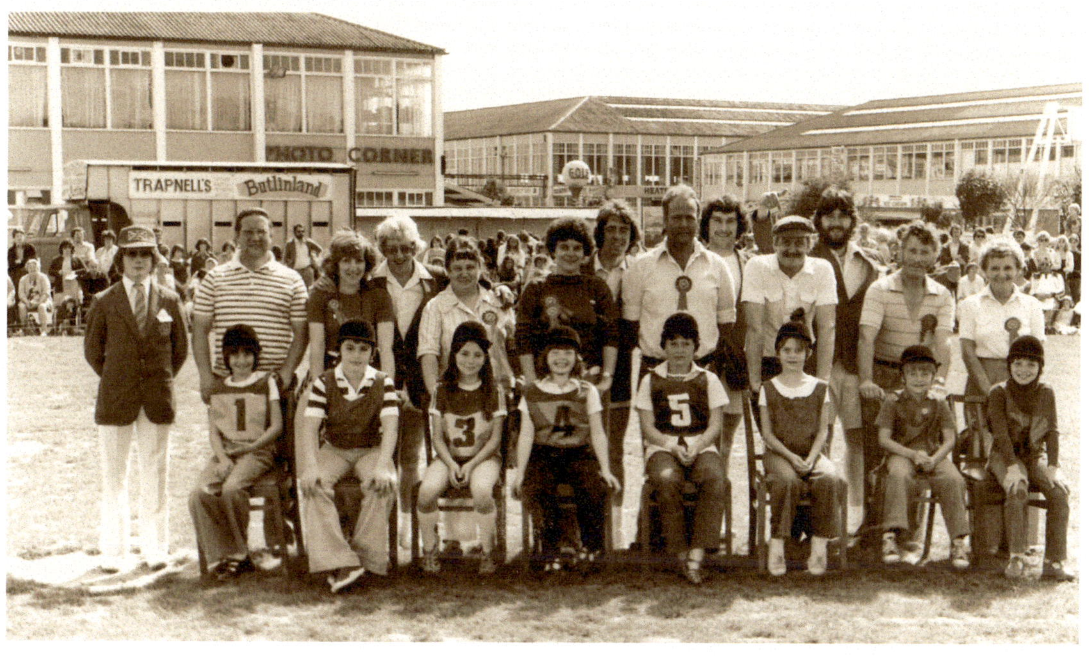

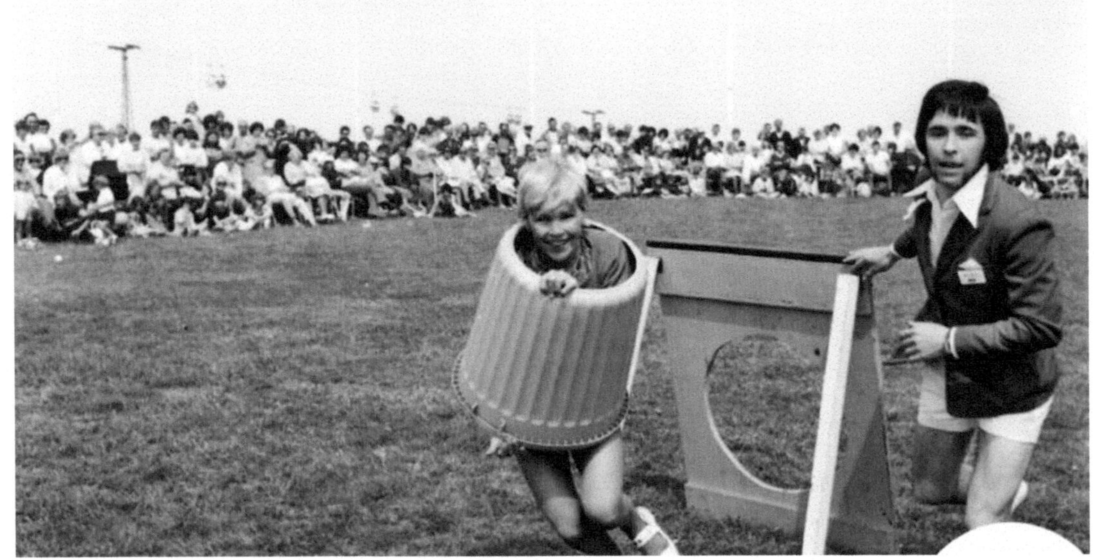

The television programme, *It's a Knockout* was incredibly popular with families and ran between 1966 and 1988. The height of its popularity was in the 1970s and Butlin's ran its own version of the game with families competing against each other. Inter-house competitions took place, which included balancing on barrels, carrying buckets of water on your head while running, and carrying your partner on your shoulders while running.

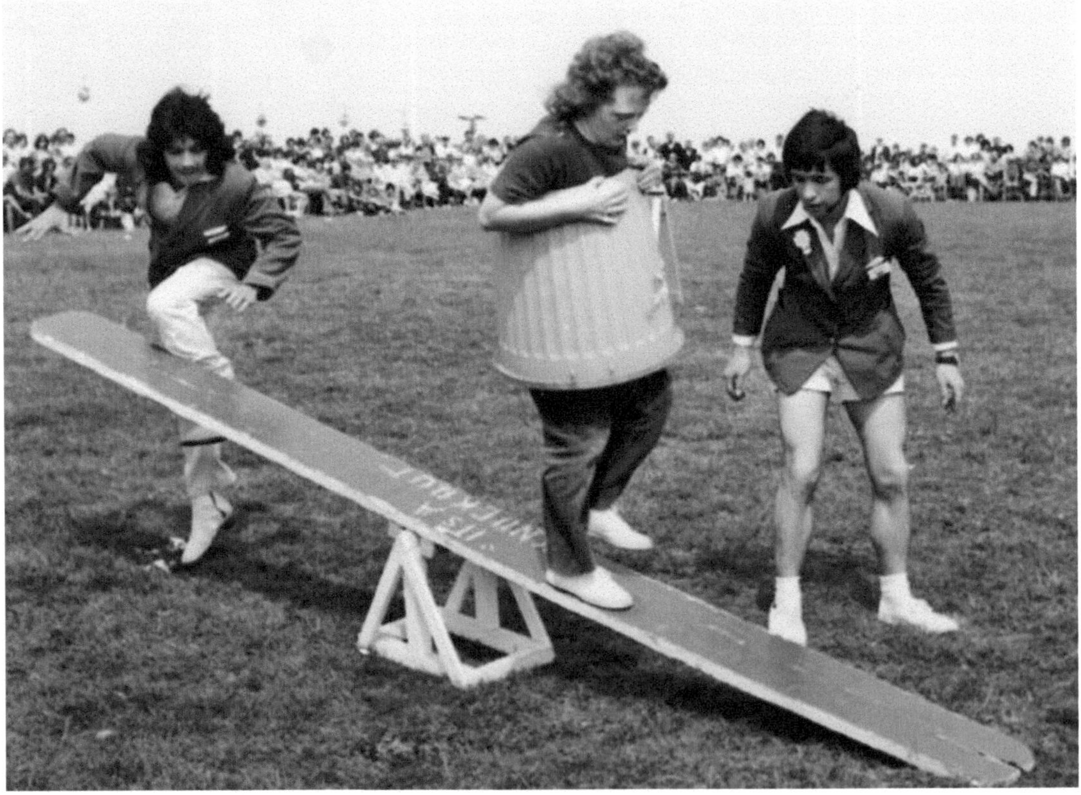

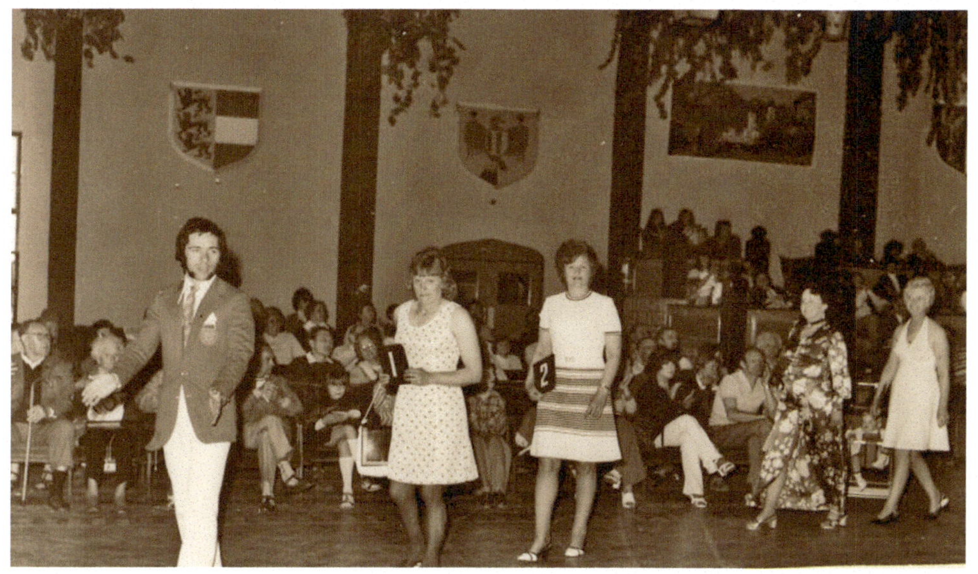

The first photograph shows a contest taking place in the ballroom on a Sunday morning. The games were designed so that everyone could join in and get to know the Redcoats as well as other campers. The second photograph shows the York team in 1973 as they line up to take part in the 'It's a Knockout Competition' which was held on the sports field.

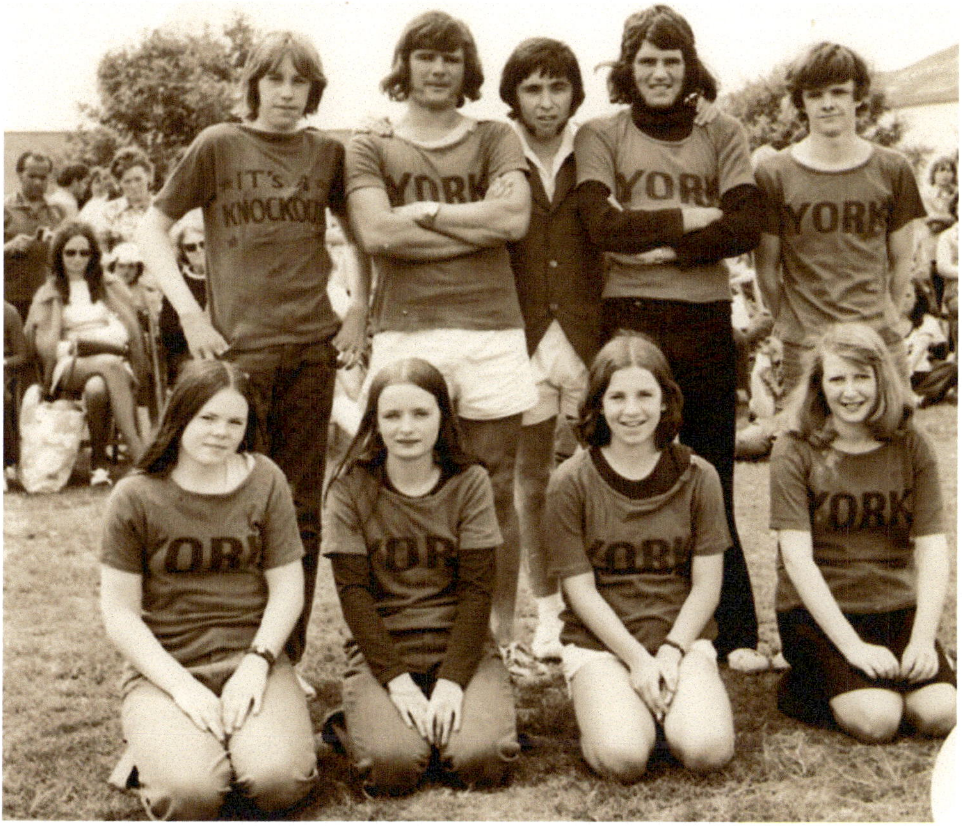

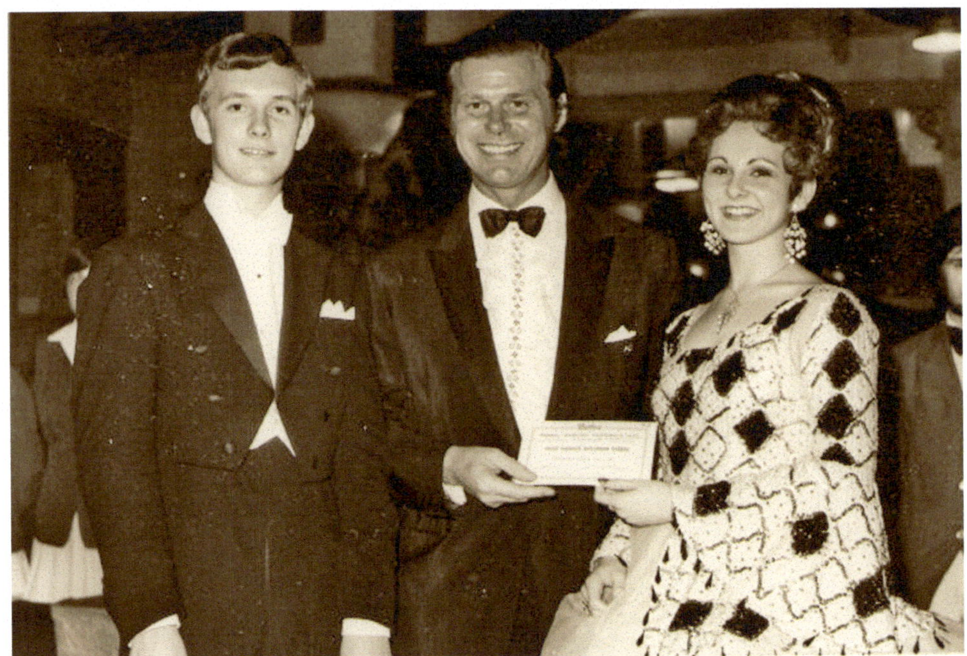

The top photograph shows Bobby Butlin presenting the ballroom prizes. In 1968, Billy Butlin retired to Jersey and his son, Bobby, took over. With the introduction of cheap package holidays abroad, Butlin's was beginning to lose money. It also suffered from poor publicity. Times had changed and many people no longer wanted to stay in small chalets and were more reluctant to take part in games organised by Redcoats. Improvements were made to accommodation and many were equipped with cookers and freezers. Lunch was no longer served and the only meals provided were at breakfast and in the evening. Together with star-studded shows and a midnight cabaret, Butlin's numbers soon increased and, by 1971, they were once again taking record bookings.

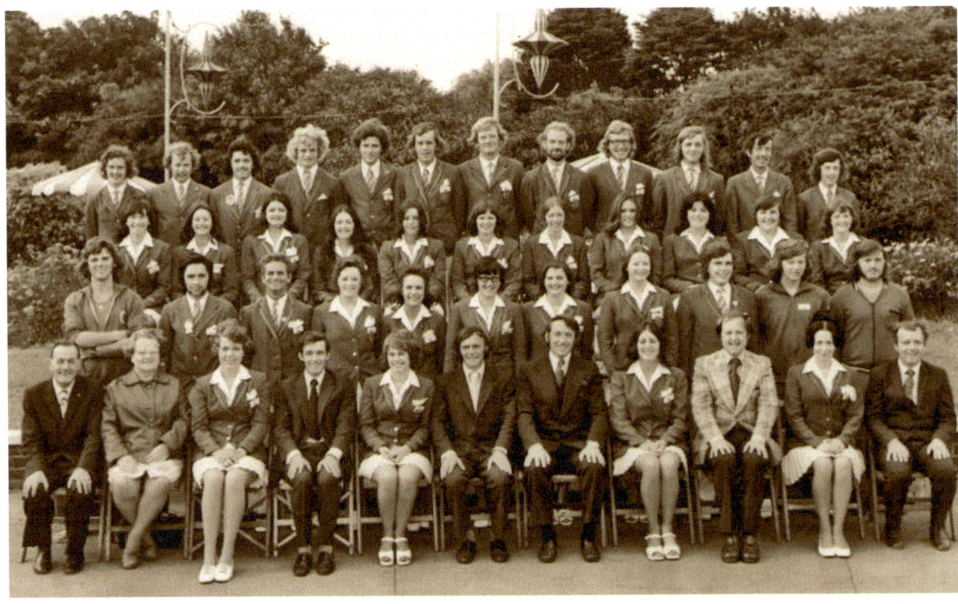

Printed and bound by CPI Group (UK) Ltd, Croydon, CR0 4YY

11/07/2026

02158879-0007